FIRES OF CHANGE:

A COMPREHENSIVE EXAMINATION OF CREMATION

SECOND EDITION

Funeral Service Education Resource Center

fSERc

Dedicated to the Advancement of Funeral Service Education

JOHN B. FRITCH, PH.D.

&

J. CHANDLER ALTIERI, ED.D.

Copyright © 2021 by Funeral Service Education Resource Center

All rights reserved. No part of this publication may be reproduced, distributed, or transmitted in any form or by any means, including photocopying, recording, or other electronic or mechanical methods, without the prior written permission of the publisher, except in the case of brief quotations embodied in critical reviews and certain other noncommercial uses permitted by copyright law. For permission requests, write to the publisher, addressed "Attention: Permissions Coordinator," at the address below.

Funeral Service Education Resource Center
3000 W Memorial STE 123, Box 241
Oklahoma City, OK 73120

Second Edition Published 2021, Printed in the U.S.A.

ISBN: 978-0-9979261-8-7

Published by:
Funeral Service Education Resource Center
3000 W Memorial STE 123, Box 241
Oklahoma City, Oklahoma 73120
Phone: 405-226-3155
Email: fnrleducation@gmail.com
Website: www.fserc.com

About the Authors

John B. Fritch, Ph.D.

Dr. Fritch holds a B.A. in Economics from the University of Kansas; a B.S. in Funeral Service from the University of Central Oklahoma; an M.Ed. also from the University of Central Oklahoma; and a Doctor of Philosophy specializing in Higher Education Leadership and Policy Studies from Oklahoma State University. He is also a licensed funeral director, embalmer and has been certified as a crematory operator.

Fritch is the chairperson for the University of Central Oklahoma, Department of Funeral Service Education. Although his full-time position at the university demands the majority of his time, he has remained committed to staying current in the funeral service profession, and continues to practice as a funeral director and embalmer when possible. His research focus centers on quality funeral service education, and what elements define such classification. In addition to his leadership role at Central, and practicing as a funeral director and embalmer, he is also the founder of the Funeral Service Education Resource Center, a company dedicated to the advancement of funeral service education.

• • •

J. Chandler Altieri, Ed.D.

Dr. Altieri earned a B.S. in Funeral Service Education from the University of Central Oklahoma; an M.S. in Management Science from Southern Nazarene University; and is a Doctor of Education specializing in higher education administration, a degree he earned from Texas Tech University. He is also a licensed practitioner in both Oklahoma and Texas.

The native of Massachusetts' South Shore moved to Texas in 1998 where he served as a faculty member and administrator in both community college and private college Mortuary Science programs. In addition to starting a Mortuary Science program, he has designed and taught numerous academic and continuing education courses (both traditional and on-line formats), including: crematory & cemetery operations, anatomy, business law, mortuary jurisprudence, history of funeral service, funeral directing practices, sociology, small business management, accounting, restorative art, technical procedures and regulatory compliance.

Dr. Altieri is President of Brenham AA Interests and Holdings, a company he co-founded in 2017, which is dedicated to cremation and related products and services. Their inventory includes one of the largest crematory operations in Southeast Texas.

Along with administration and teaching, Dr. Altieri served as Chair and member on the Committee on Accreditation for the American Board of Funeral Service Education; the programs and education committee for the Texas Funeral Directors Association; and on the Editorial Review Board for the *Journal of Funeral Service Education*. He is also a consultant specializing in funeral service accreditation; cremation operations and development; and, offers an expert opinion for legal cases.

ACKNOWLEDGEMENTS

Cremation Association of North America (CANA), no person or organization has been more supportive than CANA in the writing of this text. The sharing of expertise and resources has been amazing, the support of CANA has been central to the creation of a quality cremation textbook.

Thank you!

Bruce Kelley
Central Burial Vaults
Crematory Manufacturing & Service, Inc.
Larry Morgan, J.D.
Larry Stuart, JR.
Matthews Aurora Funeral Solutions
Mercer Adams Funeral Service
Oklahoma Mortuary Service
Poul Lemasters & Lemasters Consulting
Shannon Myott
U.S. Cremation Equipment

• • •

Chapter Authors – The following contributed as authors:

Cremation Association of North America (CANA) Barbara Kemmis
Lucia Dickinson
Jason Engler, The Cremation Historian
Glenda Stansbury

Table of Contents

Preface viii

Chapter 1 - Beauty & Light: A History of Cremation in America 1

- A Brief Look at Ancient Cremation 1
- America's First Modern Cremation 5
- Cremation Expands 7
- Architecturally Significant and Ceremonially Important ... 8
- Cremation Societies and Their Propaganda 10
- The Cremation Association of North America ... 11
- Cremation in Transition 12
- Standardizing Crematory and Columbarium Practices ... 18
- Cremation as a Personal Preference 25

Chapter 2 - Preparation of Remains 26

- Identification 28
- Viewing 29
- Identification Viewing 29
- Relationship between Viewing and Authorized Agent ... 33
- Indemnification 34
- Embalming Case Report 36

Chapter 3 - Required Authorizations 38

- Authorization to Cremate 43
- Sample Authorization Forms 47
- Authorization for Minimal Care 59
- Embalming Authorization 61
- Associated Forms 66

Chapter 4 - Final Disposition of Cremated Remains 70

- Options for Final Disposition 74
- Shipping Cremated Remains 76
- Disposition of Unclaimed Cremated Remains ... 81

Chapter 5 - The Use of Third Party Crematories 84

- Internal Policies and Procedures 85
- Due Diligence 85

Table of Contents

Chapter 6 - Recommendations for Crematory Operations — 90

- Combustion — 91
- Waste and Incinerator Classification — 92
- Crematory Component Parts — 93
- Crematory Accessories — 94
- Routine Crematory Maintenance — 96
- Cremation Process — 98
- Cremation Cases Requiring Special Care — 105

Chapter 7 - Cremation Containers — 110

- Caskets — 111
- Cremation Caskets — 113
- Alternative Containers — 114

Chapter 8 - Containers for Cremated Remains — 117

- Urns — 118
- Temporary Containers — 118
- Permanent Containers — 120
- Specialty Items — 121
- Outer Burial Containers — 123

Chapter 9 - Cremation and FTC Compliance — 126

- Required Disclosure — 127
- Required Itemized Price — 128
- Misrepresentation Prohibited — 128

Chapter 10 - The Arrangement Conference — 131

- Respond to the Pain — 133
- Engage the Stories — 134
- Articulate Options — 135
- Paint the Picture — 137
- Encourage Ceremony — 140
- Review and Refer — 144
- Follow Through — 147

Table of Contents

Chapter 11 - Alkaline Hydrolysis ... 157

    History ... 157
    Manufacturers and Machines ... 158
    Process ... 159
    Debated Pros and Cons ... 160

Chapter 12 - Understanding & Interpreting Cremation Statistics ... 162

    The Cremation Landscape ... 162
    Annual Cremation Statistics ... 163
    Milestone Project ... 165
    Roaming and Rooted ... 167

Chapter 13 - Contemporary Trends ... 171

    Consumer Preferences ... 172
    Rising Costs ... 172
    Green Alternatives ... 173
    Religion ... 174
    Changing Consumer Preferences ... 175
    Increasing Educational Levels ... 176
    Greater Life Expectancies ... 178
    Expanded Offerings ... 178
    Increased Migration ... 179
    More Socially Accepted ... 180
    Pet Cremation ... 181

Glossary ... 183

References ... 188

Index ... 196

PREFACE

• • •

When the first edition of this text was published in 2015, it was designed to fill a void in resources available to teach cremation to funeral service/mortuary science students. It was quickly discovered by the authors that the void they were feeling was universal across most funeral service educators, the book was adopted by the majority of funeral service schools across the country, and it was quickly learned that this book was doing more than assisting educators teach cremation, it was educating the next generation of funeral service professionals in the most rapidly growing segment in death care, cremation. Over the past few years the importance of this book has become apparent, we knew it was necessary to keep the content of the text both current and relevant. In many areas the authors could research various topics and make appropriate changes to the text, but in other areas it was necessary to seek out content experts in an effort to develop the most meaningful book available with respect to cremation education – we believe this edition meets that challenge. Collaboration defines this edition. We sought content experts to present new material, and worked diligently to update various sections of the first edition in order to present current and relevant information regarding all aspects related to cremation.

• • •

Read, Learn, Enjoy!

Chapter 1 – Beauty & Light:
A history of Cremation in America

Chapter Author: Jason Ryan Engler, the Cremation Historian

Chapter Learning Objectives

Upon completion of the study of this chapter students should:

- Understand the impact of ancient funeral rites on contemporary cremation.
- Be able to demonstrate an understanding of facts associated with the introduction of cremation to North America, and specifically to the United States.
- Understand why various cultures select cremation as a means toward final disposition.

• • •

Introduction

Whether for religious purposes, purification, or even outright destruction of the remains, the rite of cremation has been practiced by countless religions, sects, cults, cultures, and civilizations throughout the ages. Some cultures believed that the beauty and light of the flame encouraged the spirit toward beauty and light in the Beyond. In this chapter we will briefly explore cremation in ancient times, but will primarily focus on the modern revival of cremation which began in the 1870s.

A Brief Look at Ancient Cremation

One of the most well-documented instances of cremation in ancient times is the cremation of Patroclus, the companion of Achilles, during the Trojan war. This example, though often discounted as a work of fiction, was described in the Iliad by Homer.

The story goes that Patroclus was killed by Hector, the leader of the Trojans, while he was trying to rally the Myrmidons to fight. For days following his death, Achilles, in his deep grief, refused to allow the body of Patroclus to be cremated until one night the "shade" of Patroclus visited him in a dream. His request in the dream was that Achilles would cremate his body and place his bones in a golden vase, and that when Achilles died, that his bones would be placed within as well.

An elaborate funeral pyre was constructed, and the cremation carried out. When the fires had cooled, the bones of Patroclus were gathered and placed within the urn. On the same ground, a large tumulus, or burial mound, was raised and the urn was placed within.

Image 1.1: Greek Cremation. In ancient Greece, the cremation of a well-known person was a public event. Often, the cremation was lighted by a close friend or by the eldest son of the deceased.
Image Source: Engler Cremation Collection.

Image 1.2: Greek Vase. Following cremation, the Greeks often chose standard household objects such as wine vessels or grain storage jars. Their recognizable red or black figures told stories of Greek legend and history. The most commonly used shapes for this purpose were the Stamnos (shown here) and the Amphora – while the Lekythos was used to hold oils to aid in fueling the funeral pyre.
Image Source: a Greek vase in the collection of the Metropolitan Museum of Art, New York, photographed by Jason Engler, October, 2017.

Image 1.3: Roman Cremation. Like the Greeks, Roman cremations often took place in public and the releasing of doves was a common element of the rite.
Image Source: Engler Cremation Collection.

The Romans practiced cremation and the funeral pyre was often lighted by the eldest son of the deceased person. Following cremation, the bones were gathered and placed in urns, often to be deposited in the columbaria or cemeteries on the outskirts of Rome.

Image 1.4: Roman Columbarium. Following cremation, the Romans typically placed the remains in glass, stone or lapis urns and placed them in columbaria (from the Latin word for a dovecote) on one of the well-traveled roads on the outskirts of the city.
Image Source: Engler Cremation Collection.

The great Norse Vikings were also practitioners of cremation, as related in the Ynglinga Saga. A verse from that epic poem relates that Odin commanded that the dead "should be burned, and their belongings laid with them upon the pile, and the ashes be cast into the sea or buried in the earth. Thus, said he, everyone will come to Valhalla with the riches he had with him upon the pile; and he would also enjoy whatever he himself had buried in the earth. For men of consequence a mound should be raised to their memory, and for all other warriors who had been distinguished for manhood a standing stone."

Boats were thought to provide safe passage to the afterlife, so then the funeral pyres and sometimes grave mounds were constructed in the shape of a boat or boats were brought ashore to become part of the pyre or grave mound. Contrary to the romanticism of Hollywood, boats were not cast adrift and flaming arrows sent to light them aflame.

Cremation was also practiced by the ancient Celts, Saxons, Indians, to name a few. It is important to point out that all of these ancient and early cremations were carried out on funeral pyres – huge and often elaborate piles and structures of wood.

The first cremation performed in the United States, other than practices by indigenous Americans, was the cremation of Colonel Henry Laurens, a former president of the continental congress. His death occurred in December of 1792, and his last will and testament ordered his son to see that his body was cremated because of his fear of being buried alive. The story goes that his young daughter, stricken with smallpox, was presumed dead from its effects. Her body was removed from her bed and placed next to an open window awaiting her preparation for burial. Either the fresh cool air or raindrops from an approaching storm revived her and she lived a full life following. After his death, he ordered that his body be "wrapped in 12 yards of tow-cloth and burned."

Soon after his death, the wish was followed. A pyre was built on his South Carolina estate and his body was reduced to ashes. Following the open-air cremation, what remains could be recovered were placed in an urn and buried in the family cemetery at Mepkin, South Carolina.

• • •

Part I: Purification – Reforming Burial Customs

The modern cremation movement began in the early 1870s, when cremation had a modern revival. This began at the Vienna Exhibition of 1873 when Professor Ludovico Brunetti of Padua, Italy, revealed a furnace he had invented specifically for use in cremation. Displayed in the diorama with a miniature of the apparatus were about four pounds of cremated human remains. A nearby sign read *Vermibus erepti – Puro consumimur igni – Saved from the worms, purified by the consuming flame.*

Around this time, talk of unsanitary conditions in the overcrowded cemeteries of England piqued the interest of Sir Henry Thompson, personal surgeon to Queen Victoria. After taking much time to personally study Professor Brunetti's experiments and invention, conducting his own research, and no doubt, his experience with handling bodies after death, he wrote what would become one of the nineteenth century's most influential pro-cremation works, "Cremation: The Treatment of the Body After Death."

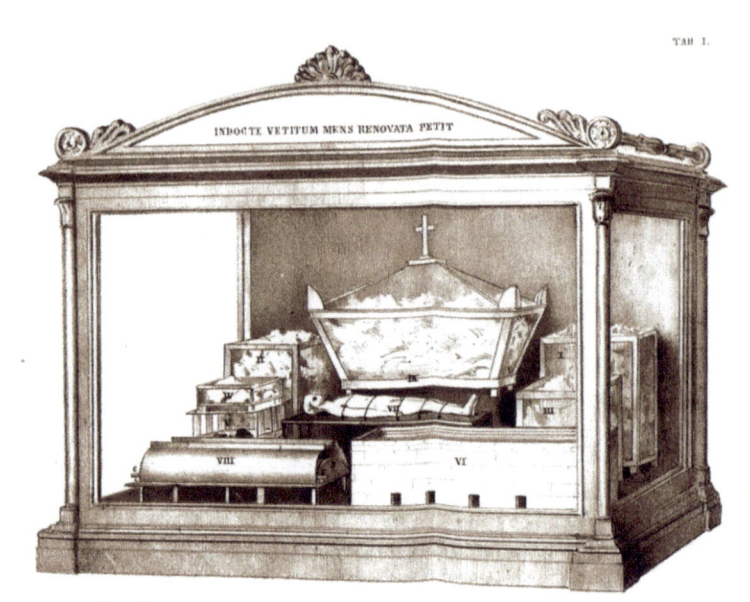

Image 1.5: Brunetti Diorama. Woodcut of the diorama showing a model of Professor Brunetti's crematory furnace and the remains of the sample cases he cremated.
Image Source: The Cremation Association Collection at the University of Chicago, John Crerar Library, Chicago, Ill.

Word of this new method of disposition spread quickly throughout Europe, then crossed the Atlantic. Across the country, periodicals, from newspapers to magazines to medical journals, published Thompson's dissertation, and many had their own articles written by experts and advocates on both sides of the "cremation versus burial" argument.

Image 1.6: Sir Henry Thompson Cremation. An artist's rendering of Sir Henry Thompson (left) researching the method of cremation by an unknown Italian inventor.
Image Source: Frank Leslie's Illustrated Newspaper in the Engler Cremation Collection.

America's First "Modern" Cremation

While Colonel Laurens' cremation was the first recorded in the US, it cannot be considered the first modern cremation in America. Modern cremation was early defined as a scientific process that takes place in a controlled chamber built for this specific the purpose. Laurens's cremation took place on a pyre in the open air.

It was a cold and rainy December day in 1876 when the Cremation movement in America made a major step forward. In the small town of Washington, Penn., Dr. Francis Julius LeMoyne, a local eccentric physician, had built small, simple two-room building with a receiving room, a furnace room which contained a crematory, designed by a local engineer. Planned exclusively for use at his own demise, the facility was constructed on his private property after the local cemetery had declined use of their grounds. The Crematory, however, could not remain idle, as it was pushed into use by Henry Steel Olcott, co-founder of the Theosophical Society of America, for the cremation of one of his followers, Bavarian immigrant Baron Joseph DePalm.

On December 5, 1876, the body of the Baron de Palm arrived at the train station in Washington, Pennsylvania. Among the party that met the train included Dr. Francis Julius LeMoyne, whose crematory was to be used, and Col. Henry Steel Olcott, founder of the Theosophical Society and executor of the Baron's estate. The cremation was a newsworthy event that was covered in almost every major newspaper in the country. On their way to the crematory, they were met by doctors of the boards of health from Brooklyn, Pittsburgh, Wheeling, W.Va., and Boston – along with about 30 reporters from various news outlets.

Image 1.7: LeMoyne Crematory. This simple structure housed Dr. LeMoyne's Crematory in Washington, Pennsylvania, a small settlement just south of Pittsburgh.
Image Source: Washington County Historical Society.

Image 1.8: Baron De Palm. The unique individual that was Baron De Palm, who turned out to not be everything he stated he was, gained notoriety as the first individual cremated in a modern cremation chamber.
Image Source: Washington County Historical Society.

The following morning, about 8 a.m., the furnace was declared ready after having been preheated for 6 hours. The body had been wrapped in a sheet saturated with alum to keep the body from igniting until the door was sealed. Various spices and evergreens were sprinkled over the body by Olcott and at 8:27 a.m., the iron cradle containing the body was placed in the retort.

By 10:45 a.m. the cremation had been pronounced completed, but the engineer in charge suggested that the fires burn a few hours longer to make sure the cremation was thoroughly complete. During the hours following the cremation being considered completed, public meetings and speeches were held in the town square where various individuals in religious, medical, and municipal fields spoke about cremation as burial reform.

When the cremated remains were finally removed from the cremation chamber, they were sprinkled with perfume and were placed in an inscribed antique vase with brass handles which was delivered to the offices of the Theosophical society. A few small apothecary vials of the cremated remains were given with permission from Olcott to members of the medical professions in attendance.

Image 1.9: DePalm Cremation. At 8:27 a.m. on December 6, 1876, Baron De Palm's body was placed in the preheated cremation chamber. This first cremation in a modern cremation chamber took more than 36 hours to complete. Coke was used as fuel and 50 bushels were consumed. The total process cost $7.04.
Image Source: Frank Leslie's Illustrated Newspaper in the Engler Cremation Collection.

The crematory at Washington, Pennsylvania, was used a mere 25 times before it announced it would no longer perform cremations for anyone outside of its own county. In total, the crematory was used 41 times before it shuttered in 1901. Notable persons cremated there included Mrs. Ben Pittman, wife of noted stenographic creator Benn Pitman, Dr. LeMoyne, founder of the crematory, and famed surgeon Dr. Samuel Gross. It was later deeded to the Washington County Historical Society, in whose care it remains to this day.

Cremation Expands

The LeMoyne Crematory remained the only crematory in the country for almost a decade when, in 1884, the Lancaster Cremation and Funeral Reform Association constructed their crematory in nearby Lancaster, Pennsylvania. Shortly after, in 1885, the earliest supporters of cremation in the U.S. organized the United States Cremation Company at Fresh Pond, Long Island, which remains the longest continuously operating crematory in the country. That same year, the sons of a physician in Buffalo, New York, opened a crematory in their father's memory.

In 1886, the first crematory operated in conjunction with an undertaking establishment was opened by Hudson Samson in Pittsburgh, Pennsylvania. The Cincinnati Cremation Company, Rosedale Cemetery Association in Los Angeles, and the Michigan Cremation Association in Detroit, founded by Dr. Hugo Erichsen, followed in 1887. The year 1888 saw the addition of two crematories, one at Philadelphia in Chelten Hills Cemetery and the other in St. Louis by the Missouri Crematory Association. In 1889, not only was a crematory built in the Loudon Park Cemetery in Baltimore, but one was also added to the Quarantine Hospital on Swinburne Island off the coast of New York.

The 1890s saw the addition of twelve more crematories and to the year 1900, 13,281 cremations had been performed in 25 crematories in the United States. The movement was off to a modest, yet impressive start.

Following this, cremation became an option for people in many major cities in the US, and the cremation rate continued to increase. By 1928, 109 crematories had been built in the U.S., and over 100,000 Cremations had been performed.

Architecturally Significant and Ceremonially Important

Very noteworthy in the early years of cremation is that the building constructed to house cremation apparatus were frequently built on a grand and beautiful scale. Among the first few dozen crematories in the U.S., only a small handful were the utilitarian structures which modern deathcare professionals are accustomed. In their architecture and construction, those at Washington and Lancaster, Pennsylvania, Pasadena, California, Swinburne Island, New York, and Middletown, Connecticut, were simplest. The remainder of these early structures could be counted as some of the most beautiful and aesthetically pleasing architectural gems in history.

Image 1.10: Gardner Earl Crematory Ext. The magnificent Gardner Earl Crematorium in Troy, New York. Gardner Earl was a strong supporter of the cremation movement, but ill health did not allow him to be able to see a crematorium completed in his area. He died at age 38 and was cremated at the Buffalo Crematory. In his memory, his parents had the most elaborate crematory building in America's history constructed in Oakwood Cemetery.
Image Source: Engler Cremation Collection.

Image 1.11: Gardner Earl Crematory Int. The committal room of the Gardner Earl Crematorium in Troy, New York, features hand-painted murals, stained glass, rich marbles, bronze and hardwoods, all to bring beauty and light to the cremation committal ceremony. The cremation chambers were discretely placed behind the bronze doors on the left wall. While Gardner Earl Crematorium is certainly the extreme, facilities at other early crematories were created in such a way as to bring ritual and ceremony to the rite of cremation.
Image Source: Engler Cremation Collection.

During the early years of cremation in the U.S., most of those who chose cremation for themselves or a loved one did so with the same regime of services as those who chose burial, so the facilities in which they conducted their services could be no less beautiful than those arranged for families choosing burial. Thus, most of the early crematories had beautiful chapels. Inlaid marble tile, frescoed walls, arched doorways, vaulted or domed ceilings, were normal features of these early facilities.

Image 1.12: Missouri Crematory Chapel. Many of the chapels in America's early crematories featured stained glass, inlaid mosaics, rich woods, and typically featured a dais or compartment where the casket was placed. This catafalque would hold the casket for the ceremony, which at a certain point would be lowered to the crematory room below or moved gently and noiselessly to an adjoining committal room.
Image Source: Engler Cremation Collection.

Cremation Societies and their Propaganda

To provide some sort of structure, cremation's earliest supporters often aligned themselves in Societies and Associations – which were fueled by the reformation of burial practices. Upon payment of their dues to their society or association, members were not only supporting the building of a crematory in their community, but they were also prepaying for their own cremation. Their membership also made them part of an important social group – meetings were often like those of other social and fraternal organizations – the only difference was that cremation was their theme.

Image 1.13: Louis Lange Fresh Pond Crematory. Many of the early followers of cremation looked at their movement like a religion, many complete with propaganda and literature, and some, like Fresh Pond Crematory in New York, complete with vestments for the crematory attendants. This image shows Louis Lange in the committal room at Fresh Pond just before a decedent is placed into the cremator.
Image Source: United States Cremation Company, Fresh Pond Crematory, Middle Village, New York.

A particularly important method for early cremationists to get their message out was by publishing what has since been referred to as propaganda. Cremation societies frequently published various booklets and pamphlets which featured reasoning for choosing cremation over burial, locations of the crematories in the US, opinions of notable persons who supported the movement, and photos of the "crematory vaults" and urn selections. A cremation society in France created propaganda that included photos of bodies in various states of decomposition after burial. Many US crematories circulated this same literature, theirs showing the gruesome images along with photos of their beautiful crematories and columbaria on the facing page. Additionally, in the late 1800s, three societies published magazines for their members – *The Urn* (published by the U.S. Cremation Company in New York), *Modern Crematist* (by the Lancaster Cremation and Funeral Reform Association in Lancaster, Penn.), and *The Columbarium* (by the Philadelphia Cremation Society), all of which ceased publication by the end of the century.

Poets and modern thinkers of the day often added their notes of support as well. For instance, the poet Arlo Bates lent his support of cremation when he wrote:

*"Let me not linger in the tainted earth,
to fester in corruption's shroud of shame,
But soar at once, as through a glorious birth
clad in a spotless robe of cleansing flame.*

*"Then wrap about my frame a robe of fire
and let it rise as incense censer swung;
until in ether pure, it may aspire
to greet the stars along the azure flung.*

*"And let me rise into a filmy cloud
and touch with gold the amber sunset sky;
or veiled in mist the driving storm enshroud
both land and tossing main – as on I fly."*

Women's suffrage supporter Frances Willard was also an ardent supporter of cremation. She stated: "I choose the luminous path of light rather than the dark slow road of the valley of the shadow of death. Holding these opinions, I have the purpose to help forward progressive movements even in my latest hours, and hence hereby decree that the earthly mantle which I shall drop ere long – shall be swiftly enfolded in flames and rendered powerless to harmfully effect the health of the living."

The Cremation Association of North America

Early on, cremationists and cemeteries who conducted cremations often struggled due to a lack of some sort of guidance and direction. There was no infrastructure or national organization to give this direction as there was in Europe where many of the crematories were operated by state and local municipalities.

Dr. Hugo Erichsen, a physician in Detroit, Michigan, and founder of the cremation society there, changed that when, in early 1913, he issued an invitation to all American cremation groups to join and form a society with a national scope. He was successful in bringing 14 delegates of the 50 or so crematories in operation together under one roof and the Cremation Association of America was born.

Image 1.14: CAA 1913 Attendees. Attendees of the meeting where the Cremation Association of America was formed in Detroit, Michigan, 1913. Dr. Erichsen is in the second from the back row, second from the right. The Cremation Association would later become CANA, which is now the undisputed source for cremation education, statistics, and information.
Image Source: Cincinnati Cremation Company Historic Collection.

While Dr. Erichsen's initial goal was burial reform, and for the first several years his focus was realized, the Cremation Association quickly developed into meetings of the businessmen who performed cremations in their communities – largely because the reform societies which built many of the early crematories in the country were taken over by them. The Association still thrives today and is unequivocally the source for cremation education, statistics, and information. The name was changed in 1975 to the Cremation Association of North America to reflect member involvement from crematories across the continent.

Image 1.15: CAA 1916 Convention Exhibit. A 1916 exhibit for the annual convention of the Cremation Association of America featured a public display of the crematories in various parts of the US, and throughout the world, along with urns from various manufacturers.
Image Source: Cincinnati Cremation Company Historic Collection.

Cremation in Transition

The modern Cremation movement in America sprang from a sanitary necessity; but over time the embalming process evolved into more common practice. This disinfection of the body, along with the advent of medicine into everyday life, the need for cremation as a means of purification after death dwindled. With sanitary concerns negated, the primary argument in favor of cremation was invalidated. New reasons to choose fire over earth needed to be enumerated, and with them, a new era in the history of cremation in America began… an era where cremation would be promoted for aesthetic reasons, and with the birth of this "memorial idea" the principles of the cremationist were strengthened.

• • •

Part II: Memorialization – Establishing the Urn Memorial

It would be impossible to pinpoint a single reason that the rite of cremation gained any acceptance during its early years in America. It was not a popular option, and tradition ruled out many areas having crematories. Many of the early crematories were built on a grand and beautiful scale, and this could have had its effect on the minds of the public. However, one could easily, after only slight research, attribute cremation's growth to an idea that gripped all areas of deathcare: the "Memorial Idea."

The memorial idea was started in cemeteries – the establishment of a memorial identity for each person who lived and died was the most important part of the rite of passage called death. Cremationists quickly adopted the idea to include cremation, and the obstacles they faced were harder to overcome than their cemeterian counterparts.

A strong cast of characters was necessary to put the idea into practice, and the crematories of the country included some of the most ardent and unique characters that could be found, some of the most notable of which were Lawrence Moore (President of the California Crematorium in Oakland which later became the famous Chapel of the Chimes), Clifford Zell (Owner of the Valhalla Chapel of Memories in St. Louis), and Herbert Hargrave (Chapel of the Light, Fresno, California) to name a few.

Clifford Zell, Sr., owner of the Valhalla Chapel of Memories in St. Louis, was the originator of the slogan of the Cremation Association of North America, a variation of which is still the mantra of our association today. It was during the 1933 convention that Clifford Zell made the statement: "There is one thought I hope that I can impress most deeply on all crematory men – cremation is not the end – cremation alone is not complete but is only an intermediate step towards the permanent preservation of the cremated remains."

The memorial idea included several tenets: No cremation was complete without inurnment, which always included ALL the following:

A. A memorial urn of imperishable material
B. The engraving of the memorial urn
C. The permanent placement of the memorial urn

A memorial urn of imperishable material:

Cremation urns have been utilized in one form or fashion since the dawn of civilization. Greeks placed their dead in urns of various materials – the legendary urn that held the cremated remains of Patroclus and Achilles was made of gold – but most were made of terra cotta. The Romans similarly placed their dead in urns of semi-precious stone and the urns were later deposited in columbaria.

After cremation's modern revival began, urns still were not uniform in size or composition. After Baron de Palm's cremation, his cremated remains were placed in an antique vase with brass handles and a brass nameplate. Prior to the turn of the century, urns were often made of pottery and some were imported porcelain. In New York, the US Cremation Company established the Art Urn Company, which offered various domestically made metal urns along with imported serpentinite stone urns from the Kingdom of Saxony, now a state in eastern Germany, and onyx and porcelain urns from other European countries. In the early 1900s, urns of various metals, including copper and tin, were frequently used, commonly made by companies that also manufactured household items – and by the 1920s, bronze urns became the norm.

Fires of Change: Beauty & Light: A History of Cremation in America

Because bronze is a semi-precious metal and cast bronze will only patina with age and will not degrade over time, it made the perfect medium to create permanent, imperishable memorials. Several companies, over time, created urns of various shapes and sizes – but most had a decorative look to them – for most were placed on display in glass fronted niches.

During this time, the urn memorial was so important to cremationists that their logos, icons, informational pamphlets, and stationery often contained illustrations of an urn. During the same period the logo of the Cremation Association was an image of an urn in a niche.

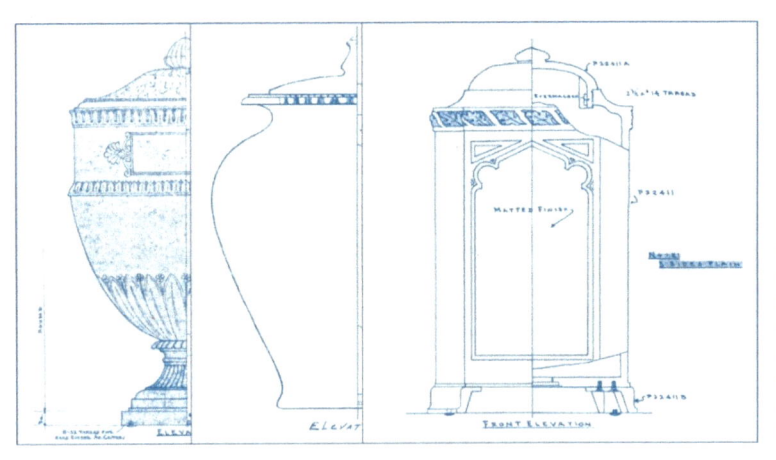

Image 1.16: Gorham Blueprints. Most urns of the era varied in their shape depending on where in the country they were placed. The Grecian shape with squared handles was one of the most prominent on the east coast, along with the footed chalice shape. Gorham Bronze, based in New York at the time, made an entire line of urns based on ancient vases found in various places in the world.
Image Source: Stephen Izzi, East Warwick, Road Island.

Image 1.17: Library of Golden Memories. On the west coast where the columbarium was most common, Oregon Brass Works, based in Portland, Oregon, debuted the book-shaped urn in the 1920s. It soon became one of the most popular styles and was instrumental in creating a common columbarium style known as the Library of Memories. This idea came to its zenith in the Library of Golden Memories Columbarium in Inglewood Park Cemetery near Los Angeles, where the rich dark granite resembled a fine library, and groupings of book urns in lighted niches gave the impression of a library.
Image Source: National Cremation Magazine, 1965. Engler Cremation Collection.

Fires of Change: Beauty & Light: A History of Cremation in America

Image 1.18: Image 1.18 Meierjohan-Wengler Urns. Meierjohan-Wengler (shown) and Michaels Art Bronze Company, both based in the Cincinnati, Ohio, area, created standard decorative urns, but also had an assortment of simpler vase and rectangle shapes that became popular in the midwestern states.
Image Source: Engler Cremation Collection.

Image 1.19: Jos. A. Mayer Urns. In the Pacific northwest, where simplicity was the precedent in cremation, much simpler containers were used. Joseph A Mayer Co. (shown), a well-known Seattle clockmaker, and Zappfe Silversmiths, manufacturer of fine serving ware, both also had popular urn lines in copper and bronze.
Image Source: Engler Cremation

Image 1.20: Hillside Chapel Hall of Peace. Interestingly, there were only a few times in history that the bronze urn rule was lifted for urn memorials in columbaria. The major exception was during World War II when brass and bronze were rationed due to their use for munitions. In their place, many cremationists had to get creative and other materials were used to make urns, including Bakelite (a heavy plastic) and ceramic. Most notably, the famous Rookwood Pottery in Cincinnati created a line of ceramic urns that were purchased by several crematories. A significant collection of this rare pottery is in the Hall of Peace columbarium of the Cincinnati Cremation Company, shown here.
Photo by Jason Engler, January, 2020.

The Engraving of the Memorial Urn

One of the major points of the memorial idea focused on establishing a memorial identity for the deceased and this was primarily done when their name was engraved, etched, or cast as part of a permanent memorial.

For cremationists, when a bronze urn was marked indelibly with a person's name and dates of birth and death, the urn became the memorial identity. The Oakland Chapel of Memories in Oakland, California, put it this way in their booklet *Cremation & Inurnment,* "These memorials are the unwritten biography of the lives of those whose earthly remains are here enshrined. In tangible form they preserve the records of lives engraved deeply in the hearts and memories of those who held them most dear."

The Permanent Placement of the Memorial Urn

It was the view of cremationists during the "Memorial Idea" period of cremation's history that every person who dies should have a permanent resting place. Just as the ancients inscribed names on the urns of their departed ones, the ancient Greeks erected Tumuli in memory of their dead, just as the Egyptians erected the pyramids, the Romans inurned in columbaria, Kings and Queens are entombed in Westminster Abbey, so the placement of the urn became the permanent memorial that cremationists required. This was the utmost concern of the cremationists who were active in the Cremation Association. The inurnment of cremated remains was not always a priority for cremationists but became their sole purpose and plight beginning in the late 1920s.

Scattering cremated remains, permanent destruction of cremated remains, and home retention of cremated remains were all in direct conflict with the memorial idea.

This impetus for inurnment resulted in some very beautiful memorials in the columbaria throughout the US.

Image 1.21: California Columbarium. The earliest section of niches in the California Crematorium's Columbarium were completed in the 1910s. The unmistakable California architecture and style would go on to become one of the larges columbaria in the country – the Oakland Chapel of the Chimes.
Image Source: Engler Cremation Collection

Fires of Change: Beauty & Light: A History of Cremation in America

Image 1.22: Odd Fellows Columbarium SF. Perhaps the most masterfully constructed columbarium in the country was the second freestanding structure for the purpose built by the Odd Fellows in San Francisco in 1897. This columbarium, with its neoclassical design, resembled an ancient temple and was complete with stained glass, rich mouldings, and niches of copper and bronze. It is one of only two places of rest left in the city of San Francisco after the city passed an ordinance moving all other cemeteries to nearby Colma.
Image Source: Engler Cremation Collection.

Image1.23: Fresh Pond Columbarium. Fresh Pond Crematory, one of the nation's first crematories, completed their columbarium and chapel in 1893. This section of the columbarium was constructed for a New York German singing group.
Image Source: United States Cremation Company, Fresh Pond Crematory, Middle Village, NY.

Standardizing Crematory and Columbarium Practices

The conventions of the Cremation Association were breeding grounds for ideas in furthering the memorial idea to those who chose cremation. Lawrence Moore was the long-time president and operator of the Chapel of the Chimes in California and was the most adamant cremationist of his time. He was the most

Image 1.24: Washelli Columbarium. On the west coast, where the columbarium truly came into its own, columbaria were places of beauty and light. The Washelli Columbarium in the 1930s was complete with comfortable seating, songbirds, and stained glass, all surrounded by urn memorials.
Image Source: Evergreen-Washelli Columbarium, Seattle, Washington.

instrumental character in the cremation world and held the accomplishment of coining the word "inurnment." Additionally, he invented the first electric-powered cremator, and a unique metallic disc used in every cremation to identify cremated remains. He also was the first to suggest using a cardboard temporary urn to encourage the selection of a permanent urn. His facility, the California Crematorium (now known as Chapel of the Chimes) in Oakland, California, is inarguably the most successful crematory and columbarium in the country. From 1911 to 1934, the California Crematorium had conducted 23,732 cremations, 53% of which were placed in bronze urns and inurned in the columbarium.

Throughout the meetings of the Cremation Association, there were frequently discussions of standardizing the practices of the crematories across the country. Many ideas were exchanged on how this could be affected to encompass the cremation customs from the east coast to the west coast and the mix of both in the Midwest. A committee was formed led by Herbert Hargrave and, after much research, in 1941 the Manual of Standard Crematory and Columbarium Practices, originally published by the Interment Association of Northern California, was adopted. This manual was considered the textbook of operations for the modern crematory and columbarium and was the catechism by which cremationists proclaimed the memorial idea.

Throughout the manual, sections dealt with all aspects of operating a crematory and columbarium, but the sections that discussed the handling of cremated remains and the permanent placement of memorial urns were the most doctrinal in nature.

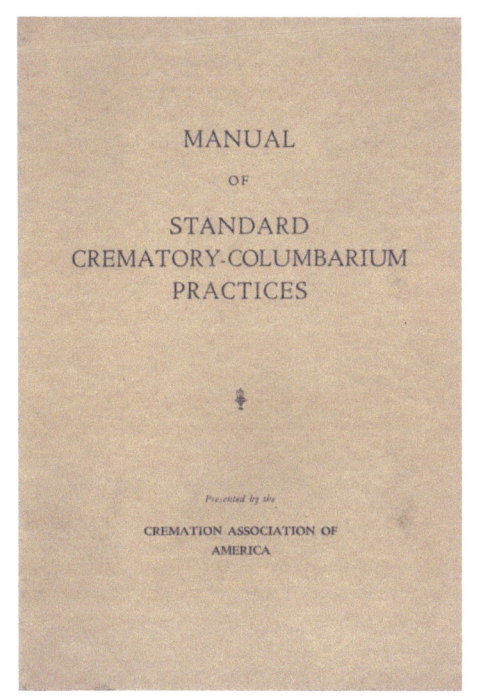

Image 1.25: Manual Standard Crematory-Columbarium Practices. The Cremation Association's first Manual of Standard Crematory-Columbarium Practices was published by the Association in 1941 and became the textbook of operations and the catechism of the memorial idea.
Image Source: Manual of Standard Crematory-Columbarium Practices, Engler Cremation Collection.

The Manual of Standard Crematory and Columbarium made its instruction clear in various sections:

"Never Crush or Grind Cremated Remains:

This is very important. We have no right to crush, grind or pulverize human bone fragments. They should be placed in the temporary container or urn, just as they were removed from the cremation vault… To do otherwise encourages desecration, gives an impression of valueless ash, and will eventually destroy the memorial idea. There is usually sentiment for the cremated remains of a loved one, but it frequently disappears when desecrated. All crematories should adopt this same policy, so the practices are the same everywhere."

This was further supported by the suggestion for reverent handling of the cremated remains:

"Cremated Remains Should be Carefully Prepared and Handled Reverently

Cremated remains are human remains and are deserving of careful and reverent handling. The attitude of the individual toward cremation is oft-times represented by the way he handles cremated remains, and the attitude of the crematory-columbarium is expressed by the way remains are prepared and handled by its employees... How can we expect a family or interested party to recognize the fact that cremated remains are human remains and are deserving of proper memorialization if, as crematory-columbarium operators we fail to express by action as well as by word and thought that the remains are sacred?"

Image 1.26: Unprocessed Cremated Remains. During the memorial idea era of cremation's history, most cremationists refused to pulverize, crush or grind cremated remains to reduce their consistency. Their reasoning was to further the need for a permanent urn and to aide in the prevention of scattering. It was the belief that the reduction of the remains to the finer consistency was a desecration to the remains and gave the impression of valueless ash.
Image Source: Cincinnati Cremation Company Historic Collection.

The admonition regarding scattering was perhaps the most doctrinal statement of the entire manual, and carried with it the most important ideal for the cremationist's purpose:

"*Never Scatter Cremated Remains.*

Cremated remains are not a powdery substance, but the human bone fragments of a loved one. They will not blow away... but will remain where strewn...

A request to scatter is frequently made with the supposition that it is the kindly thing, least expensive and least trouble for those remaining. In fact it is usually the most difficult and unkindly request that could be made. Certainly the deceased would not have requested it had they realized the possible heartaches that it would cause. There is comfort in being able to place a flower, on occasion, at the last resting place. Scattering makes this impossible. [There will be] no tangible memory where a flower may be placed in memory. When cremated remains are once destroyed, regrets cannot return them..."

The Memorial Idea period of cremation's history reads like heavy cremationist doctrine, but the cremationists were quite successful in their endeavors. This time frame in cremation's history in America caused some of the most beautiful cremation memorials imaginable to be created, and they remain beautiful to this day.

It is unquestionable that this period also revealed the heart of the cremationist in every way. It took cremation from the hands of reform societies and placed it in the care of businesses which brought the idea to life. By the 1960s and 1970s however, a new idea in cremation began to take shape. The face of cremation was about to change drastically.

• • •

Part III: **Simplification** – Cremation Transformation

As we trace the history of cremation in America for this chapter, it becomes clear that cremation now is not what cremation was in its early years. As time has evolved, so have the attitudes of consumers. This is evident in all aspects and all areas of the human life – including burial practices: change is imminent and forthcoming.

The period from the 1960s to the current day has been characterized by remarkably fast and furious change. The cremation movement has exploded with growth, especially when compared to the statistics of the previous periods discussed. An entire book could be written on the sociological impact of this change and growth, and an equal amount could be written on the effect that these rapid changes in the cremation movement have had on the funeral and cemetery professions.

Cremation's transformation began in the 1960s. Urged by many factors, this change was decidedly due to a movement of simplicity. It was in 1963 that Jessica Mitford wrote her satirical expose "The American Way of Death" – lambasting the funeral and memorialization professions. On the surface, it was primarily funeral homes that were under attack by her opinion – but all aspects of the allied funeral and memorial professions were at risk – and none were excluded from her sarcasm.

Propelled by the excitement that her book spawned, memorial societies who advocated simple direct cremation began doing business in states and cities where cremation had become popular, and these were easy avenues for those preferring minimal services.

By the late 1970s the memorial idea began to lose hold on cremation, and as it did, the cremationists did everything possible to maintain the integrity of what they viewed was the right course: the permanent memorialization of cremated remains.

The simplification process that cremation underwent was underscored by the general public's idea of death care practices. However, this movement not only affected the memorialization side of cremation – all areas of practice and procedure were affected.

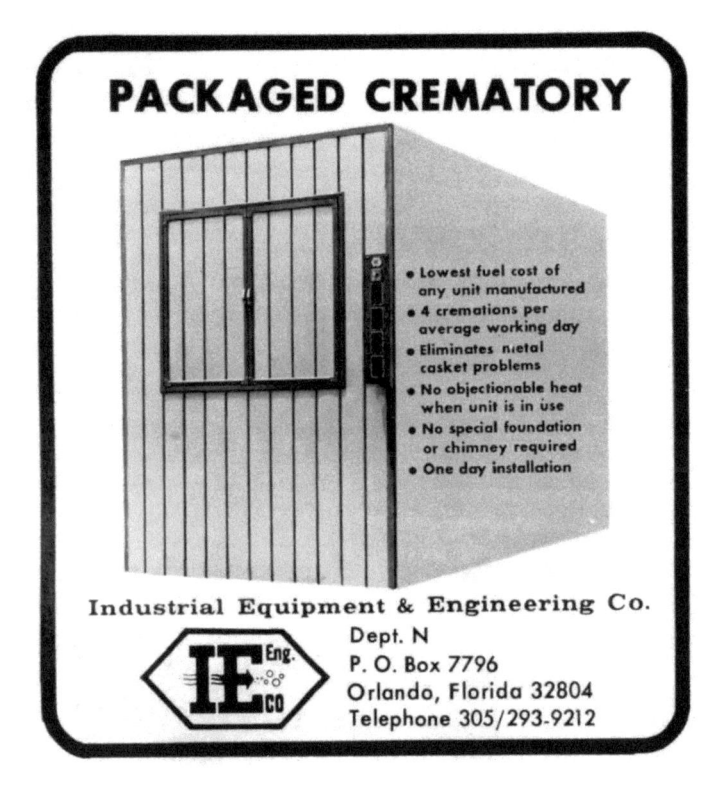

Image1.27: IEE Autumn 1968. Cremators, like this popular model from Industrial Equipment and Engineering, were no longer constructed on-site in crematories, but were made to be shipped and delivered like any other type of machinery. This cremator model has changed much over the years in appearance and operation but was the predecessor to what is now known as the Power Pak from Matthews Cremation. *Image Source: National Cremation Magazine, 1968, Engler Cremation Collection.*

Most of the early crematory buildings in the US were constructed from the ground up – including their cremation apparatus, which were often constructed onsite as part of the building structure. In the simplification period of cremation's history, cremators became equipment and were instead manufactured to ship to different locations. The simplification of purchasing, installing, and operating cremation equipment was facilitated by various companies that built it offsite and shipped it to be installed in simpler structures.

While early crematories were often placed in dignified surroundings adjoining chapels or cemetery structures, likewise during this era of cremation's history, the industrialization of the architecture of the crematory became common as well. As families distanced themselves from the process of cremation, cremation chambers were moved from chapels to garages and metal buildings.

During the transformation, the scattering of cremated remains became more and more popular. Crematories installed "cremulators" and processors to reduce the consistency of the cremated remains to facilitate scattering. Did scattering encourage processing or, as was the fear of Lawrence Moore in the Memorial Idea period, did processing encourage scattering? The answer is unknown – however the two went together during this time.

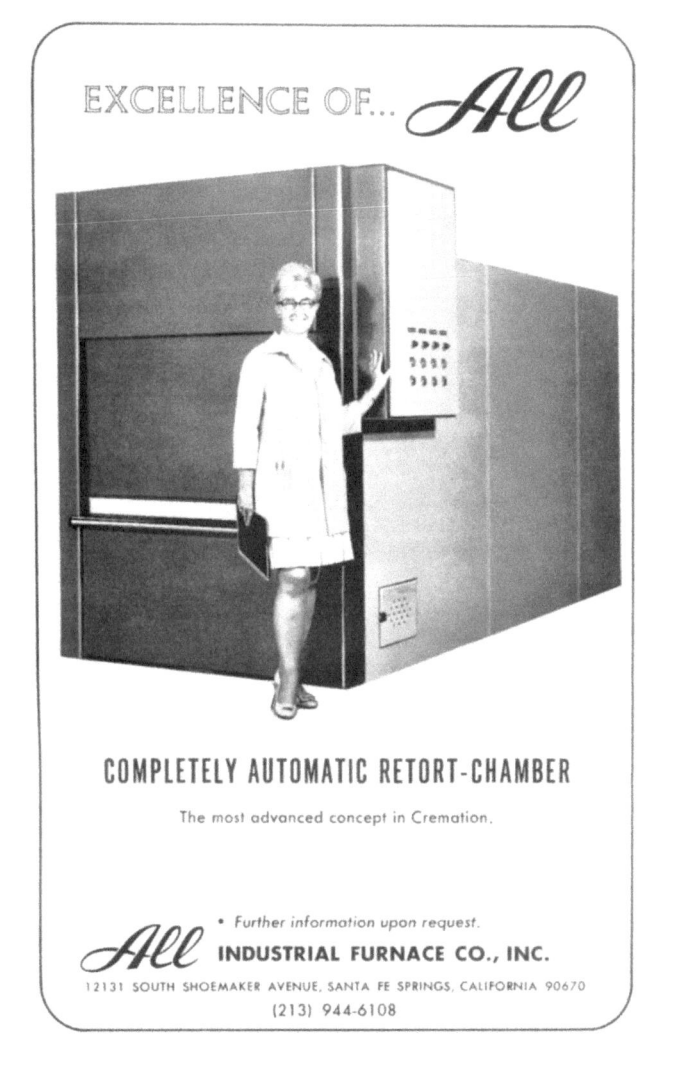

Image 1.28: ALL Crematory Summer 1974. This ad for ALL Crematory's deliverable "completely automatic retort chamber" shows that company's approach to a modern cremator.
Image Source: National Cremation Magazine, 1974, Engler Cremation Collection.

With the focus of cremation changing from memorialization to cost-conscious simplicity, the cremation memorial and urn industry changed as well. Columbarium niches went from being constructed on-site to becoming preconstructed banks of niches, shipped on a truck to be installed at the memorial property. Additionally, they became simpler in their design and were often sold from manufacturers with an assortment of urns to utilize simplicity in encouraging families to purchase a permanent memorial following cremation.

Most urns sold during the memorial idea were constructed of cast bronze. But as the trend turned toward simplicity, spun bronze, aluminum, cultured marble, and wood became popular options. Urn manufacturing in the US changed dramatically from a dozen manufacturers to dozens of manufacturers beginning in the 1970s. By the mid-1990s, cremation urns were available in a myriad of materials and from every corner of the world.

Fires of Change: Beauty & Light: A History of Cremation in America

Image 1.29: Matthews Niches 1984. To aid in selling cremation memorials, namely columbarium niches, manufacturers often sold columbarium units with a pre-selected assortment of urns to make the selection simpler for families, removing as many obstacles as possible to maintain the memorial idea.
Image Source: The Cremationist of North America Magazine, 1984, Engler Cremation Collection.

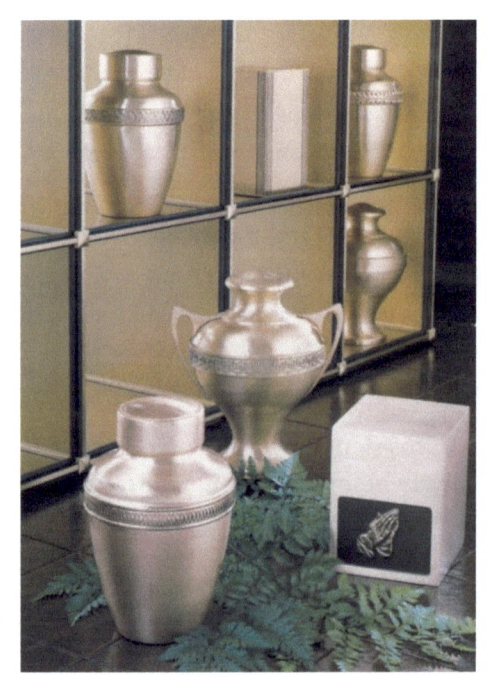

Image 1.30: Matthews Urns Ad 1982. The text part of this ad for Matthews called these urns "income producers" due to their simple sheet and spun bronze construction, low cost, and high visibility.
Image Source: The Cremationist of North America Magazine, 1982, Engler Cremation Collection.

Conclusion: Personalization – Cremation as a Personal Preference

Honoring the wishes of those who choose cremation has always been a prevalent desire since cremation's modern revival in the US. However, never has that wish been as personal as it is now.

Since ancient times and into the early part of cremation's modern revival, cremation was looked upon as a sacred rite in and of itself. While that is still the case for many of the world's religions, cremation has moreover become a means to a sacred rite. It seems that in the mind of families who choose cremation now, the disposition of the body is the least important aspect of the funeral and cremation process. Rather, it is the multitude of options that are available to them for the cremated remains. From personalized urns to keepsakes, gemstones to space travel, cremated remains have become more popular than ever.

Services, too, have become much more personalized, with celebrants, catering, personal music, and the list goes on, families now can choose what is meaningful to them almost to the limits of their imagination.

This ability for families to make the cremation movement their own now gives funeral professionals an unprecedented opportunity to use their imagination as well to create meaningful services. With that in mind, the future is ours if we will own it.

So much can be learned from the history of cremation in America. Maintaining respect for the dignified handling of remains before and after cremation, honoring the wishes of families who choose cremation, and helping those families create the most meaningful memory imaginable is what will allow our profession to thrive into the future. All those facets have been important for cremationists since cremation's modern revival in 1874 – with each era having its own approach to each. Now it is the future and an opportunity unlike any before presents itself to us as professionals. How will you respond?

Chapter 2 – Preparation of remains

Identification (importance of viewing) - Dignified and respectful preparation of deceased for identification

Chapter Learning Objectives

Upon completion of the study of this chapter students should:

- Understand Importance of viewing human remains.
- Be able to identify the relationship between a dignified and respectful presentation and identification viewing.
- Understand the importance of positive identification prior to cremation and how to achieve such identification.
- Be able to articulate the specific process associated with the identification viewing.
- Understand the importance of adhering to all local, state and federal Laws.
- Be able to demonstrate the importance of determining specific items to be removed from the cremation container prior to the cremation.
- Be able to express the relationship between viewing and the authority of the authorizing agent.
- Understand indemnification and liability with respect to inaccurate information provided by the authorizing agent.

• • •

Introduction

Cremation is an irreversible act. The enormity and finality of this one fact should be enough to guide all providers of cremation services to adhere to a strict code of body identification through viewing. Once a loved one has been placed in the cremation chamber, and the introduction of direct flames has begun the process of reducing the body to inorganic bone fragments, there is no opportunity for disinterment (such as the case when the wrong body has been interred) or reversing course once it is realized that wrong body has been cremated; it is simply too late. Yet, despite what is known about the irreversibility of cremation, and the related detrimental effects to professional reputation and the inevitable legal implications with negative publicity to follow, cases involving negligent cremation due to misidentification continue to occur.

Consider this: how you will start the conversation with the client family, with whom you have developed a close working relationship, to explain that the cremated remains in the urn you delivered to them are not those of their loved one? And this is only the beginning of the unpleasant conversations you will face in the coming days and months.

The preparation of the body for cremation is always directed by the authorizing agent(s) or their designee in writing. Directives which include cremation as a mode of disposition may include the complexity of embalming and advanced restorative treatment in order to facilitate a formal extended period of viewing/visitation, to the minimal accoutrements involved with the more informal nature of the identification viewing. It is important to note that the term "informal" should not influence our attention as funeral professionals to treat such an occasion as a casual event. This is especially true in an age where a prevalence of online cremation companies market their services as: "simple", "easy" and/or "quick." In every instance and as a general rule, the funeral professional should apply the following considerations to every human remains received at his/her facility:

1. Cause no harm, and always treat the deceased as if they were a member of your own family.
2. Consider all cases will be viewed by the family (the only exceptions being cases of advanced decomposition or trauma so advanced that viewing becomes impossible).

It is not uncommon for the funeral director to visit with the family during time of removal and hear the following response: "we want to remember our mother as she was when she was healthy. She suffered enough over the past weeks in the hospital and we all agree that we have no interest in viewing her at the funeral home." Just as universal precautions demand our attention with every deceased individual with whom we are required to have contact, funeral professionals must apply the same universal consideration and assume viewing, even through a photograph, will occur in every instance. Such a supposition will guide our preparation of the deceased when we return to the facility.

No matter what type of service is selected by the client family involving cremation as the mode of disposition, the embalming case report (see sample form 2.1) should always be utilized as standard practice for each deceased individual received into the funeral home facility. It is important to mention that with the prevalence of third-party crematory operators, best practices stipulate returning to the funeral facility immediately following removal from the place of death instead of immediately heading to the crematory. Although the third-party facility may have available refrigeration space and have the appeal of saving valuable resources, maintaining the chain of actual physical custody reigns. Most funeral professionals are familiar with the case report, as this document has been commonly used for decades in funeral facilities to record body conditions as related to the process of embalming. When minimal services (specifically in those instances when embalming has been declined) have been selected by the client family, it is still imperative to have a record of: body conditions upon arrival to the facility, attached or accompanying medical devices/prostheses and personal effects, treatments performed, and dates and times of all significant events/actions.

In his article on avoiding cremation liability, Harvey I. Lapin utilized the lessons learned from the heinous crimes committed at the Tri-State crematory. Lapin (2005) recommended employers "remind employees of their duty to handle the remains of customers' loved ones in a dignified and respectful manner." It is intriguing that we seem to have arrived at a point in funeral service where we need a reminder of that which is the foundation of fundamental practice – exemplify dignity and respect to all we encounter in the course of our duties at all times. Could it be that there is less importance placed on the treatment of the deceased for whose families select cremation? When sensational news stories and lawsuits detail instances of less-than-professional behavior at times, it may indeed be time to reiterate Lapin's advice. Preparation of the body for an identification viewing should not constitute an afterthought and instead must involve careful preparation and execution.

The verification of identification of the deceased is a continuum that begins at the place of death and ends when authorized family members receive the container holding the cremated remains of their loved one, or with final disposition. While our focus is naturally centered on the experience of the authorizing agent(s) verification of the identity of their loved one prior to cremation, Jim Starks (2014) suggested the following 10-point identification and verification procedure which details the chain of custody:

1. Verification of identity at the place of death.
2. Family identification at the funeral home.
3. Verification before leaving the funeral home to go to the crematory.
4. Verification upon delivery to the crematory.
5. Verification before placement in the cremation chamber.
6. Verification at the beginning of the clean out of the cremation chamber.
7. Verification at the start of processing.
8. Verification before the cremated human remains are placed in the urn/container.
9. Verification when the urn/container is given to the funeral home.
10. Verification before the urn/container is given to the family.

For those who utilize an off-premises, third-party crematory, steps 5 through 8 will require strict due diligence prior to and during the time cremation services are contracted as physical custody of the deceased has been transferred to the crematory. Due diligence necessitates the funeral director ensure all verification methods are strictly enforced by the crematory at all times. A well-documented (and attorney approved) due diligence assessment should be conducted before contracting with any third-party cremation provider. A key provision of the due diligence process is on-going unannounced visits to the off-premises crematory by licensed personnel. Documentation of such unannounced visits should exist which would include, at a minimum, a brief synopsis of findings. Any findings contrary to expectations should be addressed immediately.

Viewing Prior to Cremation Itself: Positive Identification of the Deceased and Documentation Prior to Cremation

Identification of the deceased by the authorizing agent(s) or their designated representative in writing is paramount when arranging a cremation. There are no exceptions (and in many states it is the law). The entire scope of identification procedures should be explained in complete and full detail, including the requirement that this must be done prior to the actual cremation (although this detail – viewing prior to the act of cremation- seems obvious to the professional arranger, client families are generally novices to the procedure). This aspect of the process should be explained to the family early in arrangement discussions with particular emphasis on the necessity of viewing their loved one in order to provide positive identification. And as with everything encountered in the cremation arrangement relationship, documentation is key.

Questions from the authorizing agent(s) regarding the entire process of identification and cremation itself should be encouraged. As with all aspects of the arrangement conference, there should never be a time when those with the authority to make arrangements are unclear and present signs of uncertainty as to what was just explained by the funeral service professional. It is the responsibility of the funeral arranger to be well-versed in every aspect of each document he/she requests a family to read and sign. Perhaps the most certain sign that later problems will occur is when we, as funeral professionals, [assume or] make assumptions that the client family understands our instructions without specifically seeking clarity.
For obvious reasons, identification of the deceased prior to cremation becomes less of an issue when embalming and/or a formal visitation has been selected by the client family. Our focus at this point is on the client family who has selected cremation without any type of viewing of their loved one.

Arrangements that are made exclusively online or at a distance serve to further complicate the process and require alternative avenues to achieve positive identification. The best advice when handling a service where minimal exposure exists between the deceased and the authorizing agent(s) is to realize beforehand that these types of experiences maximize the risk of mistakes on the part of the funeral provider. A plethora of legal documents germane to cremation are presented in the next chapter of this book. It is critical to distinguish those that are commonly signed prior to the commencement of cremation.

Identification Viewing – The Process

Identification viewing, much like a formal viewing, is an event in the life of a family that will provide a lifelong memory. Therefore, the experience should entail the highest dignity that resources and professional experience allow. To begin, identification viewing involves the authorizing agent(s) or designee physically viewing the decedent for the purpose of establishing proper identity prior to cremation. Typically, this is a purposeful time limited event, informal in nature and usually restricted to those confirming the identity. This event should not be relegated to an area of a facility not normally used for formal viewing. Additionally, it is good practice to utilize the cremation container selected by the family for the viewing. During the arrangement process it is important to explain the identification process to families so they can feel comfortable with their selection. Furthermore, the practice of identifying remains in the container selected may assist in reducing the risk of errors associated with wrongful cremation. It is imperative that funeral professionals exercise and demonstrate dignity and respect to all client families. To reiterate, there should be no difference in the treatment of cremation and non-cremation families with respect to the presentation of remains.

There will be an occasion when the funeral professional will be dealing with an out-of-town client family or a local family who chooses to complete arrangements without physically entering the funeral establishment, this reality was highlighted during the COVID-19 year. The latter of which is becoming more common in the funeral service landscape. When such an occasion occurs, and only after authority has been verified, the arranging director may have to resort to identification of the deceased through a photograph (it should be noted that identification via photograph may be the preference of families who express a desire to not physically view their loved one). However, a photograph of the deceased should never be taken without first establishing everyone with the authority to make final arrangements and receiving their written permission to take and distribute the photograph. It is assumed that when working with authorizing agents at a distance, the photograph will be transmitted electronically in digital form. Prior to releasing and sending the photograph(s) through email, it is important to establish that all email addresses are proper and accurate. Imagine the unsuspecting recipient opening an email to find the photograph of a deceased person. This is not only embarrassing to the cremation service provider, but could also present a legal problem. Additionally, a company policy on maintaining privacy for photographs should be in place.

In some situations, the client family will refuse or decline to view their deceased loved one, either in-person or via a photograph, for identification purposes. The use of a waiver, a document signed by the authorizing agent(s) releasing the funeral provider of any and all instances arising from misidentification after giving up their right to view the body, may seem to be the right choice. While this initially appears to offer a foolproof and less invasive (and labor intensive) avenue to pursue, serious liability does exist for the arranger. If all authorizing agents have not agreed to and signed the waiver, then a full and complete waiver does not exist. Also, consider the ramifications of a misidentification, as there is always another family who's deceased loved one has been handled improperly. A waiver may not be considered a prudent or desired way to conduct business. In some instances, the provider of cremation services is within his/her rights to refuse service when a family will not identify their loved one in person or via photograph (and sign the requisite document verifying the correct identification has been established).

The spectrum of identification thus far has included the actual viewing of the decedent (either in-person or by way of a photograph), to the refusal or declination of viewing by the authorizing agent(s). It should be mentioned that a compromise does exist which puts the onus on the funeral professional for identification. In this occasion, the family would provide the funeral director with a recent photograph of the decedent in order to secure proper identification. Already the difficulty in fulfilling this request should be immediately realized. By the funeral professional taking the final responsibility for certifying the identity of the decedent with whom she/he did not know or have a relationship with previously, room for error exists. The age, quality and condition of the photograph provided by the family will vary. It is recommended that the authorizing agent(s) additionally provide physical characteristics of the decedent.

The following checklist may be used to assist achieving a dignified experience when identification viewing is selected:

- Have you identified those who possess the power to authorize cremation (sample form 3.2), or their designee? If a designee has been given the power to authorize cremation by the legal next of kin, is this in writing?
- Have you detailed all aspects of the cremation process (sample form 3.4) with the authorizing agent(s) and fully explained the expectations of the identification viewing (time limited, informal, etc.)?

- Has the authorization to cremate form (sample form 3.1) been signed?
- Have you discussed and documented items (personal effects, etc.) to be removed and returned to the family? Have you documented which items are to remain with the deceased and become part of the cremation process (sample form 3.5)? Additionally, have you notified the family that certain medical devices and/or implants may need to be removed? Has permission to remove and dispose of such devices been documented (sample form 3.3).
- Is the room designated for the identification viewing in suitable condition and located in an area where viewing of all types normally occurs?
- Has the deceased been washed, groomed and positioned in a way that would suit your family (and has the body condition been documented on the embalming case report)? Please see chapter three for an extensive explanation on minimal care guidelines when embalming has been declined (sample form 3.16).
- Has the family been fully informed of what to expect regarding the condition of the body?
- Has the deceased been placed in the casket or container selected by the family for viewing (recommended)?
- If the family has elected to make the identification by way of a photograph, do you have their written permission to take the photograph? Have you discussed with the family your company policy on privacy of photographs?
- Once viewing is complete, either by photograph or in-person, has the form verifying positive identification (sample form 3.9) been signed by the authorizing agent (s) or the designee in writing?
- Are you prepared to answer questions the family may have once viewing is complete?

Adherence to All State, Federal, & Local Laws

Client-families look to the funeral service professional for guidance and rightfully assume that the person guiding them through the arrangement conference is well versed in all areas of legality pertaining to cremation. This is also the position of regulatory bodies when it comes to enforcing adherence to laws and regulations related to cremation. As mentioned, specific elements and greater detail of various authorizations related to cremation may be found in chapter three (be aware that sample forms provided in this textbook provide for a general perspective, and that specific requirements of authorizations will vary by facility and location). However, it is important to begin the discussion recognizing the fact that many states and jurisdictions have a statutory requirement for identification of the deceased. According to the National Funeral Directors Association (NFDA), at least 37 states require identification of the deceased prior to cremation. One state, for example, requires:

> The funeral director or funeral establishment shall provide a signed written statement to a crematory establishment that the human remains delivered to the crematory establishment were positively identified as the deceased person listed on the cremation authorization form by the authorizing agent or a representative of the authorizing agent delegated [and that] an authorizing agent or the delegated representative of the agent may identify a deceased person in person or by photograph. The authorizing agent may waive the right of identification.

Some states have a statutory waiting period before cremation can be initiated. Many states also require a complete death certificate or official signed document (sometimes referred to as a cremation permit) prior to cremation. Certain states will not allow the cremation of unidentified human remains. At this point, the complexity of cremation, from a regulatory standpoint, should be evident. Continual education of funeral home and crematory staff is vital in making certain the pulse of change is recognized. Also, facilities should implement extensive training programs for new and existing staff to minimize potential violations.

On the federal level, the 1984 "Funeral Rule" under the jurisdiction of the Federal Trade Commission (FTC) requires specific mandatory disclosures and price itemizations pertaining to the components of the funeral be distributed to consumers. Cremation is specifically addressed in the rule and must be included on price lists of those who offer both funeral goods and services to consumers. The Occupational Safety and Health Administration (OSHA), a federal regulatory agency, is charged with protecting employees in the workplace. OSHA may require crematory employees to be trained to avoid potential exposure to bloodborne pathogens, as well as being introduced to other workplace safety measures as a means of preventing illness and injury while on the job. Locally, some jurisdictions may require special permits that ensure cremation facilities adhere to certain practices which do not have a negative environmental impact.

Family Wishes Regarding Items to be Removed Prior to Cremation

As with all aspects of the cremation arrangement process, it is incumbent on the funeral director to leave nothing to chance. Specificity and clarity must be present in every aspect of our communication with client families, including items to be removed prior to the cremation itself. As mentioned, the tremendous heat utilized in the process of cremation does not allow any error or room for chance on our part. The destruction of personal items attached to or upon the deceased is imminent once the cremation process is started after placing the deceased into the primary cremation chamber.

A process for identification and disposal of personal effects and other items attached to, or present with, the deceased must be implemented and utilized. The process should always begin with a complete inventory of any and all personal effects as noted on the embalming case report when the body is received into custody by funeral service personnel. These records begin the chain of custody and should be available for use during the arrangement conference, whereby the funeral director can address each specific item. Chapter Three presents the *Personal Property Statement and Receipt* form (sample form 3.5). This particular form specifically requires the listing of all personal property items to be removed and returned to the authorizing agent(s) prior to cremation. The form serves as a written receipt for items returned to the family. Additionally, this form provides written evidence for the return and/or disposal of personal items, and should be included in the arrangement file. In cases when no personal items are identified, it is still a prudent practice to have the family acknowledge this in writing.

Unique to the cremation case is the emphasis on mandatory removal of specific medical devices. Certain medical devices (pacemakers, defibrillators, prostheses, etc.) implanted within, or attached to the deceased, may jeopardize the safety of cremation equipment and personnel once exposed to extreme heat. Some devices or implants containing radioactive material may pose an additional environmental and safety hazard if released. These items may need to be removed prior to the body being placed in the cremation chamber or proper precautions must be taken to prevent possible radioactive contamination of crematory equipment, the operator, and family members. The funeral professional must have a frank conversation with the family regarding these devices or implants and be able to fully explain the following language, which is taken from sample form 3.3 *Disclosure and Authorization to Remove Medical, Mechanical, or Radioactive Devices*:

> Medical, mechanical, or radioactive devices implanted in the remains of the deceased (such as pacemakers, etc.) may create a hazard when placed into a cremation chamber. I hereby authorize the staff of the crematory, funeral home in charge or the agents or representatives of each to remove such device from the body of the deceased and to dispose of such devices as said persons may deem appropriate and in their sole discretion. No notice of such removal or disposition need be provided to me, the authorized agent. I/We hereby certify that the remains of the deceased _____DO_____ DO NOT contain any type of implanted medical, mechanical or radioactive device.

Inevitably, even when written authorization has been granted, the authorizing agent(s) many times will inquire about the destination of the medical, mechanical, or radioactive devices once they are removed. Be prepared to address this issue and fully disclose the final destination of devices that have been removed.

Relationship Between Viewing and Authority of Authorizing Agent

In some states there is little option when it comes to viewing the deceased in order to establish identity prior to cremation, as it may be required by statute. As recommended, the reliance of a waiver for those authorizing agents who refuse to view, or who consider this an undue hardship, is not good practice for those seeking to refrain from becoming party to a potential lawsuit. In cases where the party who is authorized to arrange the cremation refuses to view the deceased for confirmation of identity (even by way of a photograph), it is up to the discretion of the funeral director to suggest what some consider an apt compromise: encouraging the authorizing agent to deem someone with recent familiarity of the deceased to view. In lieu of the authorizing agent(s), a close friend, other family member or clergy, could accept the duty to view. If such a case presents itself, written permission should be granted by the authorizing agent. The event should be well documented with the funeral home indemnified and held harmless by the authorizing agent in writing.

One of the rights granted to the established authorizing agent is the power to control the funeral which includes who has the right to view the deceased. The authorizing agent(s) have the power to include and exclude others in almost all aspects of the funeral process. In instances when the authorizing agent(s) express(es) a desire to view or, more specifically, witness the actual cremation of their loved one, it is incumbent upon the funeral professional to explain what is entailed when witnessing the insertion of the decedent into the cremation chamber to begin the cremation process. The ability to clearly differentiate between viewing the decedent and witnessing the cremation may serve to help avoid confusion. While it is not uncommon for the family to view their loved one prior to witnessing the cremation, clarity of expectations is required. Included in this discussion is the possibility that the experience of witnessing may be considered rather unpleasant. Sample form 3.13 *Request to Witness a Cremation* should be utilized in instances when the family makes the final decision to participate in witnessing the cremation of their loved one. Of particular importance is the confirmation by the authorizing agent(s) that they were informed about the cremation process and understand this may be emotionally disturbing and difficult to witness.

Indemnification Relieving the Funeral Director from Liability for Inaccurate Information by the Authorizing Agent

Many funeral directors will confess to meeting many families for the first time as they walked through the front door. Occasions also exist when final arrangements are conducted, for various logistical reasons, completely at a distance. These instances do not provide the opportunity to meet the family in person, and instead all necessary tasks are completed via telephone, facsimile and/or e-mail. The point of sharing these realities is to create the very real scenario when funeral directors are relying on information provided by individuals with whom they have no prior connection. Are you able to rely on the information the family provides? Is the information complete? What steps do you take to truly verify the identity of the person on the other end of the telephone? Always remember that in many situations funeral providers rely wholly upon information provided by individuals they just met, sometimes not even in person.

Black's Law Dictionary defines indemnity as "a duty to make good any loss, damage, or liability incurred by another." Funeral service personnel must rely on the information provided by the authorizing agent(s). Funeral directors are not detectives trained to ensure that all of the information for which they rely upon is completely factual. Unfortunately, when a family has left out material details, the discovery of such omissions generally occurs after the cremation is complete. Chapter three includes numerous sample forms related to cremation, including sample form 3.12 *Certification and Indemnification*. A portion of the form contains the following language:

> I/We acknowledge that the funeral home/crematory is relying upon the representations and claims being made by the party claiming to be the authorized agent(s). I/We certify that all information contained in the Cremation Authorization and Disposition documents are truthful and no oversights of any material facts have been made.

> I/We agree to indemnify, release and hold the crematory, funeral home, their affiliates, agents, employees and assigns, harmless from any and all loss, damages, liability or causes of action in connection with the cremation and disposition of the cremated remains of the deceased, as authorized herein, or my/our failure to correctly identify the remains of the deceased, disclose the presence of any implanted mechanical, medical, or radioactive devices or any other item of personal property, or take possession of or make permanent arrangements for the disposition of such remains.

While documents signed by the authorizing agent do not guarantee the funeral director will stay out of the court system and avoid legal action, a properly executed document provides powerful recourse when the authorizing agent certifies the accuracy of statements made in the course of arranging for cremation and further realizes the funeral home will move to recoup any loss from damages suffered. Again, it is the responsibility of the funeral professional to fully explain all forms requiring the authorizing agent(s) signature(s).

Conclusion

Cremation itself, the reduction of the human body to bone fragments by direct flame, is not an overly complicated process to conceptualize. However, it should be very clear at this point that the complexity of cremation exists in the myriad of authorizations, explanations and ancillary matters that surround the process and allow it to commence. Only when cremated remains have been verified and returned to the legal authorizing agent(s) or released in another manner as authorized in writing can the funeral arranger consider the family served. The inherent liability attached to a process that is irreversible and ripe for human error should cause each of us to review cremation policies and procedures, and consider opportunities for continuous training in best practices. Being vigilant and adhering to a strict ethical code, which includes respect and dignity for the body and client families, will help to relieve the possibility of a sensational mistake that will inevitably tarnish reputations and result in a potential lawsuit.

Case Study

Your funeral home received the body of a deceased 79-year-old female. When meeting with the family, you develop a good working relationship with the adult children (authorizing agents) who have arranged for cremation with a memorial service to follow at the church where their mother had been a charter member. The family requests their mother's cremated remains be present for the service and has selected a lovely bronze urn as the centerpiece for the ceremony. The family is not interested in viewing their mother prior to cremation, instead insisting that everyone in the family would like to remember her as she was in life and not how she looked while in the hospital after a long illness. You are quite confident that you received the correct remains as you personally supervised the removal process. The hospital, where the deceased died, adheres to a strict policy of not allowing transfers to be made on patient floors. Instead, all transfers must be conducted in the basement morgue. Although you clearly communicated the need to have an informal identification viewing to ensure the family's peace of mind that you indeed have custody of their loved one, the family is reluctant and refuses. The adult daughter explains, "we were all there when mom died and your staff promptly picked up mom from the hospital. We don't understand why you would put us through the trauma of having to view our mom who is finally at peace." The family is adamant and pleads to not have to view their loved one. You are aware of the idea of a "waiver" and consider explaining to the family that they may not need to view if they sign the document releasing the funeral home from all liability if misidentification were to occur. You are certain the adult children (who possess the authority to cremate) would eagerly sign the document.

1. What course of action would you take in this instance? Specifically, detail the conversation you would have with the survivors.
2. What alternatives to identification viewing are available to this family?
3. What risks are involved when relying upon the use of a waiver?
4. Do you believe refusal of service is a viable last resort if the family declines all alternatives to confirm identification of their loved one?

Consider this...

Do you have the legal authorizing agent(s) signing required cremation documents? It is not always a clean-cut determination as estrangements, multiple marriages, multiple offspring and claims of priority may complicate matters. Consider placing the exact language from your states' right of disposition, or order of priority, directly on the authorization to cremate form. By doing this the family can see for themselves what is specified by law.

Fires of Change: Preparation of Remains

Sample Form 2.1 - Embalming Case Report

Date ____-____-____

Total Time Spent:_____

Permission To Embalm: Yes ☐ No ☐
Treatment to proceed on basis of:
____ signed authorization ____ oral authorization
____ statutory 3-hr attempt to secure   Name & location where embalming procedure was performed:_____
____ orders from _____   _____

Deceased _____ Mortuary _____
Age c._____ yrs. Race _____ Sex: ☐ male ☐ female Weight c._____ lbs. Height c._____ ft. _____ in.
Date of death _____ Time ____:____ am pm Time of removal ____:____ am pm Date:___-___-___

PRE-EMBALMING OBSERVATIONS

Operation before death?   ☐ No ☐ Yes Type/Area _____
Autopsy performed?   ☐ No ☐ Yes ☐ Complete ☐ Torso/Trunk ☐ Cranial ☐ Before embalming ☐ After embalming
                                       Viscera: ☐ Retained ☐ Received
Time between death and treatment: c._____ hrs. Time between receipt of remains and treatment: c._____ hrs.
Body: ☐ Warm   ☐ Cold ☐ Refrigerated: Duration c._____ hrs. ☐ Thawed/Out of Refrigeration c._____ hrs.
Rigor mortis: Yes_____ No_____
Abdominal distension: ☐ No ☐ Yes ☐ Slight ☐ Moderate ☐ Intense ☐ Liquid ☐ Gas
Purge before embalming: ☐ No ☐ Yes Type: _____
Edema: ☐ Abdomen ☐ Thorax ☐ R. Leg ☐ L. Leg ☐ R. Arm ☐ L. Arm ☐ Face Degree _____
Discolorations: ☐ Lividity ☐ Stain _____ in; _____
Lesions: _____
Comments: _____

EMBALMING PROCEDURE

Arteries Injected: **Veins Drained:**   **Disinfection:** (Check Appropriate Areas)
Cm. Carotid R-L ____ Iliac R-L ____ Internal Jugular R-L   Eyes _____ Other body orifices _____
Subclavian   R-L   Femoral   R-L   Axillary   R-L   Mouth _____ Nose _____
Axillary   R-L   Radial   R-L   ____ Iliac   R-L   Body orifices packed _____
Brachial   R-L   Dorsalis pedis R-L Femoral   R-L   Remains bathed with antiseptic soap _____
Others _____   Others _____
Condition of: Arteries: _____   Veins: _____

Injection:
pre-injection (co-injection)   1st ____ gal.   2nd ____ gal.   3rd ____ gal.
arterial concentrate _____ (%) or (Index) 1st ____ oz.   2nd ____ oz.   3rd ____ oz.
arterial concentrate _____ (%) or (Index) 1st ____ oz.   2nd ____ oz.   3rd ____ oz.
fluid modifier _____   1st ____ oz.   2nd ____ oz.   3rd ____ oz.
humectant _____   1st ____ oz.   2nd ____ oz.   3rd ____ oz.
other _____   1st ____ oz.   2nd ____ oz.   3rd ____ oz.

Injection Method: ☐ Continuous   ☐ Alternate
Drainage: ☐ Intermittent   ☐ Continuous
Quality of Drainage _____   Quality: ☐ Heavy clots ☐ Medium   ☐ Light   ☐ None
Cavity Treatment:
Cavity fluid _____ (%) Quantity used _____ oz.   Method: ☐ Gravity ☐ Motorized ☐ Delayed ☐ Immediate

Autopsied cases: ☐ Viscera immersed   ☐ Preservative powder used   ☐ Additional treatment: _____

Other: ☐ Direct ☐ Topical   ☐ Hypodermic Treatment(Check Appropriate Areas): ☐ Arms ☐ Torso ☐ Face ☐ Legs ☐ Neck
Distribution Exceptions _____
Additional Treatment _____

Condition of Body at Completion (include comments on conditions noted above) _____

Posing Features
Mouth Closure : ☐ Suture   ☐ Needle Injection   ☐ Natural   ☐ Dentures   ☐ Cotton   ☐ Other _____
Eye Closure   ☐ Cotton   ☐ Eye Caps   ☐ Natural   ☐ Other

Identification and Treatment Reference

Indicate on chart all identifying scars, incisions, lesions and special body characteristics. Description of items marked on chart:

1. _____
2. _____
3. _____
4. _____
5. _____
6. _____
7. _____
8. _____

Date and Time case report Completed: _____

Embalmer: _____ License No. _____

Student or Provisional Licensee: _____ Provisional License No._____

"Housekeeping" post-embalming checklist (re-aspirated, dressed, etc.)

Chapter 3 – Required Authorizations

Chapter Learning Objectives

Upon completion of the study of this chapter students should:

- Understand the importance of authorization forms in funeral service, and be able to explain various forms.
- Be able to articulate the importance of ascertaining the party that holds the right of disposition.
- Understand the importance of determining the authorizing agent.
- Recognize the importance of determining who holds the right of disposition.
- Be able to explain varies aspects of Power of Attorney and Durable Power of Attorney.
- Understand appropriate structure for authorization forms used in funeral service as well as specific elements that should be contained on the authorization to cremate form.
- Be able to illustrate familiarity with various authorization forms used in funeral service.

•••

Introduction

Almost everyone in funeral service has a unique story related to their entrance into the profession. Most, after peeling through the layers, discover the essential motivation centers around serving others, and wanting to make a difference when fellow humans are suffering. An expectation exists in funeral service, that those who have chosen to earn the noble title, funeral director, shall always display reverence to the dead – and respect for the living. Seeking and receiving ALL required and appropriate authorizations related to our work shows respect for the living. Although seeking and receiving appropriate authorizations is typically a matter of compliance with the law, it is also about building a trusted working relationship with client families in an effort to meet professional standards. The key is clear communication, and to always comply with all local, state, and federal regulations. Certain authorizations are more commonly associated with cremation, for example: 1) authorization for minimum care when embalming is declined, 2) removal of medical devices, and 3) the cremation itself, secured either by the contracting funeral home or in some cases by a third party crematory.

While these authorizations (and more) will be addressed in this chapter, it is also imperative to know that virtually every authorization form utilized within a funeral home may be necessary when cremation is selected as the means of disposition. A service that includes a cremation can certainly include all elements and services typically associated with a burial service; therefore, making it appropriate to examine numerous authorizations that are utilized in the funeral industry. Although this is not to be considered an exhaustive list of possible endorsements, it is an important first step for understanding the particulars with respect to securing applicable authorizations when working with families. While it may seem initially overwhelming to the family who made the decision to select cremation, a skilled funeral service professional will be able to proficiently navigate the plethora of required authorizations to build confidence in the process and a feeling that the family made the right decision in selecting a provider.

Determining Who Has the Right of Disposition

The discussion about authorizations necessarily includes the sometimes-arduous assignment of determining the actual party that possesses legal authority to make arrangements and select the method of final disposition, and exactly how vastly this authority extends. There is no uniform national mandate concerning who holds the right of disposition. In most cases this is left to individual states to decide through legislation. Remember, although it is common for the next of kin to hold the right of disposition, it is not always a foregone conclusion. It is not adequate to simply have a working knowledge of the plethora of authorizations required and utilized in the funeral profession; one must also fully understand who actually holds the authentic right of disposition. Every funeral service provider needs to research and remain vigilant of the specific order related to who really controls the right of disposition in their own service area, and be sure to ascertain this with all client families. This is the important and crucial first step when meeting with families who express an interest in cremation. The funeral director must be comfortable asking appropriate and leading questions, a process often required in order to determine the party with the legal right of disposition. If at any point during the arrangement process the funeral director begins to feel another party may have disposition rights, it is essential to cease arrangements and diligently research to determine the person with disposition rights. And to make matters more complex, some states allow one individual from a designated class of rights holders to sign necessary authorizations.

As a licensed professional you quickly learn the numerous mechanisms available to client families concerning the party that holds rights to disposition. For example, family A has a fully funded pre-need policy and will be executing the contract for all services, or family B insists that one person has Power of Attorney while another person is claiming to be the legal next of kin, all the while, family C agrees on the legal next of kin, but a third party claims to have legal authorization to control the right of disposition. One does not need to spend much time around a funeral home to know that it is imperative to have a functional understanding of the meaning and operation of the powers associated with each of these declarations when conducting an arrangement conference; funeral directors must always follow the wishes of the party with the legal authority to make such decisions. This knowledge is essential when it is necessary to receive formal authorizations from a family to perform certain services commonly offered in the funeral service profession.

There is truth, on many levels, when people comment that pre-arranging and pre-funding funerals reduce burden. This is typically referring to decreasing the encumbrance of an emotional funeral arrangement on the surviving family. Funeral arrangements, no doubt involve numerous potentially stressful decisions that can be overwhelming for a family, but when someone makes these decisions prior to their own death, these stresses can be greatly reduced as well as offer some comfort, having the knowledge of the services desired by the deceased. These benefits extend beyond serving to comfort the family; they also can serve the funeral director. In essence, the deceased has elected to execute their own rights to determine disposition as well as associated services. While some states are very clear in granting statutory authority and precedence to directives in writing, a disclaimer is in order here that pre-need contracts may not always take precedence over the authorizing agent. One need not look further than the Iowa Supreme Court Whalen Case that states the authorized agent can negate the pre-need contract. As with all aspects of this book, it is necessary to adhere to all laws and regulations in your particular service area.

While trying to determine who has the right of disposition, it is not completely unusual to hear a statement from a member of the family or another individual who claim the right based on having the designation of power of attorney. Therefore, it is appropriate to ask the question: What is Power of Attorney (POA)? Black's Law Dictionary defines this as an instrument in writing whereby one person, as principal, appoints another as his agent and confers authority to perform certain specified acts or kinds of acts on behalf of a principal, and Black's identifies a Durable Power of Attorney (DPOA) as existing when a person executes a Power of Attorney which will become or remain effective in the event he or she should later become disabled. It is common for people in advanced age to assign someone as their agent through Power of Attorney, which may execute the durable clause. Typically, the powers executed by these orders cease upon the death of the principal. The professional funeral director should always know all particulars for the state in which they practice. First, not all states recognize POA authority, and even if your state does recognize POA, it does not mean the authority extends to disposition rights. If disposition rights are included, it is the job of the funeral director to decipher exactly what rights exist in the order. It is our professional responsibility to be knowledgeable of all legal particulars related to right of disposition as they are provided by the state in which one practices.

It is also not uncommon to be informed during the arrangement process that a decedent has named an authorized agent. In fact, it is common when funeral directors are working with clients developing a pre-arranged plan, for the funeral director to inquire if an authorized agent has been selected, and the appropriate paperwork completed and placed in the client's prearrangement file. Again, this is a process that allows a person to select someone they trust to serve in this capacity; it is also advised to have a few people assigned as reserve agents in the event that something happens to the person assigned as the agent between the time of assignment and death. Furthermore, it is vitally important to be specific with respect to the powers assigned to the agent, and to make sure the paper work includes a witnessed signature before a notary public. This document may be filed with the appropriate legal entity in your respective state if required, in order to ensure the wishes of the principal are enforced at the time of death.

This discussion beckons us to engage in a conversation specifically about determining the party that actually has legal right of disposition, as well as determining the next of kin, or primacy. Although the legal next of kin is commonly also the person with the right of disposition, this does not necessarily have to be the case. It is the funeral director's professional responsibility to understand these particulars in the state in which they practice. Almost every state (45 of 50) and the District of Columbia have laws on the books that provide specific determination of the next of kin and / or primacy (Kubasak, 2007). It is advisable to keep an updated version of this information, typically found in the state statutes from the state in which you practice, to aid in the determination of the actual party that possesses legal right of disposition. This document, when appropriate, may be shared with client families as they work to understand the legal dynamics involved. The state statutes will provide detailed direction and assist the funeral professional in understanding the determination of who actually has the legal right of disposition. Below is the verbiage from one state's statutes concerning the order of right of disposition:

1. The decedent, provided the decedent has entered into a pre-need funeral services contract or executed a written document that meets the requirements of the state
2. A representative appointed by the decedent by means of an executed and witnessed written document meeting the requirements of the state
3. The surviving spouse
4. The sole surviving adult child of the decedent whose whereabouts are reasonably ascertained or if there is more than one child of the decedent, the majority of the surviving adult children whose whereabouts are reasonably ascertained
5. The surviving parent or parents of the decedent, whose whereabouts are reasonably ascertained
6. The surviving adult brother or sister of the decedent whose whereabouts are reasonably ascertained, or if there is more than one adult sibling of the decedent, the majority of the adult surviving siblings, whose whereabouts are reasonably ascertained
7. The guardian of the person of the decedent at the time of the death of the decedent, if one had been appointed
8. The person in the classes of the next degree of kinship, in descending order, under the laws of descent and distribution to inherit the estate of the decedent. If there is more than one person of the same degree, any person of that degree may exercise the right of disposition
9. If the decedent was an indigent person or other person the final disposition of whose body is the financial responsibility of the state or a political subdivision of the state, the public officer or employee responsible for arranging the final disposition of the remains of the decedent
10. In the absence of any person under paragraphs 1 through 9 of this section, any other person willing to assume the responsibilities to act and arrange the final disposition of the remains of the decedent, including the personal representative of the estate of the decedent or the funeral director with custody of the body, after attesting in writing that a good-faith effort has been made to no avail to contact the individuals under paragraphs 1 through 9 of this section

It is clear to see the importance of maintaining current knowledge of these rights as we work with families, and always remember it is critical to only proceed with services authorized by the appropriate party. It is your professional responsibility to understand the legal parameters regarding the right of disposition set forth by the state in which you practice. Also, be aware of states that allow one member or a majority of the designated class to agree to the cremation and sign necessary authorizations. Strong objection to cremation from others within the same category determined to have the right of disposition may cause undue stress and potential problems down the road. It is a good practice to try and have everyone agree to the cremation and sign the necessary paperwork allowing it to move forward.

The importance of determining the party who holds the legal right of disposition during the arrangement conference is well documented. At times this will be quite simple, and other times it will be an enormous challenge. It is reasonable to consider the following; what if you are able to confirm who has the right of disposition, but they are unable to be located or otherwise incapacitated? Without question, this situation will offer you a distinct challenge, yet certain procedures and protocol may serve to offer you an operational plan and potential relief in these situations.

When these situations arise, it is extremely important for the funeral director to practice due diligence in the search for the party with disposition rights, and as in all operations with families, be certain to document and archive all attempts to establish communication – ultimately this trail can serve as evidence of your efforts to make contact with said party in an effort to seek appropriate authorization regarding services and disposition. It is advisable to attempt to make contact using multiple methods: telephone, certified mail, email, social media platforms, to name a few, and you must document and archive all attempts as confirmation of your attentiveness to the situation. Keep in mind that a funeral home is not a detective agency and that attempts at due diligence may only go so far. Although it is possible to conduct certain services without the authorization of the legal agent, it is imperative to receive authorization from the legal agent when dealing with viewing of the body, services with the body present, and certainly with respect to final disposition. Often, the ability to plan and execute a memorial service can aid the grieving process of family members and friends during that time when the authorized agent or other responsible party is being located. Ultimately, if the authorized agent remains unavailable, it is critical to understand the laws regarding disposition in your service area. Some states have specific statutory language offering funeral practitioners direction with respect to how to proceed when the legal next of kin or authorized agent is unavailable. It is also possible in certain situations for families to receive a court order allowing them to act as the authorized agent when the party previously named as such is unavailable. Again, although pathways exist to assist the funeral director when the party with disposition rights cannot be found, it is crucial to always utilize due diligence, document all attempts to make contact and any correspondence that may take place, and always be knowledgeable of the legal stipulations and ramifications surrounding this scenario in your service area.

Although general formats, and certain items are required to be on various authorizations it is important to remember that structure and clarity are vitally important on ALL authorization forms. As with so many elements in the funeral service profession, practitioners need to remain mindful that the majority of the families we serve will only go through this experience a few times over the course of a lifetime, and what is commonplace to us, is foreign to many of our families. These forms need to be clear, legible, and orderly as well as evoke plain language and not use what may be considered the normal vernacular of those within the funeral service profession. Each authorization should have a clear title at the top of the form declaring exactly what is being authorized, and the entire form needs to follow a standard format. Each new topic on the form should start with a new paragraph and include a heading that generally explains what that section will be addressing. These are great suggestions, but even the best worded and thought out form will typically require additional explanation by the arranging funeral director. The effective funeral director must remain cognizant of the family needs and their unfamiliarity regarding funeral arrangements – walking step-by-step through each form with the authorizing agent and taking the time to explain each item, verifying that the authorizing agent understands the form and addresses any questions, is the suggested protocol.

It is generally accepted that the best and preferred method to receive authorization is an authentic signature from the exact party that retains the legal right of disposition. Yet, in this mobile and technological society, funeral directors will receive requests to accept authorization utilizing multiple methods. Expect to have families offer to fax, email, text, as well as offer verbal authorization over the telephone. Although almost all states allow the authorized agent to sign the cremation authorization electronically, the first prudent step is to research your local service area for the laws and regulations regarding means of securing authorization, and always adhere to these standards. If fax or email (with an attachment) options exist in your area, it is suggested to have the authorized agent sign the document before a notary public prior to submitting to the funeral home, and this authorization should be followed up with the actual form that has the authorized agent's authentic signature. In many areas it is commonplace to receive initial authorization for embalming over the phone. If this method is employed, you should always follow up with an authentic signature from the authorizing agent on the authorization to embalm form. The text method of submitting authorizations should never be recognized, although this is rapidly becoming one of the most common types of communication. A funeral professional can never be certain who actually sent a text – you only know the phone which sent the message, but never the actual person sending the message. If a funeral professional makes the decision to accept an electronic signature, a process must be in place to verify the identity of the person providing the signature. The next section of this chapter discusses specific types of authorizations that may be required during a funeral arrangement, with an understanding that an authentic signature from the party that holds the legal right of disposition is always the preferred option.

Authorization to Cremate (and Related Forms)

Although it has been established that virtually every authorization utilized in the funeral profession may be appropriate and/or required when making arrangements involving a cremation, it seems appropriate to begin the discussion with the authorization to cremate. Concerns about potential liability are fundamental to this discussion. Common circumstances resulting in litigation with respect to cremation include: cremating the wrong body, cremating without authority, cremating without informed consent, and co-mingling cremated remains. Although the authorization to cremate will not eliminate every circumstance for potential litigation, it can be a very protective and supportive document. Recall from the preceding discussion the importance of determining who has the legal right of disposition. Failure to correctly ascertain this designation may result in a signed authorization that is meaningless as the incorrect or wrong signature was obtained and relied upon to move forward with the cremation.

The authorization to cremate is a required form that typically accompanies the state or local permit issued by the department of health, medical examiner, or other government entity. It is the responsibility of the funeral director to secure a legally signed and executed cremation authorization form for every cremation service provided. It is also noteworthy, that when a third party crematory is utilized, it is likely that the same authorization will be required for both the funeral home serving the family, as well as the crematory that will actually perform the cremation service. The specific length, language, and disclosures employed on these forms vary among funeral homes, but the importance and substance of this document does not waiver. It is essential that this form is both clear and specific, and ultimately assures that the party with the right of disposition understands the finality with respect to what they are authorizing. This form must explain all facets of the cremation process, the end product of the procedure, and it must engage the authorized agent in the execution of the document. Remember, when this document is carefully drafted and appropriately used, this form can be a beneficial instrument during the arrangement process. This form is considered by many to be the most important document when considering cremation services. The Model Cremation Law and Explanation approved by the Board of Directors of the Cremation Association of North America (CANA) in January 2017 indicates that a cremation authorization form should contain, at a minimum the following information:

a. The identity of the human remains and the time and date of death.
b. A unique identification number assigned by the crematory for purposes of tracking the human remains while they are in the crematory during different phases of the cremation process.
c. The name of the funeral director and funeral establishment that obtained the cremation authorization.
d. Notification as to whether the death occurred from a disease declared by the Department of Health to be infectious, contagious, communicable, or dangerous to the public health.
e. The name of the authorizing agent and the relationship between the authorizing agent and the decedent.
f. A representation that the authorizing agent does in fact have the right to authorize the cremation of the decedent, and that the authorizing agent is not aware of any living person who has superior or equal priority right to that of the authorizing agent. In the event there is another living person who has a superior or equal priority right to the authorizing agent, the form shall contain a representation that the authorizing agent has made reasonable efforts to contact that person, has been unable to do so, and has no reason to believe that the person would object to the cremation of the decedent.
g. Authorization for the crematory to cremate the human remains.
h. A representation that the human remains do not contain a pacemaker or any other material or implant that may be potentially hazardous or cause damage to the cremation chamber or the person performing the cremation.
i. The name of the person authorized to receive the cremated remains from the crematory authority.
j. The manner in which final disposition of the cremated remains is to take place, if known. If the cremation authorization form does not specify a method of final disposition provided for in Section 8 of this Act (Section 8 specifically discusses disposition of cremated remains), then the form may indicate that the cremated remains will be held by the crematory authority for 30 days before they are released, unless they are picked up from the crematory authority prior to that time, in person, by the authorizing agent. At the end of the 30 days the crematory authority may return cremated remains to the authorizing agent if no final disposition arrangements are made; or at the end of 60 days the crematory authority may dispose of the cremated remains in accordance with disposition provisions of the Law.
k. A listing of any items of value to be delivered to the crematory authority along with the human remains, and instructions as to how the items should be handled.
l. A specific statement as to whether the authorizing agent has made arrangements for any type of viewing of the decedent before cremation, or for a service with the decedent present before cremation in connection with the cremation, and if so, the date and time of the viewing or service and whether the crematory authority is authorized to proceed with the cremation upon receipt of the human remains.
m. The signature of the authorizing agent, attesting to the accuracy of all representations contained on the cremation authorization form.

n. If a cremation authorization form is being executed on a pre-need basis, the cremation authorization form shall contain the disclosure required by the pre-need provisions of the Law in Section 9 (Section 9 is dedicated to limitation of liability).
o. The cremation authorization form, other than pre-need cremation forms, shall also be signed by a funeral director or other representative of the funeral establishment that obtained the cremation authorization. That individual shall merely execute the cremation authorization form as a witness and shall not be responsible for any of the representations made by the authorizing agent, unless the individual has actual knowledge to the contrary. The information requested by items (a), (b), (c) and (g) of this Subsection, however, shall be considered to be representations of the authorizing agent and may be the representations of the funeral director or funeral establishment. In addition, the funeral director or funeral establishment shall warrant to the crematory that the human remains delivered to the crematory authority have been positively identified as the decedent listed on the cremation authorization form by the authorizing agent or a designated representative of the authorizing agent. Such identification shall be made in person or by photograph by the authorizing agent or designated representative of the authorizing agent.

Gilligan & Stueve (2011) suggest that when the authorization seeks disclosure of implanted medical devices, the form should include the authorization to remove such devices, if removal is required by the crematory. Often included in the area of implanted medical devices is an acknowledgement related to radionuclides commonly used in therapeutic nuclear medicine. Greater attention to possible radioactive contamination of the crematory, the crematory operator and those in possession of cremated remains has added an additional layer of potential litigation. Gilligan & Stueve also indicate the need to provide the authorizing agent a specific and detailed description of the cremation process (see Chapter Six for an examination of the cremation process) and the necessary process of pulverizing the cremated remains.

Much of the general public does not understand that the cremation process actually involves direct flames along with intense heat, nor do they understand that processing is required to prepare the remnants of cremation; it is the duty of the funeral director to make sure this knowledge is conveyed. There may also be an opportunity to discuss the composition of cremated remains since the use of the term "ashes" suggests what is commonly found after a fireplace or campfire has been extinguished. Some families are surprised that the majority of what remains after a cremation is bone and accompanying bone fragments. Never assume that your intricate knowledge of cremation is understood beyond the professionals by whom you are surrounded. Many cremation providers suggest disclosing elements that may be found in cremated remains other than bone fragments, such as body prostheses, dentures, dental bridgework, and dental fillings. Additionally, due to a family's lack of experience with cremation, it is imperative that the professional funeral director explains the timeline involved when the actual cremation will occur. This is the appropriate time to discuss if the family has a preference for, or would like to know, the date and time of the cremation (sample form 3.11). Culture or religious requirements may dictate the necessity of knowing or requiring a specific day and time.

It is also wise to disclose personal articles which are to be removed prior to pulverizing the bone fragments. This needs to be disclosed to the authorizing agent and authorization received to dispose of such items often found with the bone matter. Furthermore, it is prudent to include a specific statement requesting information about any personal property, jewelry, and any other keepsakes that may be sent with the deceased to accompany the body to the crematory. It is imperative that the party with disposition rights understands that the property will be destroyed during the cremation process. Any such items should be listed and authorization received in order for them to enter the cremation chamber. It is also wise to include a section that allows the family to list specific items the family wants removed prior to the cremation, as well as the specific cremation container that has been selected by the family.

Additionally, although it may be considered part of the discussion regarding the manner of disposition of the cremated remains, it is valuable to include a specific section on this authorization that indicates the container (urn or other receptacle) selected to house the cremated remains upon completion of the process. This provides an added opportunity to address the procedure or process when the volume of cremated remains exceeds the volume of the container selected by the authorizing agent or provided by the crematory. Some families may request special handling of cremated remains to include splitting or dividing them. Also, it is not uncommon for the family to request cremated remains to be mailed or shipped at the completion of the cremation process. Although the following chapter addresses the shipping of cremated remains in detail, the authorization to cremate should include a disclosure of the shipping process and the reality that cremated remains will ultimately be placed in a destructible container. These suggested procedures related to the authorization to cremate offer a window into the complexities and importance of this document. The Model Cremation Law approved by the Board of Directors of CANA and the knowledge derived from Gilligan & Stueve are without doubt important information to consider when you offer cremation services, but you MUST ALWAYS know, study, and adhere to ALL laws and standards that regulate cremation in your local service area.

This discussion has revealed the complex nature of the cremation process, and the legalities surrounding this procedure. It is necessary that the cremation authorization form is both clear and detailed. The elements contained in this form present the reality that oftentimes multiple authorizations must be secured on this one form. This is both prudent for practitioners, and can also ease the painstaking arrangement process for the client family. Different scenarios presented in the arrangement process require that the professional funeral director is prepared with the appropriate form(s) for the situation. Different schools of thought exist when it comes to the development of these authorizations; some funeral homes/crematories see the value of keeping the form to one page, while others feel it is not possible to communicate all of the required language on a single page. Form 3.1 below presents a sample of a single page authorization form. Notice how numerous authorizations are needed on this one form. Following form 3.1 you find various sample forms typically associated with cremation services. All forms presented are only intended to serve as samples. All funeral practitioners should consult their legal counsel for the drafting of official documents that will be utilized in actual practice. The following forms include:

Sample Forms

    3.1: Authorization to Cremate Remains and Release Liability
    3.2: Statement of Authenticity
    3.3: Disclosure and Authorization to Remove Medical, Mechanical, or Radioactive Devices
    3.4: The Cremation Process Explained
    3.5: Personal Property Statement and Receipt
    3.6: Processing of Cremated Remains Explained
    3.7: Disposition of Cremated Remains
    3.8: Urn / Other Container Selection
    3.9: Verification of Identity
    3.10: Ceremonial Casket Rental Acknowledgement and Release
    3.11: Time of Cremation
    3.12: Certification and Indemnification
    3.13: Request to Witness a Cremation
    3.14: Receipt of Cremated Remains
    3.15: Authorization to Commingle Cremated Remains
    3.16: Authorization for Minimum Care when Embalming Declined
    3.17: Embalming Authorization
    3.18: Authorization for Restorative Applications

Fires of Change: Required Authorizations

Sample Form 3.1
Authorization to Cremate Remains and Release of Liability

Notice: This is a legal document containing provisions concerning cremation which is an irreversible process. It should be read thoroughly and carefully before signing. You should consult an attorney if there is anything in this document which you do not fully understand.

Authorization to Cremate
The undersigned hereby authorizes Name of Funeral Home or Crematory, in accordance with and subject to its established operating procedures, to take possession of and cremate the human remains of Name of Deceased, who died at City and State where Death Occurred on the day of month, year at the age of age years, after all necessary permits required for the cremation have been obtained.

Statement of Authenticity
I/We, the undersigned, certify, warrant and represent that I/we have the full legal right and authority to, and permission from any and all other relatives, guardians or conservators to authorize the cremation, processing and disposition of the remains of Name of Deceased (hereinafter referred to as the "deceased"), further no one else has this authority.

Authorization to Remove Medical Devices, Mechanical or Radioactive Devices
Medical, mechanical, or radioactive devices implanted in the remains of the deceased (such as pacemakers, etc.) may create a hazard when placed into a cremation chamber. I hereby authorize the staff of the crematory, funeral home in charge or the agents or representatives of each to remove such device from the body of the deceased and to dispose of such device as said persons may deem appropriate and in their sole discretion. No notice of such removal or disposition need be provided to me, the authorized agent. I/We hereby certify that the remains of the deceased _____DO_____ DO NOT contain any type of implanted medical, mechanical or radioactive device.
The remains contain the following medical, mechanical, or radioactive device: _____

Cremation Process
The deceased will be placed into the cremation chamber and will be totally and irreversibly destroyed by prolonged exposure to intense heat and direct flame. I/We authorize the Crematory to open the cremation chamber during the cremation process and reposition the remains of the deceased in order to facilitate a complete and thorough cremation.

Personal Property Statement
Certain items, including but not limited to, body prostheses, dentures, dental bridgework, dental fillings, jewelry and other personal articles accompanying the remains of the deceased, may be destroyed during the cremation process. Those items still remaining with the deceased that I wish to be removed prior to cremation are as follows: _____
I/We further authorize that if any items, other than the cremated remains of the deceased are recovered from the chamber, they may be separated from the cremated remains of the deceased and disposed of by the crematory.

Processing of the Cremated Remains
Following the cremation the remains of the deceased, consisting mainly of bone fragments, will be mechanically pulverized to an unidentifiable consistency prior to placement in an urn or other container. In the event the urn or container is insufficient to accommodate all of the remains of the deceased, any excess cremated remains will be placed in a secondary container and returned together with the primary urn or container. I/We fully understand and acknowledge, that even with the exercise of reasonable care and the use of the Crematory's best efforts, it is not possible to recover all particles of the cremated remains of the deceased, and that some particles may inadvertently become commingled with particles of other cremated remains remaining in the cremation chamber and/or other devices utilized to process the cremated remains.

Disposition of Cremated Remains
I/We request the following disposition be made of the cremated remains of the deceased:
_____ Deliver cremated remains to: _____
_____ Mail cremated remains to: _____
_____ Hold cremated remains to be picked up by authorized agent or their representative: _____

Indemnify Statement
I/We agree to indemnify, release and hold the crematory, funeral home, their affiliates, agents, employees and assigns, harmless from any and all loss, damages, liability or causes of action in connection with the cremation and disposition of the cremated remains of the deceased.
Signature of person(s) authorizing the cremation of the deceased
I/We warrant that all representations and statements made herein are true and correct, and that I/We have read and understand the provisions contained in this document.
Signature: _____
                                        Print Name   Relationship

Address: _____
        Street   City   State   Zip   Phone

Witness: _____ Date: _____

Sample Form 3.2
Statement of Authenticity

Name of Deceased: _____ **Date of Death:** _____

I/We, the undersigned, certify, warrant and represent that I/we have the full legal right and authority to, and permission from any and all other relatives, guardians or conservators to authorize the cremation, processing and disposition of the remains of <u>Name of Deceased</u> , further no one else has this authority.

Signed this _____ day of _____, 20_____ at

_____

Print Name:

_____

Signature:

_____

Relationship to the Deceased:

_____

Print Name:

_____

Sample Form 3.3
Disclosure and Authorization to Remove Medical, Mechanical, or Radioactive Devices

Name of Deceased: _____ **Date of Death:** _____

Medical, mechanical, or radioactive devices implanted in the remains of the deceased (such as pacemakers, etc.) may create a hazard when placed into a cremation chamber. I hereby authorize the staff of the crematory, funeral home in charge or the agents or representatives of each to remove such device from the body of the deceased and to dispose of such devices as said persons may deem appropriate and in their sole discretion. No notice of such removal or disposition need be provided to me, the authorized agent. I/We hereby certify that the remains of the deceased _____DO_____ DO NOT contain any type of implanted medical, mechanical or radioactive device.

The remains contain the following medical, mechanical, or radioactive device(s):_____

Signed this _____ day of _____, 20_____ at _____

Print Name: _____

Signature: _____

Relationship to the Deceased: _____

Print Name: _____

Signature: _____

Relationship to the Deceased: _____

Witness: _____ Date: _____

Sample Form 3.4
The Cremation Process Explained

Name of Deceased: _____   **Date of Death:** _____

The Cremation
The deceased will be placed into a cremation casket or other container suitable for cremation, and then placed directly into the cremation chamber. These contents will be totally and irreversibly destroyed by prolonged exposure to intense heat and direct flame. The only remaining fragments include bone matter and metal items that may have been with the human remains, for example body prostheses, dental work, and jewelry, the temperatures during the cremation process may not completely consume these items. I/We authorize the Crematory to open the cremation chamber during the cremation process and reposition the remains of the deceased in order to facilitate a complete and thorough cremation.

Personal Property Statement
Certain items, including but not limited to, body prostheses, dentures, dental bridgework, dental fillings, jewelry and other personal articles accompanying the remains of the deceased, may be destroyed during the cremation process. Those items still remaining with the deceased that I wish to be removed prior to cremation are as follows: _____
I/We further authorize that if any items, other than the cremated remains of the deceased are recovered from the chamber, they may be separated from the cremated remains of the deceased and disposed of by the crematory.

Processing of the Cremated Remains
Following the cremation the remains of the deceased, consisting mainly of bone fragments, will be mechanically pulverized to an unidentifiable consistency prior to placement in an urn or other container. I/We fully understand and acknowledge, that even with the exercise of reasonable care and the use of the Crematory's best efforts, it is not possible to recover all particles of the cremated remains of the deceased, and that some particles may inadvertently become commingled with particles of other cremated remains remaining in the cremation chamber and/or other devices utilized to process the cremated remains.

Urn / Other Container Selection
Upon completion of the cremation process it is required to select a suitable container to house the cremated remains, this container is called an urn. The minimal urn capacity suitable for the average adult is two hundred (200) cubic inches. In the event the urn or container is insufficient to accommodate all of the remains of the deceased, any excess cremated remains will be placed in a secondary container and returned together with the primary urn or container. I/We, as the authorized agent(s) specify the following container to be used:
Container description: _____

Disposition of Cremated Remains
I/We request the following disposition be made of the cremated remains of the deceased:
_____ Deliver cremated remains to: _____
_____ Mail cremated remains to: _____
_____ Hold cremated remains to be picked up by authorized agent or their representative: _____

Signed this _____ day of _____, 20_____ at _____

Print Name: _____

Signature: _____

Relationship to the Deceased: _____

Print Name: _____

Signature: _____

Relationship to the Deceased: _____

Witness: _____ Date: _____

Sample Form 3.5
Personal Property Statement and Receipt

Name of Deceased: _____ **Date of Death:** _____

Certain items, including but not limited to, body prostheses, dentures, dental bridgework, dental fillings, jewelry and other personal articles, including clothing, glasses, and any keepsakes that may accompany the remains of the deceased, may be destroyed during the cremation process. Those items still remaining with the deceased that I wish to be removed prior to cremation are as follows: _____

I/We further authorize that if any items, other than the cremated remains of the deceased are recovered from the chamber, they may be separated from the cremated remains of the deceased and disposed of by the crematory.

Signed this _____ day of _____, 20_____ at _____

Print Name: _____

Signature: _____

Relationship to the Deceased: _____

Print Name: _____

Signature: _____

Relationship to the Deceased: _____

Receipt for Personal Property

Personal Property Description	Date Returned

Print Name: _____

Signature: _____

Relationship to the Deceased: _____

Witness: _____ Date: _____

Sample Form 3.6
Processing of Cremated Remains Explained

Name of Deceased: _____ **Date of Death:** _____

Following the cremation the remains of the deceased, consisting mainly of bone fragments, will be mechanically pulverized to an unidentifiable consistency prior to placement in an urn or other container. In the event the urn or container is insufficient to accommodate all of the remains of the deceased, any excess cremated remains will be placed in a secondary container and returned together with the primary urn or container. I/We fully understand and acknowledge, that even with the exercise of reasonable care and the use of the Crematory's best efforts, it is not possible to recover all particles of the cremated remains of the deceased, and that some particles may inadvertently become commingled with particles of other cremated remains remaining in the cremation chamber and/or other devices utilized to process the cremated remains.

Signed this _____ day of _____, 20_____ at _____

Print Name: _____

Signature: _____

Relationship to the Deceased: _____

Print Name: _____

Signature: _____

Relationship to the Deceased: _____

Witness: _____ Date: _____

Sample Form 3.7
Disposition of Cremated Remains

Name of Deceased: _____ **Date of Death:** _____

It is necessary to declare the final disposition of the cremated remains. As indicated on the authorization to cremate, the funeral home / crematory will only hold the cremated remains for _____ following the actual cremation.

I/We request the following disposition be made of the cremated remains of the deceased:
_____ Deliver cremated remains to: _____
_____ Deliver cremated remains to the following location and scatter remains as permitted by law: _____
_____ Mail cremated remains to: _____
_____ Hold cremated remains to be picked up by authorized agent or their representative: _____

Signed this _____ day of _____, 20_____ at _____

Print: Name: _____

Signature: _____

Relationship to the Deceased: _____

Print Name: _____

Signature: _____

Relationship to the Deceased: _____

Witness: _____ Date: _____

Sample Form 3.8
Urn / Other Container Selection

Name of Deceased: _____ **Date of Death:** _____

Upon completion of the cremation process it is required to select a suitable container to house the cremated remains, this container is called an urn. The minimal urn capacity suitable for the average adult is two hundred (200) cubic inches. In the event the urn or container is insufficient to accommodate all of the remains of the deceased, any excess cremated remains will be placed in a secondary container and returned together with the primary urn or container. I/We, as the authorized agent(s) specify the following container to be used:
Container description: _____

Signed this _____ day of _____, 20_____ at _____

Print Name: _____

Signature: _____

Relationship to the Deceased: _____

Print Name: _____

Signature: _____

Relationship to the Deceased: _____

Witness: _____ Date: _____

Sample Form 3.9
Verification of Identity

Name of Deceased: _____ **Date of Death:** _____

I/We, as the next of kin, authorized agent, or other party with legal rights to disposition, hereby confirm the identity of the above named decedent. I acknowledge that I/we were provided ample and adequate time to properly identify the decedent prior to final disposition of the decedent's remains. I/We confirm there is no doubt regarding the identity of the decedent that funeral home/crematory has in custody.

If identity of the deceased was confirmed by means other than visual identification (photograph, tattoo, scar), please specify method employed: _____

Signed this _____ day of _____, 20_____ at _____

Print Name: _____

Signature: _____

Relationship to the Deceased: _____

Print Name: _____

Signature: _____

Relationship to the Deceased: _____

Sample Form 3.10
Ceremonial Casket Rental Acknowledgement and Release

Name of Deceased: _____ **Date of Death:** _____

I/We, as the next of kin, authorized agent, or other party with legal rights to disposition, hereby acknowledge and understand that the ceremonial casket being utilized in conjunction with the visitation and funeral services for the named decedent is a rental unit which may have been used in this capacity hitherto and may so be used again. I/We understand that the funeral home/crematory provides a new insert for the rental unit in an attempt to reduce the areas contacted by the deceased, but I/we understand it is possible other remains may have come into contact with other areas of the unit.

I/We further understand that at the conclusion of the funeral services, the deceased will be removed from the rental unit and placed in an appropriate container for final disposition, I/we also acknowledge that the shell of the rental unit will remain the property of the funeral home/crematory.

Signed this _____ day of _____, 20_____ at _____

Print Name: _____
Signature: _____

Relationship to the Deceased: _____

Print Name: _____
Signature: _____

Relationship to the Deceased: _____

Witness: _____ Date: _____

Sample Form 3.11
Time of Cremation

Name of Deceased: _____ **Date of Death:** _____

_____ The undersigned hereby authorizes Name of Funeral Home or Crematory, in accordance with and subject to its established operating procedures, to take possession of and cremate the human remains of Name of Deceased, who died at City and State where Death Occurred on the day of month, year at the age of age years, after all necessary permits required for the cremation have been obtained.

OR

_____ The funeral home/crematory will attempt to accommodate a specific date and time for the cremation to take place. The funeral home/crematory will exercise their best efforts to cremate the decedent according to the schedule below:

Date of Cremation: _____ Time of Cremation: _____

Signed this _____ day of _____, 20_____ at _____

Print Name: _____
Signature: _____
Relationship to the Deceased: _____
Print Name: _____
Signature: _____
Relationship to the Deceased: _____
Witness: _____ Date: _____

Sample Form 3.12
Certification and Indemnification

Name of Deceased: _____ **Date of Death:** _____

I/We acknowledge that the funeral home/crematory is relying upon the representations and claims being made by the party claiming to be the authorized agent(s). I/We certify that all information contained in the Cremation Authorization and Disposition documents are truthful and no oversights of any material facts have been made.

I/We agree to indemnify, release and hold the crematory, funeral home, their affiliates, agents, employees and assigns, harmless from any and all loss, damages, liability or causes of action in connection with the cremation and disposition of the cremated remains of the deceased, as authorized herein, or my/our failure to correctly identify the remains of the deceased, disclose the presence of any implanted mechanical, medical, or radioactive devices or any other item of personal property, or take possession of or make permanent arrangements for the disposition of such remains.

Except as set forth in this authorization, no warranties, expressed or implied, are made by the funeral home, crematory or any of their respective affiliates, agents or employees.

I/We understand that this document does not contain a complete and detailed description of every aspect of the cremation process.

Signed this _____ day of _____, 20_____ at _____

Print Name: _____
Signature: _____
Relationship to the Deceased: _____
Print Name: _____
Signature: _____
Relationship to the Deceased: _____
Witness: _____ Date: _____

Sample Form 3.13
Request to Witness a Cremation

Name of Deceased: _____ **Date of Death:** _____

I/We, the undersigned, certify, warrant and represent that I/we have the full legal right and authority to, and permission from any and all other relatives, guardians or conservators to authorize the cremation, processing and disposition of the remains of <u>Name of Deceased</u>, further no one else has this authority. I/We further request to witness the cremation of the deceased listed above. I/We acknowledge that the funeral home/crematory has informed me/us about the cremation process and understand this may be emotionally disturbing and difficult to witness. Having been advised of these concerns, I/we wish to witness the cremation which will take place on _____ at _____ at _____ am/pm

I/We agree to release and hold the crematory, funeral home, their affiliates, agents, employees and assigns, harmless from any and all loss, damages, liability or causes of action in connection with the cremation, including any claims of emotional or physical distress that may result from the viewing of the cremation, or as the result of any aspect of the cremation process.

Signed this _____ day of _____, 20_____ at _____

Print Name: _____
Signature: _____
Relationship to the Deceased: _____
Print Name: _____
Signature: _____
Relationship to the Deceased: _____
Witness: _____ Date: _____

Witnessing of a cremation may be defined as family representative(s) are present for the initiation of the cremation process, or plan to remain for the entirety of the cremation. If the authorized agent, or other party authorized by the agent elects to witness the cremation, it is best practice to complete the request to witness a cremation form and capture the authentic signature of the authorized agent and any party authorized by the agent.

Sample Form 3.14
Receipt of Cremated Remains

Name of Deceased: _____   **Date of Death:** _____

I/We, the undersigned, certify, warrant and represent that I/we have the full legal right and authority to, and permission from any and all other relatives, guardians or conservators to authorize the cremation, processing and disposition of the remains of <u>Name of Deceased</u>, further no one else has this authority. As the authorized agent(s) we accept the responsibility to pick up the cremated remains upon completion of the cremation process. If I/we are unavailable to pick up the cremated remains, we authorize _____ to pick up the cremated remains upon completion of the cremation process.

Signed this _____ day of _____, 20_____ at_____

Print Name: _____
Signature: _____
Relationship to the Deceased: _____
Print Name: _____
Signature: _____
Relationship to the Deceased: _____

Cremated Remains Received by: _____
                                 Print Name   Signature   Date

Funeral Home / Crematory Representative Releasing Cremated Remains: _____

Sample Form 3.15
Authorization to Commingle Cremated Remains

Name of Deceased: _____   **Date of Death:** _____

I/We, the undersigned, certify, warrant and represent that I/we have the full legal right and authority to, and permission from any and all other relatives, guardians or conservators to authorize the cremation, processing and disposition of the remains of <u>Name of Deceased</u>, further no one else has this authority.

I/We acknowledge that the funeral home/crematory is relying upon the representations and claims being made by the party claiming to be the authorized agent(s). I/We certify that all information contained in the Cremation Authorization and Disposition documents are truthful and no oversights of any material facts have been made.

I/We authorize and instruct the staff of the crematory, funeral home in charge or the agents or representatives of each to make the following disposition of the cremated remains of <u>Name of Deceased</u>, which may or will involve commingling of cremated remains.

_____ Place the cremated remains of <u>Name of the Decedent</u> in a container / urn with the cremated remains of _____.

_____ Place the cremated remains of <u>Name of the Decedent</u> in _____, which contains cremated remains from pother decedent(s)

_____ Other option _____

I/We agree to indemnify, release and hold the crematory, funeral home, their affiliates, agents, employees and assigns, harmless from any and all loss, damages, liability or causes of action in connection with the cremation and disposition of the cremated remains of the deceased, as authorized herein, or my/our failure to correctly identify the remains of the deceased, disclose the presence of any implanted mechanical, medical, or radioactive devices or any other item of personal property, or take possession of or make permanent arrangements for the disposition of such remains.

Signed this _____ day of _____, 20_____ at _____

Print Name: _____
Signature: _____
Relationship to the Deceased: _____
Print Name: _____
Signature: _____
Relationship to the Deceased: _____
Witness: _____ Date: _____

Authorization for Minimum Care When Embalming Declined

One does not need to visit with many experienced funeral directors to hear stories (from the not so distant past) about how embalming in the past was the norm for most cases. When a first call was received, it was virtually assumed that the family would select embalming as part of the desired services to be rendered by the funeral home. The evolution of society, coupled with advances in technology (especially refrigeration technology and availability) has elucidated the contemporary reality that nothing is to be assumed when a first call is received, particularly the services desired or the method of disposition that will be selected. Remember that the desires and wishes relayed to the funeral service provider during the time of the removal may differ greatly from the type of service that is actually selected once the arrangement conference is complete. These modern realisms lead to other questions associated with selecting desired services. It is common practice for the professional funeral director to explain options regarding embalming, visitation, viewing, refrigeration, and other related service items in assisting families selecting options to meet their desired wishes. During this process, it may be discovered that a family prefers services that do not include embalming, but yet the funeral home should seek the authorization to perform minimum care of the deceased without the embalming procedure. Recall, it is the duty and responsibility of the funeral director to maintain both personal and public health and safety. The importance of which has become highlighted in the era of COVID-19. Although a body that is not embalmed will certainly not have the same level of disinfection as embalmed remains, minimal care does offer some sanitary elements and helps maintain a safe work environment, as well as reduce potential exposure to client families. Additionally, this service will help prepare the deceased for a respectable and meaningful viewing if the family so desires.

It may be possible that your particular service area has existing regulations that address the obligations when embalming is declined (including minimal care and refrigeration). As in all areas of funeral service, be sure to adhere to all federal, state and local laws and regulations. Additionally, funeral homes should have specific policies regarding minimal care when embalming is declined; it is important funeral directors understand and communicate all of these policies and regulations to client families. Although embalming may be declined, the professional funeral director needs to recognize the potential liability associated with every single action taken by a funeral home, this certainly includes minimal care when embalming is declined. Communication is the key. The authorized agent needs to clearly understand the procedure that will be utilized and approve this treatment. Minimal services typically include removal of medical devices, aspiration of excess fluids and gasses from the body, washing of the remains, setting of facial features and appropriately positioning the body in preparation for identification, viewing, immediate burial, or cremation. It is important to evoke the standard for receiving authorizations; it is a legal and ethical issue as well as the appropriate professional protocol. These forms are not simply devices to clutter a client file, they serve to disclose information to the consumer as well as to remove any doubt that indeed the authorized agent understands and authorizes the services being provided by the funeral professional. This is the funeral director's professional responsibility!

In many respects contemporary funeral rights are drifting away from standard practices, yet, any involvement with the body itself remain highlighted. The care and presentation of the deceased can certainly set the tone and be significant in ultimately providing a family with the meaningful memory and services they desire and deserve, regardless of whether the family elects to embalm or otherwise. The same standards of clarity and specificity discussed with respect to the authorization to cremate also exist on the authorization for minimal care when embalming is declined, as is the case with all authorizations utilized in the funeral profession. Form 3.16 below presents a Sample Authorization for Minimal Care when Embalming Declined.

Sample Form 3.16
Authorization for Minimum Care when Embalming Declined

Name of Deceased: _____ Date of Death: _____

Statement of Authenticity
I/We, the undersigned, certify, warrant and represent that I/we have the full legal right and authority to, and permission from any and all other relatives, guardians or conservators to authorize the disposition of the remains of <u>Name of Deceased</u>, further no one else has this authority.

Minimum Care Services
The undersigned has declined embalming of the above named decedent and authorizes the funeral home, or its agent(s), to provide minimum care and shelter for the body. It is understood that minimum care may include, but not be limited to removal of exterior tubes, catheters, or other medical devices; closing of the eyes and mouth by accepted mortuary practices; aspiration of excess fluids and gasses; use of surface disinfectants or deodorants; wrapping or covering the body in appropriate material; positioning of the body; housing the remains in a clean, private environment; inventory of personal effects from the body. Minimum care does not include chemically treating the body by arterial injection of chemicals and will not delay organic decomposition. Minimum care does not ensure any time for presentation of the body for viewing nor does it serve as a replacement for arterial embalming.

Indemnify Statement
I/We agree to indemnify, release and hold the funeral home, their affiliates, agents, employees and assigns, harmless from any and all loss, damages, liability or causes of action in connection with the services and disposition of the remains of the deceased.

Signed this _____ day of _____, 20_____ at _____

Print Name: _____

Signature: _____

Relationship to the Deceased: _____

Print Name: _____

Signature: _____

Relationship to the Deceased: _____

Funeral Home Representative: _____ Date: _____

Embalming Authorization

The most scrutinized authorization form commonly used in the funeral profession is, arguably, the authorization to embalm. In many ways the practice of embalming has been under fire for years, and for many people, even the mention of embalming is cause to ruffle feathers. Indeed, embalming human remains without proper authorization will be considered mutilation, and furthermore, the Federal Trade Commission's "Funeral Rule" has specified clear expectations concerning receiving the proper authority when embalming human remains. Robert G. Mayer (2012) indicates that the authorization to embalm is a form that is dichotomous in nature; this form seeks to secure authorization and indemnification for the funeral home and their agents. Mayer further suggests it is wise to include items such as who may assist with the embalming procedure, seek approval for utilizing a trade embalmer for the procedure, clearing the use of a preparation room in the funeral home or at a separate embalming facility, as well as securing authorization to complete restorative treatments on the embalming authorization form.

As is the case with all work in the funeral industry, it is imperative to document all authorizations and services. Specifically, regarding the embalming procedure, it is critical to always document and archive the pre-embalming condition of the body, as well as the professional techniques used during the procedure (an embalming case report should be completed for every case – see sample form 2.1). Additionally, never over-promise results when receiving authorization, but seek to over-deliver. It may also be tempting to offer your opinion with respect to how someone's loved one looks after embalming, cosmetic work, dressing and casketing – beware, your opinion may differ from that of the family. Let the family be the judge of your work at the first viewing, and always be near to reaffirm and offer solutions for any possible questions or problems. One of the most rewarding experiences in the funeral profession is when a family is pleased with the appearance of a loved one; always strive for excellence in this regard. It all starts with proper authorization and clear communication with the authorized agent.

As indicated earlier, the Federal Trade Commission (FTC) offers strict guidelines with respect to the authorization to embalm. Any narrative possibly provided about this topic would pale in comparison to the actual language of the FTC Funeral Rule, for that reason the following information is directly influenced by the FTC Publication, *Complying with the Funeral Rule*, published in 2019, in hopes of providing some of the important items of the Rule related to embalming in the exact language of the Rule.

Embalming is the second required disclosure on the General Price List (GPL) informing consumers that the law does not require embalming. This disclosure explains that embalming is not required by law, except in certain special cases. FTC indicates that embalming may be necessary, however, if you select certain funeral arrangements, such as a funeral with viewing. Furthermore, if you do not want embalming, you usually have the right to choose an arrangement that does not require you to pay for it, such as direct cremation or immediate burial. If a funeral home wants to add information about state law requirements, you can do so after the FTC disclosure in immediate conjunction with the price of embalming. Embalming is also one of the required itemized prices on the GPL. The Rule stipulates that the funeral home price for embalming should include use of the preparation room, as well as the professional services, equipment, and materials involved in performing embalming. FTC also discusses embalming disclosure as related to the statement of funeral goods and services selected. The disclosure relates to the need for prior approval for the embalming procedure. The Rule indicates that if a family selected a funeral that may require embalming, such as a funeral with viewing, the family may have to pay for embalming. The family will not have to pay for embalming if it was not authorized by the family, and the family selected arrangements such as a direct cremation or Immediate burial. The Rule also indicates that if you are charged for embalming, a space should be included on the statement to explain the reason embalming was selected. Remember, embalming as a specific misrepresentation is also covered by the FTC. The Rule states: Funeral directors cannot tell consumers that state or local law requires embalming if that is not true. If state law does require embalming, funeral professionals may tell the family that embalming is required due to the specific circumstances. Funeral homes must tell consumers in writing that embalming is not required by law except in special circumstances, if relevant. This is accomplished by including the mandatory embalming disclosure on the GPL.

The Rule further indicates, unless state or local law requires embalming, funeral homes may not tell consumers that embalming is required for practical purposes in the following situations: when the consumer desires a direct cremation, when the consumer wants an immediate burial, or when refrigeration is available and the consumer requests a closed-casket funeral with no formal viewing or visitation. The Rule also speaks directly about the importance of authorization. The Rule specifies that funeral homes can charge a fee for embalming, only in one of the following three circumstances. First, state or local law requires embalming under the particular circumstances regardless of any wishes the family might have. Second, the funeral home obtained prior approval for embalming from a family member or other authorized person, funeral homes must get express permission to embalm; it cannot be implied. The Rule does not require you to get the permission in writing, as long as it is expressed approval. Some states, however, may require written authorization. Third, all of the following apply: The funeral home is unable to contact a family member or other authorized person after exercising due diligence. In trying to contact the family, funeral homes must exhaust all means known, given the time constraints. The funeral home has no reason to believe that the family does not want embalming performed, and after embalming the body, the funeral home obtains subsequent approval. In seeking approval, the funeral director must tell the family that if they select a funeral where embalming would be required, they will be charged a fee, but that the funeral home will not charge a fee if they select a funeral where embalming would not be necessary. If the family then expressly approves embalming or chooses a funeral where embalming is required, the funeral home may charge them for the embalming performed. But, if the family chooses a funeral where no embalming would be required, the funeral home cannot charge for the embalming.

The explanations for the level of expectation surrounding the authorization to embalm are many, including the elaborate discussion above concerning the FTC Funeral Rule. Another compelling reason to comply with the FTC Funeral Rule, and to exercise proficiency with every aspect of the Rule, is to recognize that the maximum civil penalty for a single violation is currently $43,792. Also, the fundamental application of embalming may be perceived quite differently among people. It is common for religious or cultural norms and traditions to predetermine if a particular family will select the embalming option. Any deviance from these plans can be a source of great distress for a client family, and possibly even worse, embalming without authorization is considered mutilation. It is essential that the professional funeral director understands the intricacies and importance of seeking and securing authorization for embalming. Form 3.17 below, presents a Sample Authorization to Embalm. As with all samples in this book, this form is not intended for professional use. It is recommended that funeral home operators contact legal counsel to assist in the development of all authorizations utilized in practice.

Sample Form 3.17
Embalming Authorization

Name of Deceased: _____ **Date of Death:** _____

Statement of Authenticity
I/We, the undersigned, certify, warrant and represent, as <u>Relationship to the Deceased,</u> that I/we have the full legal right and authority to, and permission from any and all other relatives, guardians or conservators to authorize the disposition of the remains of <u>Name of Deceased</u> , further no one else has this authority.

Embalming Authorization
I/We the undersigned, authorize and direct <u>Funeral</u> Home, its employees, independent contractors, and agents (including apprentices and/or mortuary science students under the supervision of a licensed embalmer) to care for, embalm, perform restorative measures and prepare the body of <u>Deceased's Name</u>. I/We understand that this authorization includes permission to embalm at the funeral home or at another facility equipped for embalming. Furthermore, I /We further acknowledge that embalming results may vary as results depend on numerous factors, including, but not limited to the conditions surrounding the death, time lapse between death and embalming, physical condition of the body at the time of death, life-saving measures attempted, cause of death, natural elements, tissue/organ donations, and post-mortem examinations.

Indemnify Statement
I/We agree to indemnify, release and hold the funeral home, their affiliates, agents, employees and assigns, harmless from any and all loss, damages, liability or causes of action in connection with the services and disposition of the remains of the deceased.

Signed this _____ day of _____ , 20_____ at _____

Print Name:
_____

Signature:
_____

Relationship to the Deceased:
_____

Print Name:
_____

Signature:
_____

Relationship to the Deceased:
_____

Funeral Home Representative: _____ Date: _____

Authorization for Restorative Applications

The critical nature of seeking and securing authorization for various services offered in the funeral profession has been well documented thus far in this chapter. Although the difference between a major and a minor restoration is not clearly defined, as both definitions typically refer to the amount of time and skill required, definitions that are relative to the professional engaged in the practice, it is universally accepted to secure authorization for any restoration one can categorize as major. A more conservative approach is supported by Mayer (1980), when he offers that permission to undertake both major and minor restorations should be secured, and furthermore, suggests that the only restorations for which permission is not suggested are for swelling, leakages, and tissue discolorations. Most reasonable people conclude that any time your procedure involves incisions, excisions (both of which may be considered mutilation) or any other technique that may fundamentally change the appearance of the deceased, it is highly recommended and best practice to secure authorization from the party with legal rights to disposition. It is always advised to discuss these procedures with the authorized agent and secure authentic approval prior to performing these treatments. It is best to allow space on the authorization form for some specificity when disclosing the restorative procedures that will be performed in an effort to be certain that the authorized agent clearly understands the procedure and the possible outcomes. And, as discussed when seeking authorization for embalming, it is best to be realistic and to not make any binding promises to the family regarding the outcome of restorative procedures. Let the family be the judge of your work. It is, once again, important that this document follows the protocol set forth in this chapter regarding clarity of language and form. These documents need to be easy to read and understand, leaving no doubt that the authorized agent has full knowledge of the procedures authorized.

Form 3.18 below presents a Sample Authorization for Restorative Applications. It is advised that all funeral professionals have documents of this nature generated (with formal legal assistance) and prepared to use if required during an arrangement conference. The more prepared we can be as professionals, the more comfortable client families will become as we work with them to arrange a meaningful and memorable service for their loved one.

• • •

For Critical Thought…

You are working with a family that has selected a service that will include visitation, an open casket service, with a cremation to follow the funeral service. The next of kin, a spouse of 40 years, is also the authorized agent. During the arrangement meeting she indicates how much he disliked the way the tumor on his neck changed his appearance, and it is her wish to have this removed prior to the first viewing. Consider this scenario, and discuss any authorizations that would be required given the facts presented.

Sample Form 3.18
Authorization for Restorative Applications

Name of Deceased: _____ **Date of Death:** _____

Statement of Authenticity
I/We, the undersigned, certify, warrant and represent, as <u>Relationship to the Deceased,</u> that I/we have the full legal right and authority to, and permission from any and all other relatives, guardians or conservators to authorize the disposition of the remains of <u>Name of Deceased</u>, further no one else has this authority.

Restorative Application Authorization
I/We the undersigned, authorize and direct <u>Funeral</u> Home, its employees, independent contractors, and agents (including apprentices and/or mortuary science students under the supervision of a licensed embalmer) to perform restorative work on the remains of <u>Deceased's Name</u>. I/We understand that the results of restorative work vary dependent on body conditions and the exact nature of the treatments, at all times acceptable mortuary techniques will be utilized in accordance with professional standards. I/We herein acknowledge full responsibility for results of the restorative work which includes restorative applications to address the following, _____
_____

Indemnify Statement
I/We agree to indemnify, release and hold the funeral home, their affiliates, agents, employees and assigns, harmless from any and all loss, damages, liability or causes of action in connection with the services and disposition of the remains of the deceased.

Signed this _____ day of _____, 20_____ at _____

Print Name: _____

Signature: _____

Relationship to the Deceased: _____

Print Name: _____

Signature: _____

Relationship to the Deceased: _____

Funeral Home Representative: _____ Date: _____

Other Associated Forms

It is reasonable to believe that the extensive examination of the required authorizations associated with cremation services thus far has been thorough, yet, without a brief discussion of other related forms, this discussion would be incomplete. As is pointed out in many areas of this text, it is critical that cremation providers are not only familiar with the specific laws and regulations governing cremation practices in their own service area, but they necessarily must be or become experts. This is true with all cremation practices, required authorizations, as well as with other associated forms. Much like the specific state laws regarding authorizations and cremation operations, it is essential that all cremation providers are experts with respect to forms associated with cremation services. Although the names of these forms differ from state to state or in various service areas, cremationists must always remain mindful of these forms and execute these forms timely and professionally when serving a family that has selected cremation services. As with all required authorizations, it is essential to always retain and archive these documents. Below is a list of such forms. Remember, the names can vary depending on your service area.

- Medical Examiner / Coroner Permit: A governing legal entity in your service area (such as a medical examiner or coroner), upon receipt of required information will investigate the death in order to verify no need exists to perform any post mortem examination of the body. As cremation is permanent and irreversible, any information received from such an examination would be destroyed. When this governing entity is satisfied that no need exists for such examination, they will issue a permit that approves the cremation to move forward. Always remember, this permit is required in addition to all necessary and required authorizations that must be completed and signed by the authorizing agent. Not until all required authorizations and forms are completed and appropriately signed may a case be scheduled for cremation.
- Verification of Identity of Remains: As with so many elements associated with cremation, the reality of the process being final and irreversible drives many processes in order to reduce mistakes and address concerns surrounding liability and litigation. This has made the completion of the Verification of Identity of Remains form become common practice and, in many areas, a required form that must be completed and signed by the authorizing agent. Although, at times, families do not desire to view the deceased (or it may be unwise due to trauma), it is essential that the identity of the remains is verified. The best method is to have the authorizing agent actually view the remains and sign the form indicating the remains are indeed the remains at concern. If this is not possible some options may include photographs or identifying marks on the person. Every cremation provider must be aware of the approved methods of identification in their own service area, and always verify the identity of the remains utilizing an approved method and have the authorizing agent sign the form indicating this identity. This MUST be completed prior to scheduling and moving forward with the cremation process.
- Burial Transit Permit: Once again, it is necessary for all cremation providers to be familiar with requirements for their specific state and service area. Most states require funeral service professionals to secure a burial transit permit for cremated remains that will be transported out of state. Although this is more common with bodily remains, as increasing cremation rates are realized, it is becoming commonplace for states to require this permit when cremated remains will be transported across state lines for final disposition. The professional funeral director is always aware of all requirements in their service area and will secure this permit if required. If this permit is required, never make travel arrangements for the cremated remains, nor should you schedule a service at the location of final disposition, until this permit has been received.
- Death Certificate: The death certificate is fundamental to the work completed as funeral directors; although not exclusive to cremation services, it is important to mention the completion of this document as well as ensuring certification of this document for the client family. Certified death certificates may be required for the completion

of various tasks for client families and funeral directors alike. Funeral directors must assist families in completing the required information and then process the information to certify the document. Always be prepared to counsel families regarding parties that will require certified copies, and advise with respect to how to obtain additional certified copies in the future.
- Chain of Custody Form: Establishing, verifying, and documenting the chain of custody of human remains is vital for the successful funeral professional. In certain states and service areas, this may be required by laws and regulations; even if this is not required, it is certainly the best practice. This is essential for all funeral professionals, but this importance is highlighted when you consider a funeral operation that may utilize third party providers for the purposes of first calls, embalming and cremation services. As the actual funeral professional that will be contracting directly with the client family, you MUST establish protocol that ensures that you are knowledgeable of the custody of the remains at all times, this information must be documented and retained in your file archives. Families trust that the funeral home they select will care for and treat their loved one with respect from the first call until final disposition, this includes the establishment and adherence to specific protocol with respect to the chain of custody of the human remains the entire time the family has entrusted the funeral home with the care of the remains of a loved one.
- Refrigeration Log: The refrigeration log is another necessary form that is most likely required documentation in your state and service area. This log tracks the remains as they are placed into refrigeration, and also documents any time the remains are removed from this location, for example for a viewing, service, or the cremation itself. If the remains are removed and then once again placed in the refrigeration unit, this too will be denoted. This log, which should always be completed and archived in the crematory's records upon completion of the form, assists in the process of always having exact knowledge of the whereabouts of all human remains entrusted to the care of the funeral home or crematory, the funeral professional always maintains meticulous records, and the refrigeration log is certainly a document that must always be utilized and maintained when operating a crematory.
- Cremation Log: The necessity to mention the obvious may seem somewhat unwarranted, but the fundamental obligation to log all cremations makes it a must to mention this document. This is another form that is most likely required in your state and local service area, and all crematory operators MUST document all cremations utilizing a cremation log. This document will provide documentation of the exact time and day the cremation took place. This process will provide additional security regarding the identification of the remains and the chain of custody of the remains, remember, the funeral professional must always have exact knowledge as to the whereabouts of remains in his/her care, as well as where the remains are in relation to the cremation process. Furthermore, this document allows cremationists to document when the process is completed and when the cremated remains have moved into the next phase of the cremation process. The cremation log is another required document that should not only be maintained, but also saved and archived in the crematory permanent files. You should never cremate if the facility you work at does not practice the use of a cremation log.

Conclusion - Required Authorizations, Final Thoughts

As indicated at the onset of this chapter, the importance of authorizations is paramount. Yes, in most situations, securing authorizations is a matter of compliance with the law, but as presented here, when seeking and securing authorizations is completed professionally, it may also serve to build a trusted working relationship with client families. It is simply good business practice for the professional funeral director to instill confidence in the families they serve by always securing required authorizations and communicating the details associated with these authorizations during the arrangement conference. The professional funeral director will be recognized as the expert during the arrangement conference, and for that reason should be fully prepared to explain every detail and facet of each and every authorization document presented to the family.

Numerous extremely important elements associated with authorizations were covered in this chapter, one being the importance of ascertaining and securing authorization from the party that holds the legal right of disposition of the deceased. It is critical the funeral professional remains vigilant of the importance of determining this party, and always receiving authorization from this party, especially prior to viewing of the body, conducting services with the body present, and certainly when discussing the disposition of the remains. It is also the responsibility of the funeral professional to maintain an understanding of the laws regarding rights of disposition in the service area in which they practice. Retention of signed and executed authorizations may be a requirement of law or regulation, but maintaining an easily accessible archive of these documents is simply good practice and may prove to be crucial should questions arise later, which is sometimes defined by months or years.

The actual authorization documents were also discussed in this chapter, including the importance of generating a document that is clear and easy to read and understand. Each section of these forms should have a title to further aid the client family when reading these documents. Concerns with respect to receiving an authentic signature were also discussed. In this technological age it is common for families to express a desire to use numerous communication modes to complete the authorization process, and the responsible funeral professional will develop an awareness of which modes are legal and binding particularly when it comes to securing signatures. The chapter concluded with a brief discussion with respect to other associated forms when a client family selects services that include a cremation.

In our ever-changing society, it is important the funeral profession evolves with the culture. Although some authorizations are more commonly associated with a service that includes a cremation, it is critical that the funeral professional understands the importance of offering all services to all families, and not limit service options simply because a family is interested in cremation, therefore, virtually all authorization forms utilized in the practice of funeral service may apply to a service that includes a cremation. The material covered in this chapter, no doubt, are at the core of a successful and thriving cremation operation.

Consider This...

This is what happened:

The son comes in. His father had just died, and he had to make arrangements. He said, "we want to do a memorial service on Saturday, so I need to get everything done. My sister's not available, she's out of town, and I want to get him cremated, get the cremated remains back, and have the memorial service."

The funeral director says, "Here's the problem, I'm going to need both of you to sign an authorization form."

And of course he says, "She can't come; she's out of town."

"Is there any way to talk to her?"

"Yeh, we can get her on the phone and you can talk to her."

And he said, "Maybe we can fax it to her, as well."

So they called her up, she said that would be fine. They faxed the authorization form, she signed it, and it came back. They go ahead with the cremation.

Fast forward about a week. All of a sudden, the daughter calls. "What's going on with my father's funeral service?"

"We did cremation. Your brother took the cremated remains, and I believe you did a memorial service back home. What do you need?"

"I've never been contacted."

"Well, wait a second, I talked to you myself on the telephone. We faxed you the authorization form and you signed it."

"No, I've never been contacted."

The brother knew his sister did not want to have cremation and would refuse. The woman the funeral director spoke with? Guess who that was, his girlfriend.

But now we had a daughter who wanted to be involved and wanted to see her dad. We ended up settling the lawsuit for about $40,000.

There are probably a lot of people thinking, "Wait a minute. If he lied and the girlfriend lied, that's fraud, and they've got to be responsible."

You're right; they were.

And how this works is, when the son signed a cremation authorization, he said this: "I state that all these facts are true, and if they're not, I'm going to hold harmless and indemnify you." That's wonderful. The problem is, what did the daughter sign? She didn't sign anything. So, guess what; she's still allowed to sue.

Now, after we lost that lawsuit, we were able to go back to the brother and say, "Hey, $40,000 – fork it over." Do you think we got $40,000? Nope. We got a judgment. Someday – maybe.

The point is this: When you're dealing with out-of-town people, you've got to make sure you're dealing with the right people. A faxed signature is fine. Federal and state law both say electric signatures are acceptable, enforceable. If it's the right person's signature.

They don't tell you what you have to do to make sure you have the right signature. So what do you do? A lot of people will immediately say, "Let's get that thing notarized." No, a notary by itself is not enough. The notary's signature just says, "I saw him sign. I don't know who he is."

So you want that document to say something like this: I hereby notarize the signature of Jane Smith and have verified her ID by the attached identification." And then you're going to have the notary take a copy of the ID and put it on that form and sign off. That will protect you. That's what you need to handle out-of-town cases – at a minimum.

It's not the only way; it's probably one of the easiest ways. But you need to verify they are who they say. I'm sorry to break the news to you, but people will lie to get what they want.
- **This story was reprinted courtesy of Poul Lemasters and Lemasters Consulting**: lemastersconsulting.com/

Chapter 4 – Final Disposition of cremated remains & Shipping Protocol

Chapter Learning Objectives

Upon completion of the study of this chapter students should:

- Understand the challenges and complexities associated with the final disposition of cremated remains.
- Recognize various options available for the final disposition of cremated remains.
- Comprehend protocol for the transportation of cremated remains, both shipping (domestic and international) as well as other methods of transporting including air travel.
- Be able to discuss appropriate containers and packaging for transporting and shipping cremated remains.
- Understand necessary documents that must accompany cremated remains for transportation.
- Comprehend the reality of unclaimed cremated remains, as well as possible reasons and solutions to this problem.
- Understand the law and expectations with respect to the disposition of unclaimed cremated remains.

• • •

Introduction

When considering the final disposition of cremated remains the words creativity, innovative, and endless come to mind. Families often decide on a more traditional interment or entombment of the cremated remains, but it is also not uncommon for families to decide to select a more unique option. A simple web search reveals options such as becoming part of a coral reef, blending the cremated remains to become part of a tattoo, vintage style album, loaded ammunition, or fireworks display. When considering the final disposition of cremated remains the sky is truly the limit, what will be next?

This chapter explores the complexities that surround the final disposition of cremated remains including customs and restrictions, legal and otherwise; following this will be an analysis of many options available to consumers with respect to final disposition, including shipping protocol. In conclusion, a discussion will take place with respect to the disposition of unclaimed cremated remains, a common issue in funeral service. The focus of this chapter is separate from the process of placing cremated remains in an urn; specifics about urns and other related cremation merchandise will be fully studied in Chapter Eight in conjunction with the discussion of containers for cremated remains. Additionally, services associated with the disposition of remains will not be addressed here; this will be explored in Chapter Ten, with the study of the arrangement conference. The ultimate purpose here is to explore the options available for the final disposition of cremated remains and related complications.

Image 4.1: Aerial scattering over significant and meaningful locations is increasing in popularity with cremation consumers, locations like the family farm above.
Image Source: Aerial Photo courtesy of the estate of John W. Bradley

Complexities Surrounding Final Disposition

First and foremost, funeral professionals must remain mindful that cremated remains are indeed human remains, and should always be treated with the upmost dignity and respect. Furthermore, the selection and determination of the location for the final disposition of cremated remains is still ultimately the process of locating a proper place of rest for a loved one; it is a place to honor and remember a life well-lived. Unfortunately, it is common for a relaxed attitude to exist around cremated remains, an attitude that is rarely witnessed around bodily remains. Just remember, if this is witnessed by client families or the public in general, you will be considered callus and uncompassionate. Although a body has been cremated, it is still the remains of a loved one and should be treated as such.

It should come as no surprise that the final disposition of cremated remains can be marred in controversy, when the funeral director does not take proper care to be certain of family wishes, and also secure appropriate authority to carry out these requests. It is imperative that the professional funeral director receives absolute instructions from the authorizing agent with respect to the ultimate disposition of the cremated remains, including an authentic signature. The instructions for final disposition are typically part of the authorization to cremate. The *2019 Cremation Standards for Funeral Service Professionals, 2nd ed*.

published by the National Funeral Directors Association (NFDA) indicates that a few states merely call for an authorization to be signed, but most states indicate in detail the items that must be contained within the cremation authorization and disposition form. The NFDA publication further indicates that comprehensive forms are found in the state laws of Indiana, Kentucky, Ohio, and Utah, and that state laws may contain exceptions to authorization procedures. Not only must funeral directors be certain of family wishes, but they also must be sure that the final disposition of the cremated remains is completed within the parameters of the law regarding final disposition of cremated remains. It is the duty of the professional funeral director to be knowledgeable and current regarding all laws (federal, state, & local) and regulations pertaining to the final disposition of cremated remains in their own service area. It is common for state laws to require that disposition permits accompany and are affixed to the urn or other container housing the cremated remains, and if the cremated remains are being stored in more than one container, each container needs to have affixed its own disposition form. It is also a common requirement for a burial transit form to accompany cremated remains as they are being transported to their location of final disposition. Remember, as long as the funeral home or crematory operator has custody of the cremated remains, these remains are due the same respect and ethical standards that are practiced throughout the profession.

The commingling of cremated remains is also a challenge faced by funeral home and crematory operators. Two distinct situations present the opportunity to commingle cremated remains. One is during the cremation process itself, and the second is during the final disposition of the remains. Currently, we are focused on the latter, the issue of commingling during the final disposition of remains. Concerns surrounding the cremation process will be fully addressed in Chapter Six. Prior to engaging in the process of commingling cremated remains, be certain the law in your service area deems this process acceptable, and then always complete a commingling authorization form (see Chapter Three for a sample form) that details the specifics surrounding the final disposition, including an authentic signature of the authorizing agent. Options typically involving commingling of cremated remains may consist of placing the cremated remains of more than one person in a special urn, placing remains in an ossuary, or utilizing scattering as a means of final disposition. If a funeral director is requested by a family to complete the act of scattering, it is the professional responsibility of the funeral director to complete this task on an individual basis. Avoid taking cremated remains of more than one person to scatter at the same time. The bottom line is that commingling of cremated remains should never take place unless authorized by law, all regulations are followed, and express authorization from the next-of-kin or authorizing agent has been received.

Scattering is a common method of final disposition that may present challenges for a funeral director. It is common for families to express the desire to take the cremated remains of a loved one to a favorite vacation spot, or other memorable location and scatter the remains. This can certainly offer the survivors a significant "place" that signifies the life of a loved one, but it is vital that funeral directors understand and relate the restrictions that may apply, such as legal restrictions and any local customs that exist. Funeral directors must also inform client families of best practices surrounding the scattering of cremated remains. Prior to scattering cremated remains, it is advisable to encourage families to retain at least a small portion of the cremated remains that can be interred in a cemetery or placed in some other meaningful location that the family can visit to honor and remember the deceased. The family may decline, but it is our job to provide options, which is better than working with a family after the fact, when they indicate they wish they would have created a more permanent burial spot.

Scattering laws and regulations greatly vary from state to state. For example, Oklahoma at the time of this publication had no specific scattering laws, yet California has very detailed regulations presented in the *Cremated Remains Disposers Booklet: Complying with California Law (2017)*. The significance here is that funeral professionals must be knowledgeable of all local, state, and federal laws and regulations related to their service area, and this includes any that surround the act of scattering cremated remains. It is common practice for scattering to require a permit. These permits typically include specific instructions related to the authorizing agent's signature, acceptable urn for the specified scattering practice requested, as well as instructions for scattering via air, earth, water, or in a dedicated scattering cemetery. According to the *NFDA 2019 Cremation Standards for Funeral Service Professionals, 2nd ed.*, scattering or burial of cremated remains at sea may occur as long as this takes place at least three nautical miles (California Law stipulates scattering at sea cannot take place within 500 yards of the shoreline) from land, and that flowers, wreaths, and urns that are readily decomposable in a marine environment may also be disposed of with the cremated remains. The NFDA publication additionally adds that within thirty days of the scattering, a registration of the disposition must be filed with the Regional Administrator of the Environmental Protection Agency (EPA) Region by the operator of the vessel which carried the remains to the place of disposition. *The Cremation Association of North America (CANA) Model Cremation Law and Explanation approved in November 2017*, indicates that cremated remains may be scattered over uninhabitable public land, the sea or other public waterways, furthermore, cremated remains may be disposed of in any manner on the private property of a consenting owner, upon direction of the Authorizing Agent. If cremated remains are to be disposed of on private property, other than a dedicated cemetery, the Authorizing Agent shall provide the crematory authority, with the written consent of the property owner. Additionally, this practice is subject to health and environmental standards as well as the reality that the pulverization process continued until the remains were reduced to a particle-size of one-eighth inch or less. Always verify that the proposed area for the scattering is not restricted by law or personal private property rights, and no local prohibition exists. It is best practice, that any person that will scatter such cremated human remains, should file with the local registrar of births and deaths, in the county nearest the point where the cremated remains are to be scattered, a verified statement containing the name of the deceased person, the time and place of death, the place at which the cremated remains are to be scattered, and any other information that the local registrar of births and deaths may require. At this point it should be abundantly clear that the scattering of cremated remains, while enormously popular, is not overseen by clear standardized laws, regulations, and practices. The professional funeral director must remain current with respect to legal protocol in their service area, and at all times adhere to these standards.

A final comment is appropriate with respect to final disposition of cremated remains. As evidenced above, final disposition has become quite complex and burdensome with regulation. It is reasonable to predict that in the future, companies offering to serve as disposers of cremated remains will be in demand across the country. In fact, these business operations already exist in many areas of the United States, and it seems realistic that this trend will only increase as the cremation market continues to grow. If a third-party is contracted to oversee the final disposition of cremated remains, it is essential that funeral directors continue to evaluate these business relationships with the same scrutiny that all third-party providers are assessed. Ultimately, it is the funeral home's responsibility to verify that all family wishes are carried out and done so according to all federal, state, and local laws. It is critical to maintain detailed records of all business transactions, and the performance of the contracted items, including the final disposition of cremated remains, whether performed by the funeral home or by a third-party.

Options for Final Disposition of Cremated Remains

With infinite options available, it is extremely important that funeral directors never lose sight that the determination of the location and method of final disposition of cremated remains is undeniably the act of locating a place of final rest. This place can serve to honor and remember the life of a loved one. It is also essential that funeral directors, crematory operators, and companies that assist in the disposition of cremated remains, are up to date and knowledgeable of the laws and rules that regulate the disposition of cremated remains in their service area, and all final decisions are confirmed and approved with an authentic signature from the authorizing agent. When considering different possibilities for the final disposition of cremated remains, in no way can any list of possible options be exhaustive, as people are creating new options every day. Unlike bodily burial, the disposition of cremated remains may involve all or only part of the remains, and multiple locations may be involved with respect to final disposition.

Regardless of the decision reached, all federal, state, and local laws must be adhered to, and these decisions must be approved by the authorizing agent. As indicated above, it would be impossible to provide a complete list of options for the disposition of cremated remains, but here is a list of methods of disposition that have been utilized in recent years.

- Interment (Inurnment): Although numerous options exist, burial of cremated remains is a very common method of final disposition. This practice can take place in a cemetery or on private land, but always be sure to adhere to all related laws and regulations. If utilizing a public cemetery, you will also need to verify cemetery rules that may specify details about the urn used and urn vault requirements. CANA defines inurnment as the act or ceremony of burying an urn containing cremated remains.
- Entombment: The placement of the remains in a columbarium niche. These may be located in cemeteries (indoor and outdoor options exist), and it is also common for churches, and now even funeral homes, to offer a columbarium for the entombment of cremated remains. It is common practice for each columbarium to have specific urn dimensions in order to facilitate entombment, and many even require the purchase of a specific urn.
- Scattering (land, air or water): Scattering cremated remains over land, through the air, or over water as allowed by state and local law. Different options exist regarding scattering, but if a family is going to participate or actually perform the scattering of the remains, funeral directors need to inform the family what to expect and what they will witness. For example, it is important to describe the actual appearance and consistency of the cremated remains and also inform families about the medallion utilized for identification throughout the cremation process; this medallion should be attached to the plastic bag containing the cremated remains with a zip tie, or placed inside the plastic bag with the cremated remains. Also, when casting (tossing cremated remains to the wind) cremated remains over

land or water most of the remains fall immediately, but some of the dust particles will remain airborne; thus, it is important to consider the wind direction for obvious reasons. Aerial scattering requires the assistance of a professional service. As the remains are cast from a plane; a plume can be visible from the ground and can be a very powerful experience for family members. Depending on the service utilized for aerial scattering, families may be permitted to assist with the scattering itself or, at minimum, request certificates and photographs of the scattering. Scattering over a body of water also avails options, such as casting to the open wind or placing the remains in a water-soluble, biodegradable urn that dissolves and disperses the remains into the water. Remember, regardless of the option selected, always be knowledgeable of and adhere to all state and local regulations with respect to scattering cremated remains.

- Ossuary: The placement of cremated remains in a communal repository. If cremated remains are placed in an ossuary, be certain to communicate the reality of commingling and adhere to all state and local regulations. Also, as with all methods of final disposition, be sure to secure the authentic signature of the appropriate party authorizing the placement of the remains in the ossuary.
- Raking: Cremated remains are dispensed directly onto soil and raked into the earth. This is a common method in cemetery scattering gardens.
- Trenching: Cremated remains are dispensed into a superficial trench in the soil and subsequently covered. Creativity can be used in the creation of the trench to design a meaningful shape. Trenching is commonly used by families in a dedicated cemetery section. As with all methods of final disposition, be certain to adhere to all regulations.
- Sending into Space: Companies exist that offer families the ability to send small portions of cremated remains into space. Typically, only between 1-7 grams are allowed and options may include sending the remains to orbit the earth or beyond the earth's orbit into deep space.
- Underwater Reef: This is the process of mixing cremated remains with concrete and developed into a reef and submerged to the ocean floor. Companies that provide this service can create a small individual personal reef or unite (comingle) cremated remains together to create larger reefs.
- Solidified Remains: A relatively new option is solidifying cremated remains into stone. It is estimated that adult cremated remains will produce between 40 and 60 solids and the appearance of each set will vary naturally in shape, color, and texture making each collection of solidified remains unique.
- Memorialized in Art: Companies and artisans can combine cremated remains with paint, glass or other media and create various art designs, typically driven by family wishes.
- Made into Jewelry: Companies exist that will process cremated remains under intense heat and pressure to the point that component carbon is turned into a man-made diamond. Upon completion of this process, the diamond can be used in the creation of jewelry.
- Keepsakes: As indicated earlier in this chapter, it is advised to inquire with families if they would like to retain small amounts of the cremated remains for burial (if scattering) or to retain in a special place. The keepsake option is ideal for this purpose, because it allows for the housing of small portions of cremated remains. These may be mini versions of the urn selected to house the majority of the remains, jewelry pieces, or even brass rose stems. The bottom line is that keepsakes allow the cremated remains to be divided among the family members or to place a portion of the remains in a meaningful place, if the majority of the remains are to be scattered.

- Return to Family: An option selected by many cremation consumers is to bring the cremated remains home in an urn or other container, and create a special area to honor the life of a loved one. If it is the intention for the family to pick up the cremated remains, always be sure the authorized agent or other party assigned by the agent is the one to sign for and pick up the cremated remains. It is also important that the funeral home staff remain mindful that the cremated remains are indeed the remnants of the body and should be afforded appropriate respect. It is best to have the urn in a dedicated area of the funeral home, placed in a reverent and respectful way, and let the family pick up cremated remains when they are ready. Always inform the family what to expect with respect to the weight of the container and always assist with transporting the cremated remains.
- Disposal if Unclaimed: Unfortunately, cremated remains that remain unclaimed are too common. Funeral homes and crematory operators have options when they are faced with cremated remains that are abandoned by the family. This topic will be covered in some detail in the final section of this chapter.

Shipping Cremated Remains

Although shipping cremated remains is not a means of final disposition, it is often the final act a funeral home or crematory operator has with the remains, and for this reason the current process for shipping cremated remains is presented here. The United States Postal Service (USPS) policy regarding the shipping of cremated remains was updated in September 2019, consistent with the previous policy, Registered Mail service is not authorized for the domestic shipping of cremated remains. All domestically shipped cremated remains must be shipped using Priority Mail Express, and Priority Mail Express International service is available for international shipments. As carriers such as UPS, Fed-Ex and all other carriers will not accept cremated remains for shipment, it is extremely important for funeral service professionals to be aware of the current USPS guidelines for shipping cremated remains. The current USPS protocol will serve as the primary source utilized for the information contained in this section, but it is important to first discuss processes prior to the actual shipping, mainly the packaging and labeling in preparation for shipping. Suggested protocol for the packaging and labeling in preparation for shipping are presented in the Second Edition of *Cremation Standards for Funeral Service Professionals* (2019), a publication by the National Funeral Directors Association (NFDA). These protocols, in conjunction with information related to crematory operations (CANA, 2019), provide the foundation for the following suggested items regarding appropriate procedures for the packaging and labeling of cremated remains in preparation for shipping. It is always important to verify and default to the current USPS suggested procedures prior to shipping cremated remains.

1. Always place processed cremated remains in a strong and durable thick plastic bag (minimum 2 mil. thickness). It is important to capture as many minute particles as possible from the processing equipment and place in the plastic bag. If the total volume of the processed cremated remains exceeds the capacity of the plastic bag, place these remains in a second plastic bag, identifying as such.
2. The plastic bag should be sealed closed with a zip tie as twist ties can easily open and allow access to the remains.
3. Place the plastic bag containing the cremated remains in the appropriate urn/container and place a cremation identification label on either the top or bottom of the container.

4. Be certain all identification numbers match the medallion or tag number.
5. If multiple containers are required to house the cremated remains, each unit must have a cremation identification label, marked "1 of 3," "2 of 3," etc. It is also important to note on each label the number of the specific container that holds the cremation identification medallion.
6. If the capacity of the selected urn is unacceptable for the placement of the cremated remains (less than 200 cubic inches), do not force the cremated remains to fit. Notify the arranging funeral director so they can communicate with the family in order to secure an additional container to place the additional remains.
7. As a general rule, it is suggested to not place cremated remains directly into a keepsake urn. Remains should first be placed in a plastic bag. Follow the same procedures outlined above when placing cremated remains into a keepsake urn. If the selected keepsake is too small to hold the remains, notify the arranging funeral director for further instructions. These recommendations do not apply to jewelry or other mementos as these items are typically too small to attempt to first place in a plastic bag. In these cases, a portion of the cremated remains are placed directly into the small mementos. It is best to inform the family that this is the case.
8. Once cremated remains have been properly placed in the urn/container, place the urn/container in a locked secure area, inaccessible to the general public.
9. Always be aware of state regulations regarding how long unclaimed cremated remains must be held, and make certain all funeral home personnel are knowledgeable of funeral home policy regarding unclaimed cremated remains.

When the discussion turns specifically to the actual shipping of cremated remains, the prudent action is to go directly to the source, the United States Postal Service (USPS). The procedures presented here have been taken directly from the USPS publication, How to Package and Ship Cremated Remains, Publication 139, September 2019. Although these procedures were current at the time of this text, it is the responsibility of funeral service professionals to make sure they remain informed of the most current USPS guidelines regarding the shipping of cremated remains.

General Instructions

Cremated remains are permitted to be mailed to any domestic address when the package is prepared as described below and in the referenced postal manuals.

Cremated remains are permitted to be mailed to an international address when the designating country does not prohibit the contents and when Priority Mail Express International service is available to that country.

Packaging

You will need a primary inner sift-proof container, cushioning material, and an outer shipping package.

Note: A sift-proof container is any vessel that does not allow loose powder to leak or sift out. There are many options available to store cremated remains – from simple wooden boxes to decorative urns. USPS® recommends consulting with a licensed funeral director to help you select the best container.

Inner Primary Container

Domestic Shipping: **The inner primary container must be strong, durable, and constructed in such a manner as to protect and securely contain the contents inside. It must be properly sealed and sift-proof.**

Seal and Address the Inner Primary Container

In the event the shipping label becomes detached from the outer container, the Postal Service™ recommends that you put the sift-proof container in a sealed plastic bag. Then, attach a label with the complete return address and delivery address on the sealed plastic bag and the wording "Cremated Remains."

Cushioning Material

For both domestic and international shipping, place sufficient cushioning all around the inner primary sift-proof container to prevent it shifting inside the outer shipping package during transit and to absorb any shock to prevent breakage.

Outer Shipping Package

For both domestic and international shipping, cremated remains must be shipped by USPS Priority Mail Express or Priority Mail Express International Service utilizing either a USPS-produced or customer-supplied shipping package. If using a customer-supplied shipping package, it must be strong and durable to withstand transportation handling.

For convenience, the Postal Service has a Priority Mail Express Cremated Remains box that may be used for domestic or international shipments using the applicable Priority Mail Express service. The Priority Mail Express Cremated Remains box can be ordered online at the Postal Store on USPS.com® and is available as part of a kit.

Before closing and sealing the shipping package, the Postal Service recommends adding a slip of paper with both the sender's and recipient's address and contact information inside the package. This extra step will help to identify the sender and receiver in the event the shipping label becomes detached.

Labeling and Markings

To increase the visibility of mail pieces containing cremated remains, the outer shipping box (USPS produced or customer-supplied) containing cremated remains must be marked with Label 139, Cremated

Remains, affixed to each side (including top and bottom). Label 139 is available at the Postal Store on USPS.com or can be obtained at a retail Post Office™ location.

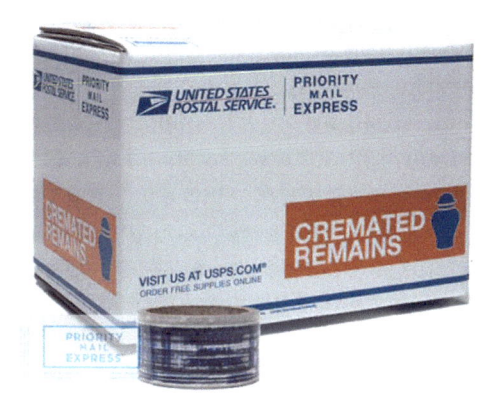

Image 4.2: Cremated Remains Human Kit 1/USPS Priority Mail Express

Image 4.3: USPS Label 139

Address Your Package

Domestic Shipping:

A complete return address and delivery address must be used. The address format for a package is the same as for an envelope. Write or print address labels clearly. Use ink that does not smear and include the addresses and ZIP Codes™ for you and your recipient.

Double check the mailing address, especially the ZIP Code. You can use Look Up a ZIP Code™ on USPS.com.

Mailers may generate single-ply Priority Mail Express labels through Click-N-Ship® or other USPS-approved methods.

International Shipping:

A complete return address and delivery address must be used. The mailer must indicate the identity of the contents (Cremated Remains) on the required applicable customs declaration form. To determine the applicable required customs form, see IMM Section 123.61.

Note: If available, the cremation certificate should be attached to the outer box or made easily accessible. The sender is responsible for adherence to any restrictions or observances noted by the designating country.

Be aware that different countries may have different and unique requirements, always verify specific requirements and make sure these are fulfilled prior to shipping. It is best practice to always contact the consulate or embassy of the destination country to ascertain current requirements and also to verify that the country, indeed, will allow the receipt of cremated remains.

In addition to the detailed USPS guidelines presented above, it is valuable to also consider the following: Prior to packaging and shipping cremated remains, be certain that you have secured all required documents for the shipment, such as certified death certificates, burial transit permits, and a funeral home affidavit declaring that only the cremated remains of the identified individual are in the shipping container. Furthermore, it is advised to always select the *Signature upon Delivery* option when shipping cremated remains. This can offer an additional level of security as you work to ensure the remains reach the correct final destination. A final note regarding the shipment of cremated remains is necessary; many funeral professionals discourage the international shipping of cremated remains. Once the package leaves the United States, the USPS loses control over the package, and it becomes quite difficult to track.

Many share stories about cremated remains never arriving at the final destination when shipping internationally; for this reason, international shipping is discouraged by numerous funeral professionals. There are a few important notes to remember when a family is not comfortable with shipping cremated remains, or simply prefers to transport the remains privately. First, remember that the family will need to maintain items such as burial transit permits, certified death certificates, and labels identifying the contents of the urn or other container, and any other required documentation, and keep them with the remains at all times. If the transport of the cremated remains involves air travel, be mindful of the Transportation Security Administration (TSA) guidelines. The Ways to Travel with Cremated Remains (TSA, 2018) document indicates that travelers are allowed to travel with cremated remains in a checked bag, however it is recommended to do so in a carry-on bag to help protect the contents from the risks associated with checked baggage. Checked bags are subjected to rapid and sometimes rough movement along a series of conveyor belts as they make the trek to and from the aircraft. TSA has a clear process for screening cremated remains. TSA officers routinely conduct these types of screenings throughout our nation's airports. Cremated remains in carry-on bags must pass through the X-ray machine to be screened. If the X-ray operator cannot clear the remains, TSA may apply other, non-intrusive means of resolving the alarm. If the officer cannot determine that the container does not contain a prohibited item, the remains will not be permitted. Remember, when passing through TSA checkpoints, the remains must NOT be in a container that is lead lined, as all packages must be X-rayed as part of the security measures. Good options include plastic or cardboard containers, although generally wood may be acceptable. If the family would like to utilize a container for the final disposition that will not pass through TSA checkpoints, one option is to pack this urn empty in their luggage, and carry the cremated remains on the plane utilizing a temporary container. The bottom line is that if the urn will not pass through the TSA checkpoint, the family will most likely be required to surrender the urn or reschedule all travel plans until other arrangements can be made for the cremated remains. It is the responsibility of the professional funeral director to ensure all client families interested in traveling with cremated remains understand the necessary requirements to travel with the remains. It is also best to check with the specific airline and receive their current regulations regarding transporting cremated remains as some airlines do not allow cremated remains in checked baggage, so check with your airline first.

One final note regarding the shipping of cremated remains is the possibility of the funeral home shipping the cremated remains as cargo on a commercial airline. The first priority is to contact airlines to determine if this option exists, and if so, what are the requirements for the shipment. Also, remember that air cargo will most likely require a representative of a funeral home to receive the cremated remains at air cargo at the destination, not a member of the deceased's family. If this type of shipping is of interest to the client family, it is the funeral director's responsibility to determine if this option exists, and if so, receive verification of requirements in order to execute and process this for the client family. It is attention to detail that can help to ensure the safe and timely shipment of cremated remains.

This section has detailed specific guidelines regarding the procedures required for shipping cremated remains. Not only must funeral service professionals be aware of these requirements, it is important to remain knowledgeable of any changes to shipping protocol that may take place that will impact these practices. Once a funeral director releases cremated remains to the USPS (or the client family) for shipment/transportation, they lose direct control over the care of the remains. This is why great care must be taken to make sure all guidelines have been followed, appropriate documents filed, and labels affixed in order to provide the best opportunity for the cremated remains to ultimately arrive at the correct destination in a timely fashion.

Disposition of Unclaimed Cremated Remains

It is common to discover an area in a funeral home dedicated to unclaimed/abandoned cremated remains. One can only guess why this has become such a common occurrence, but it is important to consider why this is happening and examine possible solutions to this problem. The issues of dealing with unclaimed cremated remains is pervasive and common, as a result, most states have implemented laws to assist funeral homes and crematory operators in the disposition of these remains. In the following section we examine possible reasons cremated remains are unclaimed, as well as steps that may be taken to reduce the commonality of this practice. The final section of this chapter will cover laws and expectations regarding the disposition of unclaimed cremated remains.

Conceivable Reasons and Solutions

One can only speculate why so many cremated remains are unclaimed and left for funeral homes and crematories to make a decision regarding final disposition. Were the remains simply forgotten, or did the family truly believe they had adequately addressed final disposition when cremation was selected? As with any problem, it is important to consider if actions or inactions of participants may have contributed to the problem. So, we must consider if the discussion of final disposition actually took place during the arrangement conference, and if options for such disposition were presented to the authorizing agent.

Funeral directors need to remember that most families are relying on us to lead them through this process, and if we do not ask appropriate and necessary questions, it is reasonable to conclude that certain elements will be overlooked and forgotten. Closely related to this is the duty of the funeral director to explain to client families what options exist, and what decisions must be made when cremation is selected. It is possible for a family to believe that when cremation is selected, no further decisions are required with respect to dealing with the physical body of a loved one. The general public is relying on funeral directors to lead them, provide options, and explain required elements surrounding both services and final disposition of a loved one. When considering unclaimed cremated remains, it is also possible that at the time of death no survivors exist, and prior arrangements have not been made for the final disposition of the cremated remains; they may ultimately wind up being unclaimed.

It is interesting to consider possible reasons for the reality of unclaimed cremated remains, but now we must consider possible solutions. First, when working with a family that selects cremation, always determine the final disposition of the cremated remains, and have the authorizing agent sign the agreement indicating the choice selected. The authorization for final disposition typically accompanies the authorization to cremate (see Chapter Three) and should be discussed during the arrangement conference. Furthermore, information regarding the funeral home policies and procedures for unclaimed cremated remains can be placed on the authorization to cremate. This section, which will be signed by the authorizing agent, indicates the decision for final disposition must be made and executed, or the funeral home policy regarding final disposition will be enforced. In conclusion, every funeral home/crematory needs to have a written policy regarding cremated remains that is communicated to all employees. This policy needs to be included on the authorization to cremate form, and directors must address this concern with every family that selects cremation and always secure the authentic signature of the authorizing agent. This will provide the funeral home the ability to act accordingly with the families wishes, or after a specified length of time, enforce the funeral home's written policy regarding unclaimed cremated remains.

Laws and Expectations Regarding the Disposition of Unclaimed Cremated Remains

The reality of unclaimed cremated remains has led many states to implement laws that allow funeral service professionals the ability to move forward with the final disposition of these remains. Historically, it was the expectation of funeral service professionals to house these remains for an indefinite period of time. Laws vary from state to state, the second edition of *Cremation Standards for Funeral Service Professional* published by The National Funeral Directors Association (NFDA) in 2019, indicates that the amount of time a funeral home/crematory is required to hold cremated remains varies greatly, from as little as 30 days (North Carolina and South Dakota) to four years (Maine). The bottom line is that these laws permit funeral service professionals the opportunity to proceed with the final disposition of cremated remains if the authorizing agent fails to claim and take possession of the remains within a specified period of time. Funeral service professionals must be knowledgeable of the laws with respect to final disposition of unclaimed cremated remains in their own service area, and always adhere to these laws and regulations. The NFDA publication also states that funeral directors should observe any religious practices or preferences specified by the authorized agent when exercising the disposition of unclaimed cremated remains. Although not state law, the *Cremation Association of North America (CANA) Model Cremation Law and Explanation which was approved by the CANA Board of Directors in November 2017*, specifies that if after a period of 60 days from the time of cremation, if the Authorizing Agent or their representative has not specified the ultimate disposition or claimed the cremated remains, the Crematory Authority or person in possession of the cremated remains may dispose of the cremated remains in any manner permitted by law, and of course as long as this time period is in accordance with state law in your particular service area.

The problem of unclaimed cremated remains is real and prevalent; this is a reality that all cremation providers will need to address. As indicated in this chapter, steps can be taken to help prevent cremated remains from joining the unclaimed ranks - mainly written policy, authorization forms, and an effective arrangement conference. Even with diligent efforts, some cremated remains will ultimately be unclaimed. For this reason, laws and expectations with respect to storing and disposing of cremated remains have evolved and changed over time to help alleviate this burden on the funeral service profession. It is the duty and responsibility of every single funeral home and cremation provider to be knowledgeable of current laws regarding the disposition of cremated remains (including unclaimed remains) in their respective state and service area.

Conclusion

This chapter explores the complexities surrounding the final disposition of cremated remains as well as presents various options for final disposition. Specific options for final disposition include interment, entombment, scattering, placement in an ossuary, raking, trenching, sending into space, placement as part of an underwater reef, solidifying into stone, memorialized in art, made into jewelry, or simply returned to the family. Although this is a somewhat lengthy list, it is in no way an exhaustive list as new and creative ways to celebrate loved ones are being realized at a rapid pace. Also included in this chapter are the specific procedures related to the shipping of cremated remains, it is necessary for funeral service professionals to remain knowledgeable with respect to the intricacies of shipping and the packaging process. The final section of the chapter discusses unclaimed cremated remains including possible reasons for this reality, as well as some potential solutions. As we study cremation it is necessary to stay current on the various and emerging trends related to the disposition of cremated remains and also be knowledgeable with respect to the specific protocol related to the shipping of cremated remains.

• • •

For Critical Thought...

During an arrangement conference a client family indicates a desire to have their father's cremated remains shipped to a relative in another city and state. They communicate the relative will be taking the remains to a cemetery so they may be interred with their mother. Describe the exact process for preparing the remains for shipping and actually mailing the cremated remains, and also consider the forms that will be required in this scenario.

Now consider the family wanted to transport the cremated remains themselves, and they intend air travel. At a minimum, what instructions should you communicate to the family? What forms are required in this scenario, and what documentation should be provided to the family?

Chapter 5 – The Use of Third Party Crematories

Chapter Learning Objectives

Upon completion of the study of this chapter students should:

- Understand the necessary procedures to develop and foster professional relationships with third party crematories.
- Recognize the importance of establishing internal policies and procedures with respect to cremation practices.
- Understand the essential elements of due diligence.
- Be able to discuss suggested crematory interview questions.
- Comprehend appropriate items to be included on a crematory inspection checklist.

• • •

Introduction

Explaining to a family why their loved one was not transported directly to the funeral home after death is challenging at best. Imagine entering the arrangement room, before you even have the opportunity to greet the family, being questioned, "We did not trust the people that came to the house last night, so we followed them, and they did not even come here, they went to an industrial area on the other side of town, please explain." Certainly not an ideal way to start an arrangement conference. It is absolutely critical that funeral directors are completely transparent regarding business practices, which includes when a funeral home elects to utilize third party operators, including third party crematories. The practice of informing client families of such matters goes a long way in building a relationship of trust. The importance of utilizing best practices in the relationship between third party crematories has been substantially documented. It is essential that funeral service professionals understand that measures can and should be taken to reduce concerns in the use of third party providers. As long as the client family is contracting with a specific funeral home, the third party provider should be considered an extension of the services of the contracting funeral home. It is important that funeral homes disclose the use of third party providers to families. It is critical that funeral homes practice due diligence in an effort to ensure that third party providers operate according to funeral home standards, both professionally and ethically. The Tri State Crematory findings in Nobles, Georgia in 2002 forced funeral professionals to focus on due diligence with respect to third party crematories. As a result, these findings compelled lawmakers and funeral professionals to address methods necessary to ensure that third party crematories perform cremations as required by the law and in accordance with human decency. The fundamental goal of this chapter is to present a suggested pathway for building a successful relationship with third party crematories. This presentation includes the importance of establishing funeral home policies and procedures, obtaining the records of any crematory utilized, and ongoing interviews of crematory staff and management, as well as crematory inspections.

Internal Policies & Procedures

The CANA Crematory Operations Certification Program manual, 4th edition (2019) identifies a four-step due diligence process when a funeral home is considering using a third party crematory. The first step is internal due diligence, any funeral home that offers cremation services must examine their own cremation policies and procedures. Funeral homes should have specific policies and procedures in place that dictate protocol, procedures and policies surrounding the use of third party crematories. If none exist, the first step is to create such protocol. It is essential that these protocols include a minimum standard for identification and the preparation of remains. Also necessary are appropriate and required authorization forms and permits, instructions for final disposition and merchandise selection of alternative cremation containers, urns, as well as appropriate training for how to handle a cremation arrangement conference. If these standards are not drafted and adhered to in a funeral home, the development of such policies and procedures would certainly be a necessary first step when a funeral home makes the commitment to offer cremation services. The importance of each of these items is evident, so the inclusion of independent chapters or sections has been included in this text, but the focus of this chapter is specifically related to third party crematories. Once a funeral home determines that appropriate internal policies and procedures exist for cremation services, the search for a third party crematory will make more sense.

When selecting a third party provider, funeral home ownership/management can consider their own internal policies and procedures in order to determine if the operations of the third party provider align with the specific funeral home. Upon selection of a third party crematory, it is wise to enter into an agreement or contract that specifies funeral home policies and procedures for cremation services, and the expectation of services that will be provided. It is important to specify the rules and responsibilities included in this agreement, including the need for appropriate insurance. An agreement of this nature will help to ensure transparency with respect to policies and procedures as well as establish direct oversight of the chain of custody of human remains. Once these agreements are finalized, it is suggested that these records be kept in a safe place in the funeral home. Furthermore, always document all steps taken to ensure that third party providers/suppliers meet service expectations of the contracting funeral home. Items to consider should include, crematory records, ongoing interviews of crematory ownership and operators, and proper documentation of ongoing crematory inspections. Collectively these documents may be seen as vital elements in practicing due diligence.

Due Diligence

Due diligence is certainly the cornerstone of establishing and maintaining a good working relationship with a third party crematory. Gilligan (2011) presented the importance of routinely investigating third party crematories, including crematory records requests, interviewing crematory management, and physically inspecting the crematory. CANA (2019) supports the Gilligan approach, but adds the importance of first examining the funeral homes internal policies and procedures to make sure the selection of a third party will support the firms established policies and procedures.

Records Request

When establishing and maintaining a relationship with a third party crematory, it is essential to ascertain that the crematory is operating and complying within legal parameters as well as meeting professional standards. The expectation is that the funeral home will seek and receive crematory records as requested. These records should include appropriate certifications and licenses as well as detailed operational records which will indicate the policies and procedures which the crematory follows. Upon receipt of the requested documents, the funeral home ownership/management must examine the documents and determine if the records reveal that the crematory is operating under acceptable terms and within the confines of the law of the particular service area. If protocol is in alignment with the contracting funeral home's expectations it is safe to assume that the crematory can be considered a candidate to provide services.

At a minimum, the records requested should include verification that the crematory is appropriately licensed in the state in which it operates. Comprehensive documentation should also include the identification of the actual owner of the establishment, proper documentation of all certified personnel who are qualified to operate the crematory, and a formal policies and procedures manual should be made available upon request. Additionally, verify at this time the forms and authorizations required and utilized by the crematory, and always keep copies of these forms at the funeral home, as an authentic signature from the authorizing agent will be required on these forms. It is also considered best practice to verify that the crematory maintains adequate liability insurance as a third party crematory. It is best to secure these documents, and analyze all data prior to entering into an agreement with a third party crematory. If a crematory fails or refuses to provide the funeral home with the documents requested, it should be considered problematic, and indicates the crematory has something it would rather you not know about their operation – it would be best to continue the search for an operator that is in line with the funeral home's service expectations. Upon the receipt and evaluation of the requested information, a decision can be made to move to the next step in the evaluation process. If ultimately a service agreement is established, it is suggested that you request and reevaluate the crematory records on an annual basis, unless service indicates otherwise. Remember, it is extremely important that the funeral home establish, maintain, and archive all records and involvement with the third party crematory. All records, in total will help to serve as evidence of the funeral home's due diligence when selecting a third party crematory.

Interviews

The crematory records are indeed a valuable and necessary tool for evaluating third party crematories, but they will not tell the entire story, more information is required in order to make an informed decision and maintain a positive relationship with a third party crematory. Detailed and formal interviews with the management and staff of the crematory are a necessary and valuable step for funeral homes in an effort to model best practices and ensure due diligence when contracting with a third party crematory. When a contracting funeral home interviews third party crematory management, it will help the contracting funeral home to make an informed decision and further establish a business relationship with the provider. Determination of ownership and operations policies as well as procedures can be discussed during this meeting. Additionally, information about the actual equipment and personnel will be considered and can help with insights into how the crematory operates and if, indeed, it makes sense for the funeral home to use the crematory as a service provider. In preparation for the interview process, it is critical to develop a list of questions (see suggested questions below) to be covered during the interview process. Always practice professional courtesy when scheduling the interview with management. Again, it is essential to document all interactions and responses received during the interview process. Once again, add this to the appropriate file at the funeral home. It may seem quite obvious, but if anything is revealed during the interview process that concerns the funeral home representative, discuss this with the crematory management and seek resolution immediately. If adequate refutation is not received in ample time, it may be necessary to seek another service provider. It is advised to list these concerns on paper and provide them to the crematory management so these concerns can be formally addressed. The concerns and subsequent responses should be maintained in the permanent file in the funeral home.

Suggested Crematory Interview Questions

This is not to be considered an exhaustive list, but a starting point upon which to reflect, as funeral home representatives prepare for the interview process.

- Who owns the crematory and how long have they been the owners?
- How many crematory operators are employed and what training/certification is required?
- If licensure does not require a background check, does the crematory require background checks?
- Does the crematory have refrigeration? If yes, what is the capacity?
- What types of crematories are available? Include manufacturer and age of unit, as well as service schedule.
- What type of processing unit is utilized? Include manufacturer and age, as well as service schedule.
- Does the facility have an alarm system?
- What identification standards are utilized to identify remains throughout the process?
- How many cremations are performed annually?
- How are cremations scheduled?
- How are bodies stored while waiting for cremation?
- Describe the requirements for cremation containers
- How does the crematory deal with commingled cremated remains dust?
- What paper work (forms and authorizations) are required?
- What is the crematories policy regarding personal effects and medical devices?
- Does the crematory perform pet cremations?
- What are the crematories procedures for identifying and labeling processed cremated remains?
- What is the crematories policy for dealing with unclaimed cremated remains?

Much like crematory records, the interview process garners necessary and valuable information to be used in the decision making process, yet, these two together are not sufficient to make an informed selection for a crematory provider, nor do they alone establish due diligence. Contracting funeral homes should physically inspect potential third party crematories.

Inspections

It is natural for business owners and managers to put their best foot forward when attempting to secure and maintain clients. This reality will no doubt influence the interview process, making it necessary to conduct periodic inspections of crematories that serve, or may serve as third party providers. It is extremely important to conduct unannounced inspections, and these need to take place annually, at a minimum.

Theses inspections should take place during normal business hours. If a potential provider refuses to allow the inspection of their facility, it should be considered a red flag. The funeral home should continue the search for a crematory service provider that has no objection to inspections. In order to perform a qualified inspection, the funeral home representative must utilize a checklist of items (see below for suggested items to be included on the checklist) that need to be assessed during the facility examination. This form will serve as documentation of the process. Again, it is important to archive these forms in the funeral home records. Shortcomings and concerns documented during the process must be recorded and shared in writing with the management/ownership of the crematory in an effort to rectify deficiencies. In the event that modifications are not made, it can be seen as further evidence that the provider is not practicing in accordance with the contracting funeral home's expectations, and it would be best to seek the service of a different third party provider. No doubt, much can be learned through the inspection of records and the interview process, but seeing is believing, or in this case, seeing is confirming the policies, procedures, and operations of a crematory. The inspection process allows funeral homes beneficial insights that would be otherwise unavailable.

It is always best, prior to entering into a service agreement with a third party crematory, to practice due diligence and ensure that best practices are being utilized by all parties concerned. Upon verification that a crematory operates within the expectations of the funeral home, it is critical that a contract between the parties be generated (with the assistance of an attorney) and signed by both parties. It is this contract that serves to formally establish the expectations of the third party crematory by the contracting funeral home. Furthermore, this contract can serve to hold the crematory accountable to the desired level of service expected and can also serve as a final document supporting the due diligence of the funeral home in establishing a positive working relationship with the provider.

Suggested Items for Inclusion on the Crematory Inspection Checklist

This is not to be considered an exhaustive list, but a starting point upon which to reflect, as funeral home representatives prepare for crematory inspections.
- Appropriate licenses and permits are posted
- Crematory operators are dressed appropriately and operating in a professional manner
- Facility is clean and orderly
- How are human remains held prior to cremation, are remains covered and handled in a dignified manner

- Is the holding area dignified and clean
- Operational condition of crematory
- Operational condition of refrigeration unit
- Operational condition of processing unit
- Identification practices prior to cremation, while in the crematory, while being processed, as well as post-processing storage protocol
- Cremation log practices, and is the log up to date
- Crematory schedule, and is the schedule up to date
- Equipment maintenance schedule, and is the schedule up to date
- Is the facility secured by an alarm system
- Is the facility appropriately staffed to handle the volume of business

Conclusion

Practicing due diligence regarding selection and retention of a third party crematory is a four step process.

These four steps are:
1. Evaluation and review of the funeral home's internal policies and procedures.
2. Review and evaluation of the crematory's records.
3. Interviews with crematory personnel at all levels of the organization.
4. Physical inspection of the crematory site.

Each of these items independently offers valuable insight into the operations of any particular crematory, but only collectively can one ascertain if a particular facility offers the level of professional and ethical care congruent with the funeral home's culture and mission. Therefore, it is essential that funeral homes practice this level of due diligence when considering the use of a third party cremation provider. Furthermore, upon the selection of a cremation provider, parties must practice due diligence in order to maintain best practices in their working relationship.

• • •

> *For Critical Thought...*
>
> - You have been named the manager of ABC Funeral Home, and your first duty is to locate a crematory to handle the cremations for the funeral home. What are all the required steps you must take to be sure you employ due diligence throughout the process?
> - What are appropriate questions to ask during an interview of crematory management?
> - What are appropriate items to verify during a crematory inspection?

Chapter 6 – Recommendations for Crematory Operations

Chapter Learning Objectives

Upon completion of the study of this chapter students should:

- Understand the basic operations of a crematory and how the process works.
- Comprehend the classifications of wastes and incinerators.
- Be able to identify various crematory component parts and accessories.
- Understand basic crematory maintenance protocol including routine maintenance.
- Comprehend the cremation process including: receiving remains, cremation containers, cremation schedule, evaluation of containers and remains prior to cremation, and the cremation process itself.
- Understand the removal of cremated remains, cleanout, and processing procedures.
- Be able to discuss cases requiring special care including: Obese cases, infant and stillborn infant cases, cases with pacemakers, and cases with infectious diseases.

• • •

Introduction

Consistent with the spirit of this book, it is necessary to include a chapter examining the actual operations of a crematory. This is a new aspect regarding textbooks, and only limited empirical content exists in this regard. Therefore, in an effort to offer best practices, the foundation of this chapter is information gathered from the Cremation Association of North America (CANA) Crematory Operations Certification Program and the associated training manual, as well as direct correspondence with Larry Stuart, Jr.

As we turn the page to examine recommendations for actual crematory operations, it has become increasingly difficult to attempt to rank the importance of the chapters in this book, all material presented in this text are of great value to funeral service professionals. Entire curriculums and certification programs have been developed related to crematory operations. Even when veteran crematory operators attend certification programs, they learn specific best practices they have never practiced. The reality is that many crematory employees are simply trained by previous operators and never receive formal training from the manufacturer or a program such as training programs offered by the Cremation Association of North America (CANA), the National Funeral Directors Association (NFDA), or the International Cemetery, Cremation and Funeral Association (ICCFA); no doubt these programs improve operations and help create a safe working environment. Insurance underwriters may also require those operating crematory equipment to be formally trained. The fundamental purpose of this chapter is to present an overview of elements associated with the actual operation of a crematory. This will include an analysis of the basic cremation process including information on combustion and cremation equipment, an overview of the actual cremation process and basic maintenance required, as well as a presentation dealing with special cases and handling potentially hazardous objects. The chapter also includes an examination of appropriate containers for use during the cremation process, as well as those that are to be avoided. It is the goal for all readers to receive a solid foundation of information regarding crematory operations.

Image 6.1: Classic-XCEL Human Cremation System
Image courtesy of U.S. Cremation Equipment

Combustion

In order to grasp an understanding of crematory operations it is once again important to revisit elements typically included in the definition of cremation. Items such as the reduction of human remains to bone fragments by extreme heat and direct flame, followed by the pulverizing of these remains to granulated particles suitable for final disposition. Most can comprehend this description, but what is actually taking place is combustion, which is defined by the Cremation Association of North America (CANA) Crematory Operations Certification Program Manual as the act or instance of burning, and involves a chemical reaction in which oxygen is rapidly combined with fuel, giving off heat. The oxygen combines with carbon, hydrogen, sulfur, and/or certain other components of the fuel, changing them into different gasses. The components of the fuel that are not burned remain as ash. Perfect combustion is identified as the result of mixing and burning the exact proportions of fuel and oxygen so that no unburned fuel or oxygen remains. This combustion process involves two phases, a primary combustion in the ignition chamber (most cremationists refer to this as the primary chamber) and secondary combustion, here the products of the combustion process settle and are further combusted, and ultimately the remaining gasses will discharge from the crematory stack. Time, temperature, and turbulence are three elements of the cremation process deemed critical for the successful combustion that takes place in the secondary burner. The products of combustion need to be allotted enough time in the secondary chamber to be consumed, the temperature in the secondary chamber should be in the 1400 to 1800 degrees Fahrenheit range (many states require the secondary chamber be preheated to an acceptable level prior to igniting the main chamber), and the importance of effective turbulence in order to help the gasses involved properly mix in order to aid the consummation of the products of cremation prior to entering the atmosphere. A term commonly associated with the emissions of a crematory is opacity, which may be defined as the degree to which light is reduced when viewed through a smoke plume or visible emissions. The Environmental Protection Agency (EPA) identifies opacity testing standards; these limits vary among the states. It is important to know that visible emissions which consist of smoke and flame are indicators of improper combustion and excessive particulate emissions; this reality indicates that adjustments need to be made by the operator or a trained service technician. Preventative maintenance as suggested by the manufacturer may help to prevent or reduce repeated occurrences of prolonged opacity. For the purpose of classification of wastes and incinerators see the two tables below.

Classification of Wastes: Data retrieved from the CANA Crematory Operations Certification Program Training Manual.

Waste Classification	Waste Description
Type 0	A mixture of highly combustible waste, primarily paper, cardboard, wood, boxes, and combustible floor sweepings; mixtures may contain up to 10% by volume of plastic bags, coated paper, laminated paper, treated corrugated cardboard, oily rags, and plastic rubber scraps. Commercial and industrial sources.
Type 1	A mixture of combustible waste such as paper, cardboard, wood scrap, foliage, floor sweepings, and up to 20% cafeteria waste, commercial, and industrial sources.
Type 2	Rubbish and garbage. Residential sources.
Type 3	Animal and vegetation waste from restaurants, cafeterias, hotels, etc. Institutional, club, and commercial sources.
Type 4	**Human and animal remains consisting of carcasses, organs, and solid tissue wastes from farms, laboratories, and animal pounds.**
Type 5	Medical waste including sharps and pathological, surgical, and associated infectious waste materials.
Type 6	Department store waste.
Type 7	School waste with lunch programs.
Type 8	Supermarket waste.
Type 9	Other wastes not described here or which have variable or unknown BTU content that may be verified.

Classification of Incinerators: Data retrieved from the CANA Crematory Operations Certification Program Training Manual.

Class I	Portable, packaged, direct-fed incinerators with a capacity of up to 25 pounds per hour of Type 1 or Type 2 refuse.
Class IA	Portable, packaged, or site assembled, direct-fed incinerators, with a capacity from 25 to 100 pounds per hour of Type 1 or Type 2 refuse.
Class II	Chute-fed apartment house incinerators, where the refuse chute also acts as the flue for the products of combustion.
Class IIA	Chute-fed apartment house incinerators, having a separate flue for the products of combustion.
Class III	Direct-fed incinerators, with a burning rate of 100 pounds per hour or more, suitable for Type 1 or Type 2 refuse.
Class IV	Direct-fed incinerators, with a burning rate of 75 pounds per hour or more, suitable for Type 3 refuse.
Class V	Municipal incinerators, with a burning rate of 1 ton per hour or more.
Class VI	**Crematory and pathological incinerators, suitable for only Type 4 refuse.**
Class VII	Incinerators designed for specific Type 5 or Type 6 by-product waste.

Crematory Component Parts

When considering crematory operations, it is important to identify certain component parts that are included in most crematories. This list can provide some basic terminology in order to better understand the workings of a crematory. The information contained here can serve as a spring board into a more detailed conversation about operations with a crematory manufacturer or professional crematory operator. Two basic types of crematory designs exist, the retort design and the in-line design. Although the word "retort" is used somewhat universally to describe a crematory, it is actually only describing a specific design of crematory. The difference between these two designs rests in the flow of gasses during operation. In the in-line design gasses flow from front to back and then out; the exhaust does not recirculate beneath the hearth. The air flow in the retort design is from front to back, then underneath the hearth prior to exiting through the stack. Although many similarities exist in the design of these machines, the air flow is the defining factor if a machine is a retort or in-line design crematory.

Crematory Parts Defined

- Charging Door: **The door to the primary chamber typically electrically or hydraulically operated.**
- Control Panel/Station: **Houses control equipment to operate the function of the crematory unit.**
- Primary Chamber: **Where the actual cremation takes place. In this chamber heat and air are mixed creating combustion. 1400 to 1800 degrees Fahrenheit has been identified as the acceptable range for the operation of the primary chamber. With so many variables, it is difficult to determine an optimal temperature, but in most cases the ideal temperature at a consistent and controlled rate of combustion is around 1600 degrees Fahrenheit.**

- Secondary Chamber: **Holds the unburned combustion from the primary chamber until complete combustion is achieved, and also allows for proper and controlled air flow to the stack. 1400 to 1800 degrees Fahrenheit is the acceptable range for secondary combustion, with 1650-1700 being more ideal. It is important that the secondary chamber run at least 50 degrees hotter than the main chamber for drafting and air flow perfection.**
- Hearth: **The floor of the crematory.**
- Refractory Material: **Specialized material designed to withstand high temperatures. This material lines the interior of the crematory.**
- Burners: **Introduce flame by delivering fuel and its combustion air at desired velocities and turbulence. The purpose is to establish and maintain proper ignition and combustion of the fuel. Burners are located in the primary and secondary chambers. The main burner will ignite within the primary chamber and start the cremation process, while the secondary burner is located in the secondary chamber and maintains temperatures so that complete combustion can take place.**
- Thermocouple: **A heat-sensing device, typically crematories have two thermocouples, one in each chamber.**
- Pollution/Opacity Monitoring System: **A device to detect gases exiting the stack which alerts the operator and the unit when gases contain a level of opacity greater than an acceptable level.**
- Stack: **The final discharge point where the products of combustion are released to the environment.**

Crematory Accessories

In addition to the major mechanical machines required to offer cremation services (crematory, refrigeration, and processing unit) numerous other supplies are required to properly execute the cremation of human remains. Crematory manufacturers offer many accessories for use in conjunction with the cremation process, and it is common for certain states to require crematories to utilize many items described as accessories in this text. Remember, it is essential to research and maintain a thorough

Image 6.2: Crematory Accessories.
Image courtesy of Larry Stuart, JR., & Crematory Manufacturing & Service, Inc.

understanding of the laws and regulations regarding cremation in your specific service area, and always adhere to these practices. Below is a list of items associated with the cremation process. As with all aspects of cremation, the technology and accessories available are constantly changing; for this reason, it is important for crematory operators to remain current on technology and accessories available to help ensure optimal operation of a crematorium.

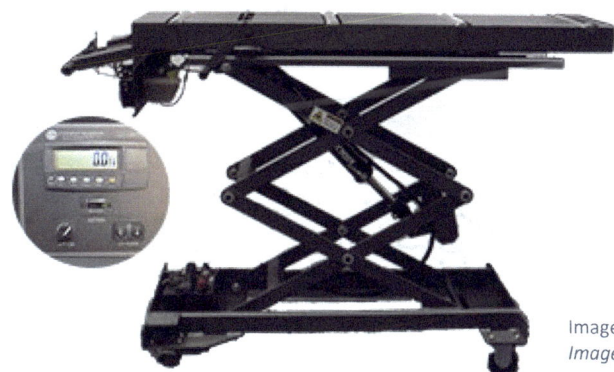

Image 6.3: Electric Hydraulic lift table & weight scale.
Image courtesy of U.S. Cremation Equipment

- Loading Device to assist with safe and appropriate placement of remains in the crematory.
- Electronic Scale is used to weigh the decedent, a crucial element for proper cremation scheduling and prevention of fire hazards. It is not uncommon to have a scale integrated with a loading device.
- Fire Extinguisher, this is critical in order to ensure a safe environment in the event of a fire.
- First Aid Supplies, should include a burn treatment.
- High Density Cardboard Rollers to aid in the smooth movement of the cremation container into the cremation chamber; these will help to prevent damage to the refractory materials on the floor of the cremation unit.
- Cremation Pan to help contain remains when cremating infant cases. A typical pan is constructed of 12-gauge stainless steel with a diameter of 20 inches and a height of 4 inches.
- Wire Brushes/Rakes with appropriate length of shaft to clean the crematory floor.

Image 6.4: Roller
Image Credit: Larry Stuart, JR., & Crematory Manufacturing & Service, Inc.

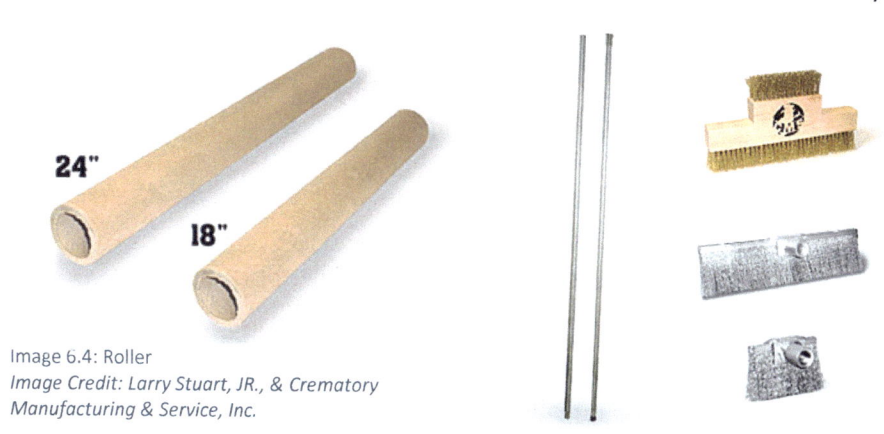

Image 6.5: Wire Brushes
Image Credit: Larry Stuart, JR., & Crematory Manufacturing & Service, Inc.

- **Collection Pan** to retrieve the cremated remains prior to processing.
- **Cooling Rack,** a unit to allow ventilation or air movement around a collection pan to assist with the reduction of heat of cremated remains.
- **Hand Magnet** to locate and initiate the removal of any ferrous metal prior to processing.
- **Heavy Duty Plastic Bags** to place cremated remains in after processing, these bags should be a minimum of 2 mil. in thickness.
- **Temporary Containers** to house cremated remains prior to placement in a permanent urn.

Image 6.6: Hand Magnet
Image Credit: Larry Stuart, JR., & Crematory Manufacturing & Service, Inc.

Image 6.7: Temporary Container
Image Credit: Larry Stuart, JR., & Crematory Manufacturing & Service, Inc.

- **Funnel** to assist cremationists with the placement of cremated remains in certain containers.
- **Mortar and Pestle** to process the cremated remains of small cases.
- **Zip Ties** to secure the heavy-duty plastic bags closed once cremated remains and placed in the bags.
- **Identification Medallions** (stainless steel) to identify remains.
- **Vacuum System** for total removal of cremated remains and to help maintain a dust-free work environment. It is important to make sure the filter bag is flame-resistant.
- **Personal Protective Equipment (PPE),** including items appropriate for handling human remains and PPE more specific to cremation operations. These items include:
    - Heat Resistant Apron
    - Heat Resistant Face Protection
    - Heat and Flame-Resistant Gloves
    - Eye Protection
    - Ear Protection
    - Dust Mask/Respirator
    - PPE such as latex gloves, impermeable gowns, face shields, shoe covers and face shields when working directly with human remains.

Basic Crematory Maintenance Protocol

First and foremost, regarding crematory maintenance, it is critical to follow manufacturers suggested protocol. It is imperative for crematory operators to have good working relationships with manufacturers and to utilize these resources in order to improve the daily operation of the crematory and extend the overall life span of the machine. Crematory operators need to be proactive regarding machine maintenance - anticipating when problems may occur in order to provide necessary maintenance. It is of extreme importance for crematory operators, in tandem with manufacturer's recommendations, to develop a system of basic maintenance that is detailed and routine. Like any complex machine, certain basic maintenance is appropriate for operators to address, and other maintenance requires a trained technician. If during the process of routine maintenance the operator becomes unsure of appropriate care, it is important to contact the manufacturer or technician and seek professional advice and assistance. The first step is to establish a routine maintenance schedule that includes both processes appropriate for operators and those that will require a trained technician. A technician trained by the manufacturer will be able to provide advanced diagnostics and will generally provide a report of the overall condition of the unit at the conclusion of maintenance and/or repair services. Also, remember that not all machines will require exact maintenance as basic maintenance schedules are typically a derivative of the level of usage, based on the number of cremations performed.

Routine Maintenance Schedule Items

- First, always refer to your crematories owner's manual and maintenance schedule. Some basic maintenance such as replacing thermocouples may be safely accomplished by operators, but always adhere to manufacturers suggested guidelines. Preventative maintenance is essential in avoiding unexpected costly repairs and unnecessary operational down time. Factoring the cost of preventative maintenance into each cremation may help alleviate the financial burden associated with this area of cremation operations. Also, some maintenance tasks may require the unit to be completely cooled down and off-line for an extended period of time.
- As with all machinery, maintaining a clean work environment is essential for the efficient operation of a crematory and the processing unit. This is certainly a maintenance step that can be undertaken by operators and is central to the routine maintenance schedule, as the crematory needs to remain both clean and dust free for safe and optimal operation.
- No area of the crematory holding facility should ever be used for storage. For many reasons this is dangerous and inappropriate - the most obvious being the reality of a fire hazard. Additionally, as a result of the vibration of the machine, cremators have a tendency to shift during operations – as a result a six-inch clearance must be maintained at all times where the stack penetrates the ceiling.
- Inspection of the external stack is advised at least monthly, and some manufacturers recommend more frequent inspection to ensure the proper alignment and no external damage is observed as a result of weather conditions or other unavoidable circumstances.
- The refractory material should be inspected prior to loading every case into the crematory. Damage to the refractory material may prevent the crematory from operating efficiently and depending where the damage is located, may result in the unsafe operation of the machine. Refractory material discovered during the clean-out process may be an indication of a greater problem and should be explored further. When the refractory material is damaged, the best practice is to notify your manufacturer and seek professional assistance.
- Included in the maintenance schedule should be the routine inspection of the refrigeration unit. Be sure the unit is cooling properly (40 degrees Fahrenheit is suggested) and ensure the unit is clean. Some refrigeration units are equipped with a sensor that alerts operators when temperatures are above a preset threshold for a prolonged period.

It is true that major maintenance will need to be addressed by trained crematory technicians; yet, successful routine maintenance can improve the operations of your machine and extend the life of the crematory. Some of the appropriate steps for this schedule are identified above, but always refer to your specific manufacturer's maintenance guidelines, budget appropriately, and if you ever have concerns or questions about maintenance or the operation of your crematory, immediately contact the manufacturer and seek professional assistance.

The Cremation Process

Although similarities exist among cases, each client family and the services selected can be as unique as a finger print. For the purpose of this chapter, the cremation process is referring to a point in time when a body is received for the cremation, with an understanding that any visitation and memorialization with the full body remains physically present have been concluded, and the remains are being received directly by the crematory for the cremation. A couple of poignant elements should be mentioned at the onset of this presentation. First, it is a fact that cremation is an irreversible process and a permit to cremate is required by a governmental body (check your service area for the appropriate authority and required forms); thus, it is suggested to allow at least 48 hours from the time of death until cremation, and never proceed with cremation until all required forms, permits, and authorizations have been received. Although different states may stipulate different requirements, 48 hours is a suggested minimum time period to wait prior to performing a cremation to ensure any necessary investigations have been able to take place, and necessary forms and authorizations have been secured. Second, it is possible for a crematory to refuse to receive human remains for cremation in certain cases. For example, incomplete paperwork, questionable identification, unsuitable cremation container are examples that would make it inappropriate to accept remains for cremation. Establishing and maintaining high standards is essential for the crematory operator. These standards include items such as demanding complete paperwork, enforcing a stringent identification processes, and clear expectations regarding cremation containers. If these standards are not met, it is important to refuse the case until the crematory standards have been met; otherwise, the established crematory protocol have been compromised. If the established protocol is violated the propensity for errors will undoubtedly increase. These established standards are simply non-negotiable.

Below is an orderly procedure suggested for the cremation process, from the point of receiving the human remains until the cremated remains have been placed into an urn or temporary container. This presentation will include an examination of necessary processes when working with special cases such as dealing with large cases, infants and stillbirth children, as well as a few comments regarding dealing with cases with infectious diseases. Furthermore, a discussion about pacemakers, radioactive materials, other hazardous materials, and dealing with medical implants are also included. The importance of establishing standards, and processes is highlighted in this section; the successful crematory will institute clear standards and all employees must adhere to these procedures for each and every case.

Receiving Remains

As we walk through the steps involved in the cremation process, it is important to indicate that these are general descriptions, and once again encourage all crematory operators to seek out a certification course in order to better understand the exact procedures suggested for operating a crematory. It is valid to remind all parties that employees that deal directly with the cremation process should be limited to licensed, registered, certified, or otherwise formally trained personnel. Furthermore, remember that it is a Federal requirement to post on doors entering both the crematory and refrigeration areas, identifying the existence of biohazards. With these understandings, it is essential to have a predetermined process for receiving remains, including protocol of which all employees are trained to execute and enforce. As indicated above, in certain cases it may be necessary for a crematory to refuse remains until required standards are met with regard to paperwork, appropriate cremation container, and identification of the remains. When receiving remains, the crematory personnel must ensure that the identity of the deceased is not in question, that appropriate paperwork has been completed without error, that all authorizations and permits are intact and enforceable, and that the remains are encased in an appropriate and combustible container that has not been compromised and is not leaking. Upon determination of these requirements, the remains can be added into the crematory log, assigned a crematory identification number and stainless-steel medallion with matching identification number; at this time, the remains may be formally accepted into the custody of the crematory. Minimum information that should be part of the receipt of remains include the name of the deceased, date and time of death, date and time of arrival at the crematory facility, the funeral director delivering the remains, an inventory of any personal effects delivered with the decedent, as well as the identity of the authorizing agent, and a note specifying the final disposition of the cremated remains. It is critical that a copy of this information remain with the body until the actual cremation. The official paperwork will need to be placed in the permanent record file of the deceased.

Cremation Container

Human remains must be delivered to the crematory in a container that is appropriate for cremation, one that has not been compromised, and the container must not be leaking any contents (see chapter 7 for a complete explanation of cremation containers). In order to be considered appropriate, a container should totally encase the remains, be both combustible (interior and exterior) and rigid in order to assist in the loading process, contain less than 0.5% chlorinated plastic (this plastic is often found in PVC components, plastic casket components and body disaster bags) of total weight. The goal is to take steps to ensure a successful cremation, eliminate the release of toxic and hazardous elements, as well as protect the machine and the environment. Common materials used for the construction of containers appropriate for cremation include corrugated cardboard, particleboard, and wood; while materials such as fiberglass, Styrofoam, plastic, and polystyrene are not appropriate, and these containers should not be cremated. The high BTUs these products contain may be damaging to the unit and pose a fire hazard; and the toxic substances they release may be damaging to the environment. Although some crematories will cremate human remains in a metal casket, this practice is not advised. First, prior to electing to cremate a metal casket, verify that this practice is approved by regulating boards and governmental agencies in your specific service area, then check with the manufacturer of your machine and verify this as a viable option, and determine the best practice for your specific machine. Also consider how the metal casket will be disposed of at the completion of the cremation.

Although it may seem like common sense to use an appropriate container to encase human remains in preparation for cremation, it is critical to establish and adhere to appropriate standards regarding containers that will be accepted by the crematory. This necessary step will not only assist in the proper functioning of the machine, but also serve as elements of safety to the client family, crematory operator, the cremation facility, and the environment as a whole. Loading an inadequate or compromised cremation container into an 1800-degree Fahrenheit machine in not just dangerous, but may be life threatening. The professional funeral director understands the importance of an appropriate cremation container and will skillfully explain the need for certain standards and present options to client families.

The Cremation Schedule

To people outside of the funeral service profession little thought would be given to the importance of appropriate scheduling of cremations. Many would assume that the cremation schedule would be based on a first in, first out principle; nothing could be further from the truth. Although funeral directors do have certain obligations to the families they serve to cremate their loved one in a timely manner. So, upon completion and receipt of all necessary documentation, it may be necessary to prioritize by death order. Yet, the completion of all required authorizations and the receipt of required permits do not automatically place a certain case as the next body to be cremated. Large (obese) cases or cases that will be cremated in highly varnished containers should always be the first cremation of the day, in order that the cremation begins in a cool chamber. These cases burn extremely hot and, in some cases, ignite prior to starting the primary burner in a hot crematory. Scheduling these cases as the first cremation of the day will help provide safety to operators and machinery alike. Always review the manufacturer's procedures for obese cases and when cremating a varnished container. Scheduling is also important if you plan to cremate a metal casket, this must be the final cremation of the day, as the unit will not be fully consumed and an extended period of time will be required to cool off the contents remaining after the cremation.

It is also possible for families to desire to be present at the beginning of a cremation, sometimes referred to as witnessing or insertion. As with all aspects of the funeral service profession, attention to detail is essential to be successful, this is the case when a family desires to be present at the cremation. If this is to take place in a professional manner, all funeral directors and crematory operators need to work together as a team and establish and maintain open lines of communication. All parties must be on the same page, and understand the day and time the planned, witnessed cremation will take place. Scheduling for this type of service becomes even more crucial if other cremations are to take place on the same day, using the same cremation unit.

It is irrefutable that in order to cremate human remains all required authorizations and permits must be received and authentic signatures secured, but this is not the end of the story with respect to scheduling the cremation. The professional funeral director and crematory operator should always be prudent in their scheduling etiquette as many times, unique elements associated with a specific case will require that the cremation will take place at a specific time, or in a specific order. Without question, scheduling is an important element of the overall operation of a successful crematory.

Evaluation of Container and Remains Prior to Cremation

Attention to detail is vital to the successful operations of a crematory facility. One aspect of the operations that requires consistent and dedicated attention to detail is the necessary evaluation of human remains and the container in which they are encased, prior to the actual cremation. Although this assessment will take place somewhat simultaneously, they are indeed unique.

As discussed above certain expectations exist regarding the cremation container, what materials are appropriate for cremation as well as others that do not meet acceptable standards. Always adhere to this standard and never compromise when concerning these criteria. Additionally, it is important that the crematory operator is aware of the contents of the container, beyond the human remains. This can be problematic in some states as law prohibits the inspection of the contents of the container unless a reason exists to question the contents. If you practice in a state with this law, it is imperative that you demand full disclosure from the funeral home regarding the contents of the container, and examine these documents to be certain items that should be removed have, indeed, been removed, and items that are to remain are appropriate to enter the crematory, and will not be problematic for the operation or safety of the machine, environment or personnel. If you practice in a state where it is allowed to inspect the contents, this is a valuable practice. If any items are questionable, always error on the side of caution and verify with the family or funeral home with respect to any items of concern, and always insist on signed authorization in these cases. Other items of particular concern are pacemakers and other medical devices powered by lithium batteries, radioactive seeds, as well as personal effects of the deceased and their family; items such as jewelry, personal letters to the deceased, and family heirlooms to name but a few. If any of these items are inside the cremation container, verification must exist concerning the families wishes regarding personal effects and crematory requirements with respect to materials and items that may be dangerous if they enter the cremation chamber.

One of the first items of which crematory operators are trained is that if human remains contain a pacemaker, or other medical devices operated with lithium batteries, these devices must be removed prior to cremation. The removal of such devices will require an incision, making it essential to receive written permission to remove the device from the authorizing agent. These devices must be removed prior to cremation to avoid an explosion in the cremation chamber that can damage the crematory and in extreme cases injure crematory operators. If a funeral director/embalmer discovers such a device, after receiving authorization, the device should be removed prior to cremation. Medical implants should be removed by embalmers in a preparation room, it is not appropriate for crematory operators to remove these devices at the crematory facility. Pacemakers are considered permanent implants by the Federal Drug Administration (FDA), so the appropriate process after removing a pacemaker is to sterilize the device and return it to the manufacturer, as the FDA regulates the distribution of these devices.

As indicated above, the evaluation of not only the human remains prior to cremation, but also the container and the contents of the container are critical for the successful and safe operation of a crematory. All operators must be trained and required to use these procedures, and always pay great attention to detail when employing these standards.

The Cremation

As we begin the conversation regarding the actual step by step cremation process, it is important to engage in the conversation about simultaneous cremations (the cremation of more than one human body at the same time within the same crematory) – a service you may be requested to perform in the future. As with so many matters in funeral service, the first question to address is if this practice is legal and permitted in your state/service area, as this practice may be prohibited in your service area. If this practice is permitted in the service area, make certain that all criteria established by the regulating board in your service area have been met and all appropriate authorizations have been secured prior to proceeding with the cremation. Even if simultaneous cremations are permitted in your service area, ultimately the decision to perform such services rests with the crematory operator. Operators should verify with manufacturers prior to electing to move forward with a simultaneous cremation, as the machines we utilize in funeral service are designed for single cremations. The simultaneous process certainly will impact the cremation process and may cause damage to your machine. We all must make decisions with respect to the services we will offer to our consumers; the key is to always adhere to all established laws that regulate our profession, and in the case of cremation, always consult your manufacturer when considering unique cases such as simultaneous cremations. The average cremation takes between two and three hours, but with so many variables it is difficult to provide an exact timeframe for a complete cremation to take place. No doubt, if you were to engage in a simultaneous cremation, the timeframe would exceed this average timeframe.

Now it is time to present the orderly progression of the cremation process. Below is a list intended to introduce the usual step-by-step process utilized during cremation.

- Verify the unit is prepared for cremation by opening the charging door and inspecting the primary chamber. The unit should be clean and no visible remnants of previous cremations should be detected. It is also important to inspect the refractory material to make sure it is not damaged. Extreme caution should be used when inspecting a hot cremation chamber. After this inspection, close the door.
- Start the purge cycle. This cycle will replace the air in the chambers of the cremator with fresh air, this will help to ensure that the air in the chambers have no flammable contents, prior to this exchange of air the chambers are also pressurized.
- Preheat the secondary chamber. As indicated earlier in this chapter, preheating is not only suggested, but also required in many states. This process prepares the secondary chamber to combust the products of combustion that take place in the primary chamber.
- Once the secondary chamber has been preheated, transport the cremation container to the staging area. Complete all cremation log information as well as all required paper work associated with this step in the cremation process, including identification procedures, it is common to utilize a stainless-steel medallion to track human remains throughout the process, including while in the crematory;

usually this disc is placed just inside the crematory. In preparation to load the container into the machine, place a cardboard roller on the floor inside the crematory to assist with the smooth loading of the container into the crematory.

- Using an appropriate loading device, position the container, load the container into the cremation unit and close the door.
- Ignite the primary burner and perform the cremation according to manufacturer's guidelines. The monitoring of the cremation process is of extreme importance, never start a cremation and leave; the operator must monitor the process and be available in the event something goes astray. The first 30 minutes are very important; the operator must keep a watchful eye on the temperature, emissions, and any other factor that may stray from normal operation.
- Monitor the cremation process, it is important to keep a keen eye on temperature fluctuations and any visible emissions from the stack (opacity). The air flow through the machine is controlled and extremely important for successful combustion. For this reason, it is important not to open the charging door for at least an hour after the cremation has started, and furthermore, only leave the door open to load, reposition, or unload the remains. If it becomes necessary to reposition the remains during the process, minimize this movement and be certain all matter has been removed from the repositioning device prior to removing it from the cremation unit. At no time should the operator leave the premises or leave the crematory unattended while a cremation is in progress. Once the cremation cycle is completed, open the door and verify that the process has been successful, if this is the case, close the door and begin the cool down phase of the procedure.

Removal of Cremated Remains, Cleanout, & Processing

As with all work in the funeral service profession, always don the appropriate Personal Protective Equipment (PPE), when working with cremation, prior to the procedure, during the cremation, and after. Following an adequate cool down period as determined by the crematory manufacturer, the operator will open the door of the primary chamber to begin the process of removing the cremated remains. First, the operator must reevaluate the remains to make sure the cremation was complete. Once this has been determined and the tray to recover the remains is secured in place, the cremated remains can be removed utilizing hand tools such as brooms, rakes, hoes, and push rods which are often provided by the manufacturer of the machine or by an automatic removal system, if your cremation unit has this option. Recall, it was advised to examine the condition of the refractory material prior to the cremation, specifically the floor. Damage to the floor of a crematory can cause the loss of up to 10% of the cremated remains; therefore, it is critical to keep up the maintenance on the floor of the cremator on a regular basis (CANA Crematory Operators certification Program, 2019). Using the hand tools or the automatic system, the cremated remains are placed into the recovery tray with great diligence in an effort to recover all cremation residues, upon completion of this task, the remains are prepared for processing. Take great care to remove any non-combustible material from the bone matter either by magnetic device, or elements that are visible to the operator. Ferrous material can be removed by a hand-held magnetic device, but non-ferrous material must be removed by hand. Typical items found include staples, steel buttons, surgical prostheses, dentures, and any non-combustible items from the cremation container. Operators should refer to local and state requirements related to the disposal or recycling of these items. At this time, it is important to identify the contents of the removal tray with the established identification system, including the stainless-steel medallion that has been with the remains from the time they were received into the custody of the crematory. After the successful removal and identification of the cremated remains, it is critical to reexamine the cremation chamber to verify that NO visible residue remains on the floor. This step is crucial if a crematory is going to take every possible step to minimize the unavoidable commingling with other cremated remains from other cremations, as it is not possible to recover all residues and every fragment for processing and pulverization. At this point, and after verifying remains have cooled to an appropriate or recommended temperature, the cremated remains are ready for pulverization. Pulverization can take place immediately, or, if necessary, at a later time. If the pulverization will not take place immediately, follow the crematory protocol with respect to storing and securing cremated remains pending pulverization.

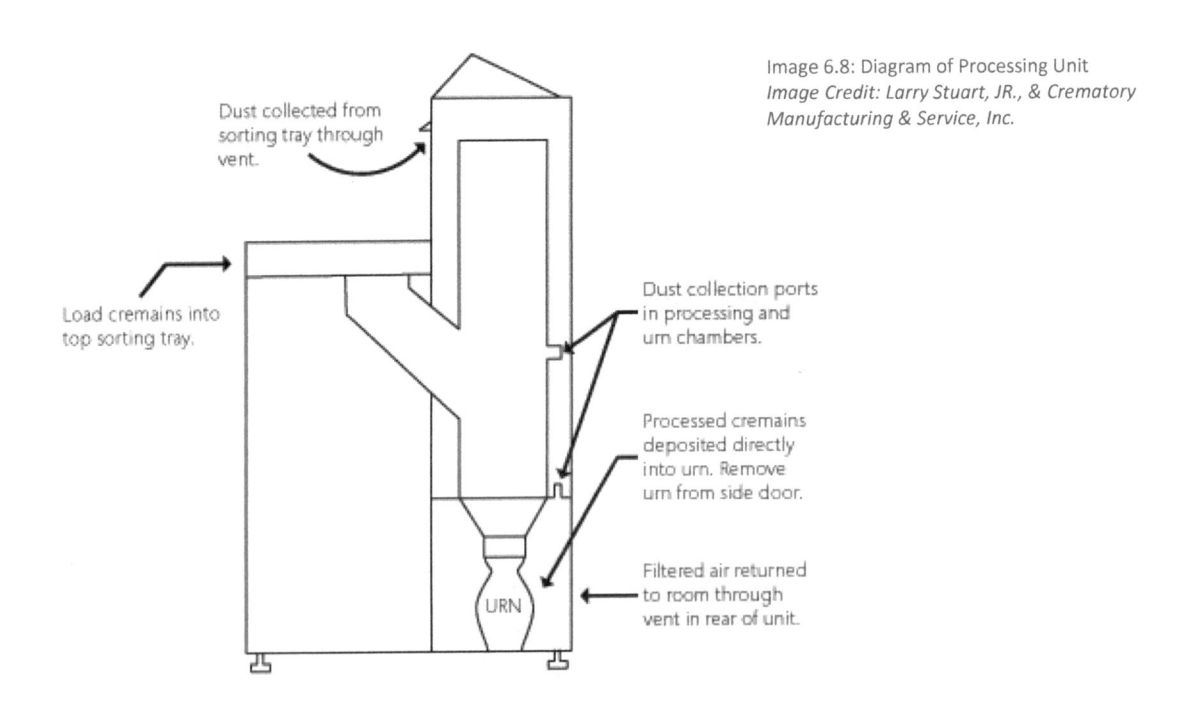

Image 6.8: Diagram of Processing Unit
Image Credit: Larry Stuart, JR., & Crematory Manufacturing & Service, Inc.

Dust collected from sorting tray through vent.

Load cremains into top sorting tray.

Dust collection ports in processing and urn chambers.

Processed cremains deposited directly into urn. Remove urn from side door.

Filtered air returned to room through vent in rear of unit.

URN

Prior to the actual pulverization, it is best to again verify the identification of the remains and make sure the identification codes match all documents associated with the remains. Once the identification of the remains is confirmed, and non-combustible material has been removed, the cremated remains can be transferred to the pulverization unit. This machine should reduce the cremated remains to a uniform size no larger than 1/4 inch, unless the cremated remains are scheduled to be scattered, the standard for these remains is no larger than 1/8 inch. Some states have specific requirements regarding the size of pulverized remains.

Upon conclusion of the processing and pulverization of the cremated remains, they should be placed into a clear plastic bag that is at least 2 mils thick and closed using a zip tie closure, as twist ties are unreliable.

Continue with the crematory identification protocol. Often the stainless-steel medallion is placed inside the plastic bag with the remains, and others choose to thread the zip tie through this identification disc and have it remain outside of the plastic bag. The bag containing the cremated remains should now be placed and secured in an appropriate urn/container (200 cubic inches) for storage in a secure and inaccessible location until the remains are picked up or scheduled for final disposition. It is vital that all identification standards of the crematory are adhered to and that the urn/container has an affixed identification label that corresponds with the ID number that matches the stainless-steel disc that has been with the remains throughout the cremation process. In the instance when there is too great a volume of cremated remains to comfortably fit into the urn or container, follow the above procedures by placing excess into a clear plastic bag which is properly closed and placed into an additional container, generally a temporary urn. It is crucial to place or attach identification to the bag and the additional container or urn. Furthermore, crematory records should indicate that there is an extra urn or container holding excess cremated remains.

It is common for cremation facilities to conduct numerous cremations every day. As the days get long, and the employees become weary, it is essential that the established protocol regarding crematory operations are observed on each and every case. A culture of attention to detail must be established in a crematory facility, and strict protocol developed. The expectation must always be to successfully adhere to this practice. No room for error exists when you offer cremation services. The development and implementation of quality standards is an essential step in this profession.

Cremation Cases Requiring Special Care

Although a great deal of the following information was explained above, the reality of dealing with certain cases that require special care, coupled with the importance of executing appropriate procedures warrant the following bullet point presentation regarding large (obese) cases, infant and stillborn infant cases, cases that have pacemakers or other hermetically sealed implanted medical devices powered by a lithium battery, cases treated with radionuclides, as well as cases with infectious diseases. In an effort to ensure an understanding of the circumstances surrounding these special cases, the following information is provided.

Large (Obese) Cases

- Obese cases should be the first cremation of the day or only after the unit has been cooled down per manufacturer's instructions, as these remains will themselves become a source of fuel for the combustion process which can significantly increase the heat during the cremation process. If the cremation unit is already hot, the process might cause the temperature to rise to an unsafe and inappropriate level for a successful and safe cremation. A serious fire hazard exists when instructions for cremating large cases are not strictly followed.
- As with all cases, preheat the secondary chamber to the appropriate level (1400-1800 degrees Fahrenheit).
- Some manufactures recommend large cases be placed into the crematory head first. This is necessary with some units in order to position the remains further from the primary burner. It is important to

ensure appropriate clearance between the body and the walls of the crematory exists prior to loading and once the body has been loaded into the cremation unit.
- As with all cases, it is extremely important to monitor the process meticulously to make sure the cremation process remains safe; and expect these cases to take longer for the cremation to successfully conclude. With large cases, after igniting the cremation container it is important to watch the temperature, and as it approaches 100 to 200 degrees turn off the cremation burner, but maintain monitoring, because if the temperature stops increasing, it may be necessary to reignite the burner once again. Additionally, during the monitoring process, be mindful that the rate and temperature of combustion may cause visible emissions from the stack. If this is the case, the secondary burner should be adjusted to make sure complete combustion is taking place in the secondary chamber.
- If necessary, an air tray may be used as the base of the cremation container for obese cases. It is not uncommon for traditional alternative containers to not be rigid enough to support the load of a heavy case; this may deem it necessary to utilize an air tray for additional support.

Infant and Stillborn Infant Cases

- Cremating cases of this nature provide unique challenges; foremost being the reality that due to the lack of skeletal structure, the amount of recoverable cremated remains may be minimal and it may be possible that no recoverable remains will exist at the conclusion of the cremation. It is essential that families understand this reality, but they should also be reassured that you, as a funeral professional, will take all steps possible to work to perform a cremation that will allow for recovery of cremated remains, as small as the amount might ultimately turn out to be.
- Crematory operators must do everything possible to allow for the recovery of cremated remains at the conclusion of the cremation, this includes utilizing a special cremation pan for use with small cases, which should be available from your crematory manufacturer, and never place the pan with the remains directly beneath the primary chamber burner, as this would significantly increase the possibility of consuming all of the remains, making recovering cremated remains impossible. It is advised to place the pan with the remains to the side of the burner, and after 20 minutes, verify the remains have indeed ignited. In most cases, the entire process will take less than one hour.
- After the successful completion of the cremation, allow adequate time for the cooling off process, taking all steps possible to retrieve any recoverable cremated remains. After recovering the remains, never use a machine to pulverize these delicate remains, instead manually process when dealing with these cases. A mortar and pestle are commonly used for this purpose.
- As with all cases, be vigilant regarding required paperwork, authorizations, and identification standards.

Cases with Pacemakers - (Or Other Implanted Medical Devices Containing a Lithium Battery)

- Pacemakers, defibrillators and other hermetically sealed, battery powered implanted medical devices should be removed prior to cremation; failure to do so will damage the crematory equipment, alter the cremation process, and possibly injure crematory personnel, as the device will explode as a result of the intense heat.

- It is required to receive written authorization from the authorized agent prior to removing any implanted medical device.
- It is best practice for pacemakers to be removed by licensed embalmers prior to the remains arriving at the crematory facility. Crematory operators at the crematory facility should not engage in this practice.
- After the removal of a pacemaker, it is advised to sterilize the pacemaker and return the device to the manufacturer. The Federal Drug Administration (FDA) classifies pacemakers as permanent implants, regulates the distribution of these devices, and tracks them. Crematory operators are not classified as pacemaker distributors, so crematory operators are only authorized to return these devices to the pacemaker manufacturer.

Cases Treated with Radionuclides or Containing Radioactive Implants

A review of the literature reveals little research, discussion and recommendations regarding cremation of cases involving nuclear medicine procedures whereby radionuclides (or radioactive substances) are used in the treatment and diagnosis of certain diseases, particularly cancer. However, this issue was highlighted in 2019 when a crematory operation in Arizona gained national attention after sampling by scientists revealed measurable levels of radioactive contamination in crematory equipment and the crematory operator. In this instance, traces of the intravenous radiopharmaceutical used to treat a decedent days before his death was detected in the retort and other crematory equipment; while the operator had traces of contamination from a completely different radioactive compound not used in treating the decedent while he was a patient. The implications of this discovery should be far reaching when consideration is given to almost 19 million nuclear medicine treatments performed annually in the United States.

A somewhat new treatment for prostate and breast cancer, called brachytherapy, involves the implantation of radioactive seeds either into or a short distance from a tumor. These seeds have different spans of time in which they remain active. Typically, if the seeds have been implanted within the past 12 months, it is recommended not to cremate the remains until the seeds have been removed by a medical professional, or until the required time has passed so the seeds become inactive. It is imperative to have good communication with the family and to have a section of the cremation authorization which clearly addresses radionuclide treatments. If any question exists about the date of implantation, it is best to not cremate until more information is available and an informed decision can be made by the funeral professional. It is advised that if bodies contain radium, iridium-192, or tantalum-182, the radioactive material should be removed by a medical professional prior to cremation. It should be noted that a radionuclide therapy is different from receiving radiation treatments, which the latter uses a beam of intense radioactive energy to shrink or kill a tumor.

Cremation of a body treated with radiopharmaceuticals may require the use of special protective equipment and processes. Protective equipment commonly used for cases treated with radiopharmaceuticals include: a respirator with an appropriate dust filter, a rubber apron and rubber or vinyl gloves. Disposal of protective items may include placing items in a container specifically intended for such a purpose. The pulverization process may need to be delayed in some instances and the storage of possibly contaminated remains may need to be placed in a lead or metal container during this time. The continued use of an exhaust fan while pulverizing and processing remains is recommended. Also, the scattering of cremated remains, as well as placement of remains in keepsake jewelry may be restricted or not recommended. Again, it is important to know exactly which radiopharmaceutical was used, the date of last use, and when cremation is recommended from that date. A frank discussion and open communication with health professionals concerning a decedent treated with a radiopharmaceutical is the recommended course of action. The following table offered by the Canadian Nuclear Safety Commission presents some suggested time frames for taking precautions when a decedent has undergone treatment with radiopharmaceuticals. In some instances, the family (and the crematory operator) may decide that cremation is not a reasonable choice depending on the circumstances.

Nuclear substance used in prior medical procedure	Recommended time frame for taking precautions*			
	Autopsy	Embalmment	Cremation	Alkaline hydrolysis
Strontium-89	1 year	2 weeks	1 year	1 year
Yttrium-90	6 weeks	1 month	6 weeks	6 weeks
Phosphorus-32	6 months	6 weeks	6 months	6 months
Iodine-131	4 months	1 month	4 months	4 months
Samarium-153	3 weeks	2 weeks	3 weeks	3 weeks
Lutetium-177	3 months	2 weeks	3 months	3 months
Radium-223	3 months	2 weeks	3 months	3 months
Iodine-125	2 years	1 month	2 years	2 years
Palladium-103	3 months	1 month	3 months	3 months

Table 6.1: Suggested time frames for taking precautions when a decedent has undergone treatment with radiopharmaceuticals. Table provided by Canadian Nuclear Safety Commission

Cases with Infectious Diseases

- As with all cases, practice Universal Precautions.
- Minimize exposure to bodily fluids and airborne droplets.
- Utilize disposable personal protective equipment (PPE) to minimize any contact with infectious fluids.
- It is advised to perform these cremations as soon as possible, but always adhere to all regulations.
- Concerns with the Ebola Virus led to specific information from the Centers for Disease Control and prevention (CDC) regarding handling these specific cases. The CDC, regarding mortuary care advised the following: Do not embalm, do not open body bags, do not remove remains from the body bags, mortuary personnel should wear PPE, in the event of leakage of fluids from the body bag, thoroughly clean and decontaminate areas of the environment with Environmental Protection Agency (EPA) registered disinfectants, which can kill a broad range of viruses in accordance with label instructions. The CDC further advises that remains should be cremated or buried promptly in a hermetically sealed casket.

• • •

Conclusion

No room for error exists in the operation of a crematory; for this reason, attention to detail is central to the successful operator. This chapter has presented in great detail elements associated with operating a crematory. This included a discussion about developing and executing appropriate protocol for the successful cremation, and continued with discussions about the actual cremation procedure, essential machinery, and component parts required to provide these services, as well as a discussion about recommended maintenance that can serve to improve operations and help extend the lifetime of cremation equipment. Readers then examined the actual step-by-step process of a cremation, as well as considerations for special cases.

Fundamentally, this chapter has presented a window into the actual daily operations of a crematory. With increasing cremation rates across the country, a profound understanding of cremation, cremation services, and operations are critical for all funeral service professionals, regardless of whether you work in a facility that operates a crematory or otherwise.

• • •

For Critical Thought...

- What considerations are important when scheduling cremations? What type of case should be scheduled for first of the day?
- What is the appropriate temperature range for the primary chamber? Why? What is the appropriate temperature range for the secondary chamber? Why?
- Today, you are the managing crematory operator. As you receive human remains for cremation, what considerations should you give to the cremation container? What elements are essential for a container to be considered appropriate for cremation?
- You notice that your work today includes an infant cremation, how will this procedure be different from an adult cremation?
- The crematory has taken custody of an obese case, what considerations and procedures must be employed in the cremation of this case?
- What medical devices must be removed prior to cremation? Who should remove these devices? Where should the removal take place?
- As a crematory operator, describe any times when it would be appropriate to refuse to take custody of human remains for cremation.

Chapter 7 – Cremation Containers

Chapter Learning Objectives

Upon completion of the study of this chapter students should:

- Understand the complexities associated with burial caskets utilized for cremation.
- Have a basic understanding of the types of burial caskets which may be considered appropriate for cremation and those that should be avoided.
- Be able to express the evolution of cremation caskets and why these units are appropriate for cremation.
- Be able to discuss appropriate construction materials for cremation caskets and why.
- Recognize construction materials that should be avoided for cremation caskets and why.
- Be able to explain what alternative containers are and how they are used in funeral service.
- Understand appropriate construction materials for the construction of alternative containers, and materials that should be avoided and why.

• • •

Introduction

This is a new generation for funeral service. Challenges faced by contemporary funeral providers are numerous, and each service seems to offer its own set of unique challenges and opportunities. Fundamental to the continual success of funeral directors is the adaption to the current service environment. It is indisputable that services associated when cremation is selected plays a critical role today, and will in the future with respect to general business success. When considering the multitude of service opportunities for cremation families, the cremation container is central to the discussion. During the arrangement process, it is not only necessary to provide client families all of the available options, but it is required to explain the necessity of a cremation container to assist in the delivery of the services selected. The purpose of a cremation container can be considered three-fold: to provide a dignified option for viewing the remains, as an encasement for the remains when a service is planned where the remains will be present, and finally, as a container to assist with the loading of the remains into the cremation chamber itself. Today, a multitude of options are available for families that select cremation, and it is the task of the funeral professional to present all options, and help families make informed decisions that best support the desired services selected. This chapter presents alternatives available when considering cremation containers, both construction materials and functionality will be addressed as we work our way through the various items. In the following section, you will find a presentation on burial caskets, cremation caskets, and ceremonial (rental) caskets, followed by information about options for alternative containers. Collectively, these serve as the container possibilities available when making cremation arrangements.

Fires of Change: Cremation Containers

Image 7.1: Ceremonial Caskets (similar to the one shown here) are popular choices for families that select cremation services.

Image 7.2: Also, many new options are available for families that select cremation, units that are both cremation friendly (100% combustible) and suitable for viewing of remains, as the cremation container shown here.

Caskets

When considering caskets in conjunction with cremation services, it is important to remain mindful that some funeral directors and cremation providers will accept many traditional caskets intended for burial as suitable containers for cremation. As explained previously in the chapter on crematory operations, challenges exist; and although many times traditional burial caskets are not the ideal container when selecting cremation, they may remain options. When considering the use of these types of units, it is best to always consult the crematory manufacturer's best practices for such a cremation with your specific machine. It is important to note that there are special caskets constructed that may be a better option when cremation is selected. In this section we present information on three categories of caskets - burial caskets, ceremonial caskets (rental caskets), and cremation caskets, all of which may be considered containers suitable for cremation services.

Burial Caskets

Burial caskets are typically grouped in two major categories, those constructed of metal, and those constructed of wood. For a number of reasons, wood burial caskets are more appropriate for cremation than their metal counterparts, but many challenges are presented when traditional wood burial caskets are utilized for cremation services. Traditional construction materials for wood caskets include hardwood species (broad-leaved deciduous trees such as pecan, oak and cherry), as well as softwood species, which are coniferous trees such as pine and cedar. Although the main construction component is, indeed, wood, these caskets contain a great amount of metal including screws, staples, hinges, hardware, and the spring system that provides support for the bedding. These components are not combustible in crematories, and will present additional challenges when removing and processing the remains after the completion of the cremation. It is also noteworthy that at the temperatures reached in a crematory chamber, zinc in large amounts will produce thick white smoke and may cause the anti-pollution equipment of the crematory to malfunction, causing a glitch in the entire cremation process. Although most caskets do not contain zinc at levels high enough to be problematic, it is best to remove casket components containing zinc prior to cremation. It may be necessary to contact the casket manufacturer to ascertain this information. Furthermore, many wood burial caskets have a highly polished varnish, which will burn extremely hot, and will require additional care by the crematory operating staff. Given these concerns, it is now rare for families to select a burial casket in conjunction with a cremation service. It is suggested to have the authorizing agent sign for and authorize the cremation of this casket, as it will be irreversibly destroyed during the cremation process.

Metal caskets, classified as ferrous (any metal formed from iron), including steel and stainless steel or non-ferrous (metal not formed from iron), including bronze and copper make up the majority of the metal offerings in selection rooms across the country. Although some funeral homes and crematories may allow the cremation of metal caskets, these caskets pose great challenges and often lead to policies that do not provide for this as an option. In addition to the concerns about zinc addressed above, it is necessary to acknowledge that galvanized caskets, and those constructed of bronze should never be cremated, as they contain high levels of zinc. Also, many of the difficulties mentioned above regarding wood caskets are also true when considering metal caskets. These caskets, beyond the shell of the casket, contain a great deal of additional metal including hinges, hardware, and the spring system that support of the bedding. Again, these components are not combustible in crematories and will present additional challenges when removing and processing the remains after the completion of the cremation. Metal caskets will also offer considerable challenges for the crematory operator, for they must be scheduled as the last cremation of the day, as it will take considerable time for the remaining shell to cool off enough to handle the material safely. Furthermore, once the operator has completed the arduous process of separating all remains from the metal casket components, it will be necessary for the crematory operator to both safely and within laws and regulations discard the casket shell that remains after the cremation process. Some funeral homes and crematories may still allow metal caskets as an option for families that select cremation, but the challenges are numerous and many crematories opt to not offer this service. Always consult the manufacturer of your specific machine for the suggested best protocol if you elect to cremate metal caskets.

Ceremonial (Rental) Caskets

"Necessity spawns invention," a well-known saying which is certainly applicable to the now commonplace rental casket (see Image 7.1). The brilliant invention of the rental casket includes a beautiful exterior casket shell with a removable insert. This allows families that select cremation the flexibility to honor their loved one as they deem appropriate, without the financial burden of purchasing an expensive casket. The insert, which is removed from the exterior shell for cremation, includes all parts of the interior that may come in contact with the remains, including a removable and disposable pillow, extendover, overlay, and overlay skirt. In fact, the insert includes all the necessary lining in order to have a dignified visitation and open-casket funeral. Following all visitation and funeral ceremonies, the insert is removed and covered with the included container enclosure in preparation for cremation. A new insert is then placed in the casket shell preparing the unit for reuse.

Cremation Caskets

As cremation rates continue to rise, grieving families are demanding more options when they select cremation as the means toward disposition. We must make sure families understand that they can create a meaningful and appropriate tribute to their loved one when they opt for cremation, utilizing all options available to those selecting burial services. Cremation families expect merchandise that specifically meets

Image 7.3: Cremation Casket
Image Source: Matthews Aurora Funeral Solutions

their needs, and this includes caskets explicitly designed for cremation. Casket manufacturers have addressed these demands and offer numerous units that are uniquely designed for cremation - cremation caskets. In order for a cremation container to be considered appropriate, the container should totally encase the remains, be combustible (interior and exterior), rigid in order to assist in the loading process, contain less than 0.5% chlorinated plastic of total weight, and not emit hazardous or toxic elements when combusted (CANA, 2019). The goal is to take steps to ensure a successful cremation, eliminate toxic and hazardous elements, as well as to protect the machine and the environment. Common materials used for the construction of containers appropriate for cremation include corrugated cardboard, particleboard, and wood; while materials such as fiberglass, Styrofoam, plastic, and polystyrene are not appropriate, and these containers should not be cremated. Cremation caskets address the concerns identified with respect to burial caskets by eliminating most metal utilized in the construction of the casket interior such as staples, hinges, and spring bedding support, replacing these with combustible materials such as wood, corrugated cardboard, and straw. The shell of these caskets is constructed of appropriate materials such as wood, particleboard, and corrugated cardboard in an effort to create a 100% combustible unit that offers families the opportunity to select a casket that meets cremation standards, while maintaining an appearance that will allow for a dignified presentation of the body for both visitation and funeral ceremonies but will not be reused as with a rental casket.

Alternative Containers

An alternative container as defined by the Cremation Association of North America (2019) is the case in which the human body is delivered to the crematory and in which it is cremated. General requirements for the container: Be composed of a suitable combustible material, be rigid enough for handling ease, assure protection of the health and safety of the operator, as well as provide proper covering for the remains. In essence, an alternative container is a simple, combustible container intended to meet basic requirements for encasing and supporting human remains into the cremation chamber. Again, the evolution of the cremation market and increasing cremation rates have led to the development and distribution of numerous products that are available to consumers who are considering alternative containers. Always remember the intended purpose, and requirements for such a container, as families might select an option that may not fully encase or be rigid enough to allow for appropriate positioning in the cremation chamber, and may also put crematory operators in an unsafe environment. Every funeral home and crematory should communicate the fundamental purpose and the requirements of these containers, as well as have

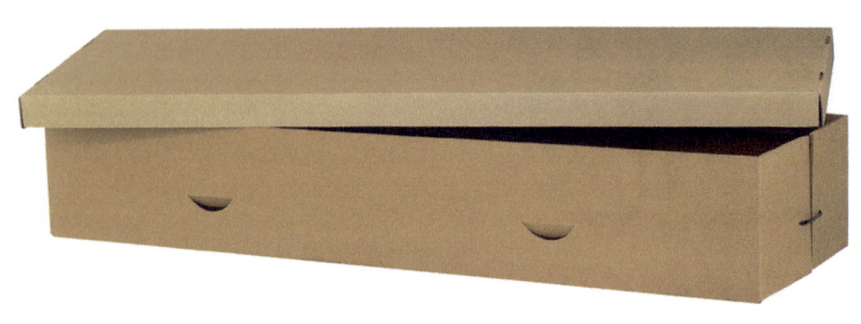

Image 7.4: Alternative Container
Image Source: Matthews Aurora Funeral Solutions

information available regarding appropriate containers for those interested in cremation. In the following section, we present a brief synopsis of appropriate materials for the construction of containers that may be considered alternative containers, as well as identify concerns with certain encasements that may not be fully appropriate to serve as an alternate container.

Appropriate Construction Materials

When considering what materials are appropriate for the construction of alternative containers we need not look further than the elements contained in the definition: The material must be rigid, combustible, cover the remains, and provide adequate safety measures for crematory operators. These descriptors make materials such as corrugated cardboard, basic wood, both plywood and particleboard, appropriate for the construction of these containers. It is also possible for families to simply purchase the insert from the rental casket without utilizing the shell. They may feel it is warmer and more dignified than the plain corrugated cardboard container. It is common for funeral homes and crematories to offer the basic corrugated cardboard container to serve as the simple alternative container, with other options available if client families so desire. An important note should be made here; in order for a container to be appropriate, it should not only be combustible and rigid, but it should also encase the human remains, allow a proper covering for the remains, and ensure the safety of the operator. The professional funeral director will always provide all options so families can make selections that will best meet their needs, this includes explaining the purpose, requirements, and alternatives available concerning containers required when selecting a cremation service.

Other Materials and Containers Sometimes Considered

As indicated above, central to the definition of an alternative container is that the container is combustible. For this reason, plastics and metals are not appropriate for the construction of alternative containers. Furthermore, it is best to eliminate metal nails, screws, and staples in the construction of wood alternative containers. It is also becoming common for families to consider containers that are more environmentally friendly "green", such as wicker burial containers, cremation pouches, and shrouds. Again, it is important to recall the definition of an alternative container and the fundamental purpose. Many times, green options meet the requirements for an alternative container, but in other instances they do not. For example, a cremation pouch or green burial shroud will certainly cover the body, but will not be rigid, and allow for the safe and successful placing of the remains into the cremation chamber. Some families select to place their loved one in a burial shroud, and then place the shrouded remains into a basic corrugated cardboard container to meet all crematory requirements. As the cremation consumer is becoming more astute, funeral directors must do the same. One option some cremation families appreciate is when a funeral home offers to place the remains of their loved one in a cremation shroud during the removal. The family finds comfort in the knowledge that their loved one is secure in a dignified pouch while arrangements are being made for the cremation and other services. The importance of explaining requirements and options to families is once again highlighted. Funeral personnel must be ready to meet the ever-changing demands of the contemporary consumer.

● ● ●

Conclusion - Chapter Content Review

No shortage exists when considering the options available regarding cremation containers. This chapter examined the appropriateness and practicality of different options as cremation containers, including burial caskets, cremation caskets, and rental caskets. Suitable construction materials were discussed and advantages and challenges for different containers were presented. The final section of the chapter considered alternative containers. Again, appropriate construction materials and various options were presented, maintaining a focus on the fundamental purpose and requirements associated with selecting a cremation container. Times are changing and so are funeral consumers. The professional funeral provider must embrace the new environment and work to provide the goods and services required in order to paint a meaningful memory picture of a family's loved one, which includes having a vast knowledge of products and services associated with cremation services.

•••

> *For Critical Thought...*
>
> - How would you describe a container that is appropriate to serve as a cremation container?
> - If a family is interested in a service that includes viewing and an open casket funeral with a cremation to follow, what options exist with respect to the cremation casket/container?
> - What concerns exist regarding inappropriate containers for cremation?
> - What materials are considered inappropriate in the construction of cremation caskets/containers?
> - What is the difference between a cremation casket, rental casket, and an alternative container?

Chapter 8 – Containers for Cremated remains

Chapter Learning Objectives

Upon completion of the study of this chapter students should:

- Be able to discuss urns, both temporary and permanent containers.
- Understand functions of different containers used to hold cremated remains.
- Be able to identify appropriate construction materials for the different containers.
- Be able to identify appropriate container capacities for the cremated remains of adults, children, and infants.
- Be able to discuss specialty items used in funeral service including keepsake items, jewelry, thumbprint impressions, and other options available for cremated remains.
- Understand outer burial containers used in conjunction with cremation, including urn vaults, and urn grave liners.
- Be able to identify appropriate construction materials utilized for outer burial containers associated with cremation.

• • •

Introduction

The importance of explaining to client families the decisions that must be made when arranging a cremation has been well documented throughout this text, included is the selection of a container for final disposition. As with so much of the cremation market, demand has driven suppliers to develop and offer an extensive arrangement of containers suitable to serve as containers for the final disposition of cremated remains. It is beneficial at the start of this chapter to make a simple point that will serve all directors as they work with families that select cremation, the importance of pre-counseling before the arrangement conference. Just as funeral directors advise families prior to the arrangement conference that they will need to select two containers, a casket and an outer burial container, when working with families that select cremation, funeral directors should counsel families that they, also, will need to select at least two containers, a pre-cremation container such as a cremation casket or alternative container, a post-cremation container such as an urn, and possibly an urn vault. This chapter will explore the options for containers for final disposition; the presentation will include information about temporary containers, permanent containers, specialty items, as well as outer burial containers for the cremation consumer.

Urns

An urn, defined as a receptacle designed to permanently encase the cremated remains (CANA, 2019), can take many forms and be constructed using numerous materials. Additionally, the fundamental purpose of the urn can drive the decision-making process and encourage consumers to select certain urns. For example, entombment into a niche in a columbarium may require the purchase of a certain container as each space in the columbarium was designed to house a specific urn. It may also be the case that the client family intends to scatter the cremated remains in the future, and require a scattering urn, or want to construct the permanent urn themselves, but need time to do so; in this case a temporary urn may be the more appropriate selection at the actual time arrangements are being made. It is also appropriate to consider one of the most difficult aspects of our profession, working with families that have lost a child; again, these cases will no doubt necessitate the selection of merchandise appropriate for the situation. Regardless of the situation or consumer need, options now exist for these families, and all families should have the opportunity to examine all available alternatives when making arrangements for a loved one. In order to fully survey the various urns available, this section has been divided into three sections; temporary containers, permanent containers, and specialty items.

Image 8.1: Numerous urn options are now available for the cremation consumer. An example is unique and personalized wood urns like the one above.
Image Credit: Matthews Aurora Funeral Solutions

Image 8.2: Numerous urn options are now available for the cremation consumer. One example is a marble style container such as this companion urn which has the capacity for the cremated remains of two people.
Image Credit: Matthews Aurora Funeral Solutions

Temporary Containers

It is not uncommon for families to select services that are best served by choosing an urn that is actually classified as a temporary container. A temporary container, a receptacle for cremated remains usually made of cardboard, plastic, or similar material designed to hold the cremated remains until an urn or other permanent container is acquired (CANA, 2019). Examples of when a temporary container is necessary may include families that are waiting for a special urn to be constructed, or the shipment of the permanent container has not yet been received. It is also true that a temporary urn may be necessary if a family plans air travel with the cremated remains, as temporary containers are constructed with materials that allow X-Ray to be possible, and the Transportation Security Administration (TSA) will require this of all materials that are carried on to airlines (see chapter 4 for complete details). As indicated in the definition above, these containers are typically constructed of corrugated cardboard or plastic and are very simple in design. In addition to the definition above, specific scattering urns are also only intended as temporary containers. For example, when a family intends to schedule a time in the future to scatter the cremated remains but needs a temporary container to house the remains until the scattering takes place, funeral homes/crematories often offer specific scattering urns. These urns are designed to hold the cremated remains for a brief period of time between the cremation and the scattering of the remains. These urns are more durable than a standard temporary container, usually constructed of wood, wood by-products, or spun bronze. Although these urns are more significant than standard temporary containers, they are presented here, with the intended purpose to only house the cremated remains for a temporary period of time.

A special note is necessary when discussing the scattering of cremated remains. When a family is considering scattering, funeral directors need to be sure that families understand that scattering is an irrevocable act, and once scattered, the remains will not be recoverable. Additionally, it is necessary to make the family aware that no formal place will exist to go visit after the scattering takes place. For this reason, funeral professionals should make these families aware of options available with respect to permanent memorialization in a cemetery or columbarium. Even if the family opts to scatter the cremated remains, the funeral director can offer options such as a memorial bench, even without the cremated remains present; this will offer a permanent memorial site to honor the deceased's life, and allow a "place" for the family to visit. Finally, in addition to receiving written authorization to scatter cremated remains, funeral directors should contact the family prior to the actual scattering to ensure that they still wish for the cremated remains to be scattered.

Beyond the basic needs and functions of a temporary container, it is important to mention that these containers exist for both adult and child cremations. When considering adult cremated remains, the appropriate capacity for the cremated remains of an adult is 200 cubic inches. Although this is considered sufficient for the cremated remains of most adults, you will encounter cases that will require more than the standard capacity, this is another time it will be necessary to guide families with respect to options that exist for the additional remains. When this reality occurs always carefully place the additional remains in an appropriate heavy plastic bag, zip tied, and place in a second temporary container that is appropriately identified and labeled until the family has made a final decision regarding the total of the remains. When considering infant and child containers, no exact appropriate capacity is identified, as the size of each child varies. Although no set appropriate capacity exists, most child containers are 70 cubic inches or less in capacity, and most infant containers are less than 30 cubic inches in capacity.

One final note regarding temporary containers is the reality that these containers, like permanent urns, may be purchased from the arranging funeral home/crematory, or the family may elect to actually provide the container. It is possible that families want to construct the container, or simply found what they believe to be a suitable container elsewhere. When this is the case it is extremely important to have a candid conversation with the family about the required capacity for a container to serve as an urn, and always have families bring the container into the funeral home/crematory and perform the transfer into the urn as a service to the family. With respect to situations of this nature, it is probable that the description, 200 cubic inches, will mean very little to most consumers, so it is more informative to put this in terms that are more descriptive, allowing families to successfully select an appropriate container. One funeral home owner indicated that in an effort to assist families with this task they will explain to families that the capacity required is similar to the capacity of a five-pound bag of flour, giving the family a tangible concept to consider when selecting a container.

The funeral service profession is a service industry, and it is our task to provide families with the best and most appropriate goods and services to meet their needs, offering counsel and assisting families in the selection of an appropriate container for cremated remains given each scenario is part of the funeral directors' job. At times this may include the placement of cremated remains in a beautiful bronze urn for inurnment in an urn vault, or it may mean utilizing a temporary container, as it should always be about what best meets the needs of the family.

Permanent Containers

Permanent containers (cinerary urns) are exactly what the name indicates, a container which will permanently house the cremated remains. Regardless of whether the remains will be interred, entombed, stored in a home, or some other option selected for final disposition. Capacity concerns and the reality that consumers may elect to provide their own permanent containers, for the most part, concludes the similarities between temporary and permanent containers. Urns can be designed to hold the cremated remains of a single adult with a minimum capacity of 200 cubic inches, two adults in one or two separate chambers with a minimum capacity of 400 cubic inches (see Image 8.2), or they may be designed to house the remains of infants or children with considerably less capacity. These urns are provided in numerous shapes and are constructed of various materials. The following section presents many of the appropriate materials that are suitable for the construction of permanent containers, and will be followed by specialty items offered to the cremation consumer.

These urns are intended to be permanent containers, and as such it is important that they are constructed of strong and durable materials. Although it is difficult to provide a comprehensive list, common materials used in the manufacturing of urns include: woods, metals, marble, plastics and polymer resins. When considering wood and metal, you see similar materials as those used to construct caskets. Appropriate woods for urn construction include pine, cherry, oak, walnut and mahogany. As with wood caskets, wood urns are considered warm, beautiful, and unique, as the wood grain is visible on stained and unstained wood urns. Metals appropriate for urn construction include bronze, copper, steel, and pewter. Although these urns are typically considered cold, they are also a vision of strength, and the production process for metals allows for the construction of unique designs that may reflect the life of a loved one. For example, an urn can be designed in the shape of a golfer, boat, or a plethora of additional other meaningful casts. It is common for funeral providers to offer urns constructed of marble, plastics, polymer resigns, and for that matter many other materials including iron, glass, granite and cloisonné, to mention but a few. Most materials mentioned above are also appropriate for infant and child urns. In addition to offering the same qualities but in an appropriate size, these urns are also available in appropriate themes when families are experiencing the loss of a child. For example, urns for children come in the shape of hearts or building blocks with the letters of the alphabet embossed or imprinted on the urn. It is also possible to purchase stuffed animals that include a small urn that can be placed permanently inside the animal once the cremated remains are placed in the urn. One only needs to use his or her imagination to envision the color schemes and shapes that are available to house the cremated remains of children. Increasing urn options are appearing on a regular basis to meet the needs of the ever-increasing cremation market, and the professional funeral provider must stay very much in tune with new options that become available for the families they serve.

Another category of urns, classified as permanent containers, that is growing in popularity are biodegradable urns. As many consumers are inspired by environmentally friendly "green" options, this category of urn has increased in demand. Typically, these containers will break down quickly in the presence of water, specifically designed for families that intend to conduct a water scattering of the remains. Options include papier-mâché and crushed oyster shells assembled together. These urns will take on the water and quickly dissolve and release the cremated remains into the water. Other biodegradable urns are also designed to easily break down and become organic material when buried directly into soil. A Bios Urn was developed that placed the cremated remains in a biodegradable urn with pine seed; when buried, the contents of the urn will actually become fertilizer for the seeds and aid in the growth of a tree.

Although many options for urns and containers for final disposition have been presented here, it is essential that funeral providers remain current with new options that are arriving on the market on a regular basis, you do not want to find out about consumer options from a client family that has researched viable options, it is our professional responsibility to be on the cutting edge with respect to options for grieving families; remember, we must be the experts.

Specialty Items

Although many items that will be introduced in this section could be identified as permanent containers for cremated remains, their unique and varied nature has landed these items in the specialty section. As with

Image 8.3: Keepsakes and specialty items are available for cremation consumers.
Image Credit: Matthews Aurora Funeral Solutions

so many items associated with cremation services, the sheer volume of products can be overwhelming to client families. Again, we are reminded that funeral professionals must be prepared to explain options and provide appropriate and truthful information about all products and services that will allow grieving families to make informed decisions that best suit their specific wants and needs. In this section, we will present items that are intended to house smaller portions of cremated remains, and other items associated with cremation services. These items include keepsake "mini urns" and jewelry options that only hold a tiny portion of cremated remains. Additionally, we will present options such as thumbprint impressions; artwork developed utilizing cremated remains, fireworks and the development of synthetic diamonds, to mention a few. As we venture into the new and interesting world of cremation services, we must always remain mindful that it is our task to offer options and help educate consumers regarding all goods and services available and then work earnestly to provide the desired selections professionally and timely.

Keepsake, "mini urns", were specifically designed so that families that select cremation have the opportunity to divide cremated remains and retain a small portion of cremated remains while the majority of the remains are interred, entombed, scattered, or disposed of by other means. The capacity of keepsake containers varies greatly, it has been suggested that the range is from 2 to 70 cubic inches, but this is truly an estimate. Most containers that are classified as keepsake urns are offered individually or as a set. Often each member of the surviving family expresses a desire to retain a small portion of the cremated remains. These "mini urns" are often replicas of full-size urns, allowing family members to have the same design as the main urn that contains the majority of the remains. As with other aspects of cremation services, numerous keepsake designs and color schemes are available for family selection, once again, we recall the importance of providing families with various options in order to best meet their needs.

Another common option for keeping small portions of cremated remains offered to families is referred to as cremation jewelry. These charms only hold a tiny portion of cremated remains (amount varies by design) and are intended to be worn by family members as a necklace, bracelet, rings, or earrings. This jewelry is designed using the same material as traditional jewelry including gold, silver, gold vermeil, brass, glass, pewter, and wood. Numerous pendant designs exist; common shapes include hearts, crosses, tear drops, interlocking rings, angels, and tiny urns. The majority of these items allow for personalization through an engraving process. The option to select cremation jewelry can be both a unique and meaningful way for family members to honor loved ones.

The study of cremation certainly presents the reality that cremation families have the distinct opportunity to personalize each and every aspect of a service; no doubt, the immense volume of cremation merchandise can certainly be included in these personalizing options. For this reason, it is important to mention several available items that many in the funeral profession offer in conjunction with cremation services. It is now quite common for funeral/cremation providers to offer thumbprint impressions of the deceased which can then be utilized to create items such as jewelry or art pieces. Many funeral homes capture the thumbprint of each deceased case (after receiving permission from the authorized agent) in preparation of a future desire to purchase this merchandise. By scanning and archiving these prints families have the option to design and purchase these items at an undetermined time in the future. Another option that seems to be receiving more attention is utilizing portions of cremated remains in the development of artwork. For example, mixing a portion of the cremated remains with paint and commissioning an artist to paint a portrait of the deceased, or employing a portion of the cremated remains in the production of a blown glass vase or even in the creation of a stained-glass window. Add to the list the ability to add cremated remains into a firework display or into a bullet that will be scattered when the bullet is fired, or added to the ink coloring used during the tattooing process these options certainly highlight the vast possibilities that avail the cremation consumer.

Outer Burial Containers

Regardless of whether the remains are casketed or cremated and placed into an urn, the fundamental purpose for an outer burial container is to support the weight of the earth (help prevent the collapse of the grave which can be a maintenance, appearance, and safety issue), and to protect the contents of the urn or casket. Although many families might decide to purchase an outer burial container without being required to do so, it seems that the majority of the time consumers select an outer burial container as a result of a cemetery requirement. Consistent with outer burial containers designed for casketed remains, outer burial containers intended for urns are available in two distinct types: vaults and grave liners. The following section describes these two options and offers the similarities, differences, and any advantages or disadvantages of the selection of an option from either category.

Urn Vaults

The essential advantage of a vault over a grave liner is that vaults offer sealing qualities and are lined to aid in the deterrence of the entry of water, soil, and the contents of soil into contact with the urn. Urn vaults are typically constructed of concrete, metal, or polymer plastics and are generally constructed in the same fashion, and by the same companies, that construct full-size burial vaults. It is common for concrete urn vaults to have a synthetic liner as well as an additional polymer plastic, stainless steel, bronze or copper secondary liner. These vaults typically have tongue and groove sealing qualities that also utilize an adhesive

Image 8.4: Image Courtesy of Central Burial Vaults

to secure contact and ensure that the vault is appropriately sealed. Another design for urn vaults includes vaults constructed of steel, copper, polymer plastics, or aluminum, and this design utilizes what is described as an air seal (a method of sealing that utilizes air pressure created by placing the dome cover of the vault onto the base of the vault). These materials are not permeable, so they are not lined as is described when discussing concrete urn vaults. Regardless of construction material or the design of the seal, urn vaults are intended to both support the weight of the earth and protect the contents of the urn from water, soil, and other contents of the soil.

Urn Grave Liners

Although similarities exist, the key difference between urn vaults and grave liners is that urn grave liners do not seal and are not lined. These outer burial containers are designed strictly to support the weight of the earth without offering any additional protective qualities. These containers are typically constructed of concrete and meet minimal requirements for most cemeteries. As these liners are constructed of concrete, and concrete is permeable, it is fact that water, soil and other contents of soil that come in contact with the liner will eventually come into contact with the urn. Although this is true, it is also the case that these liners will support the weight of the earth and assist with the maintenance, appearance, and safety of the grounds of the cemetery.

• • •

Conclusion - Chapter Content Review

The mission of this chapter is to present options to encase cremated remains for final disposition. It is important that funeral directors present these options to client families during the arrangement conference in an effort to better serve families and ensure they understand all options regarding services and merchandise that are available. Containers presented included urns, both temporary and permanent containers, as well as specialty items such as keepsake urns and cremation jewelry. The analysis of containers for disposition concluded with an examination of outer burial containers offered for inurned remains.

The choices surrounding cremation options can certainly be overwhelming for client families, and it is important that funeral professionals are mindful of this reality. The professional funeral provider must explain all options and assist families as they walk through this difficult process. It is common for service decisions to drive merchandise selections, but at all times funeral directors must remain mindful that we are here to serve families, and maybe in some way make this difficult time more bearable, and help develop a meaningful and memorable service to honor the life of their loved one. In order to effectively achieve these expectations, funeral professionals must always be knowledgeable of all items related to cremation including legal and regulatory processes, available services, and merchandise, and this no doubt includes expertise related to containers for disposition of cremated remains.

For Critical Thought...

- What is the appropriate capacity for an urn that will accommodate the remains of two adults?
- You are working with a family that has selected cremation. They inform you that they own a niche at a columbarium at a local church and they intend to entomb the remains in that space. What is an appropriate conversation to have with this family regarding the container for final disposition?
- During the arrangement conference you learn that the family desires to scatter the cremated remains at a later date, what container options exist for this family? What additional information should be communicated to this family?

Chapter 9 – Cremation and Federal trade Commission (FTC) Compliance

Chapter Learning Objectives

Upon completion of the study of this chapter students should:

- Understand basic information about "The Funeral Rule" including date it went into effect, who must comply, and in general what the rule prohibits.
- Be able to identify specific aspects of "The Rule" that pertain to cremation.
- Be able to explain the required disclosure with respect to alternative containers.
- Be able to identify the required itemized price on the General Price List (GPL) regarding direct cremation.
- Be able to explain the misrepresentation prohibited by "The Rule" with respect to requiring a casket for direct cremation.

• • •

Introduction

As with all aspects of funeral service, when talking cremation, it is essential to study, comprehend, and comply with the Federal Trade Commission (FTC) Funeral Rule. For this reason, this chapter is dedicated to the elements of the FTC Funeral Rule that focus directly on elements related to cremation. The most appropriate way to cover this material is to go directly to the source, FTC documents. The content of this chapter is taken directly from Complying with the Funeral Rule, a document published by the Federal Trade Commission in April 2019. The intent is to assist students of cremation with compliance of the Rule. Following you will read a brief introduction to the Funeral Rule as well as who must comply with the Rule. Following this presentation, three distinct areas of the Rule that deal directly with features of cremation are presented; these include a required disclosure, itemized price, as well as a misrepresentation prohibited by the Rule.

Introduction to the Funeral Rule

The Funeral Rule went into effect on April 30, 1984. The Federal Trade Commission revised the Rule early in 1994; revisions became effective later that year. The Funeral Rule requires you to give consumers accurate, itemized price information and various other disclosures about funeral goods and services. In addition, the Rule prohibits you from:

- misrepresenting legal, crematory, and cemetery requirements;
- embalming for a fee without permission;
- requiring the purchase of a casket for direct cremation;
- requiring consumers to buy certain funeral goods or services as a condition for furnishing other funeral goods or services; and
- engaging in other deceptive or unfair practices.

Furthermore, if you violate the Funeral Rule, you may be subject to penalties of up to $43,280 per violation. The nature and intent of the Rule is evident from these statements lifted directly from the FTC document; Complying with the Funeral Rule is about consumer protection.

Who Must Comply with the Funeral Rule?

The FTC Funeral Rule commands that all "funeral providers" must comply with the Rule. You are a funeral provider if you sell or offer to sell both funeral goods and funeral services to the public. The Rule states that funeral goods are all products sold directly to the public in connection with funeral services and explains that funeral services are services used to care for and prepare bodies for burial, cremation, or other final disposition; and services used to arrange, supervise, or conduct the funeral ceremony or final disposition of human remains. The Rule clarifies by declaring that you are a funeral provider if you sell or offer to sell funeral goods **and** both types of funeral services. You do not have to be a licensed funeral director and your business does not have to be a licensed funeral home to be covered by the Funeral Rule. Cemeteries, crematories, and other businesses can also be "funeral providers" if they market both funeral goods and services.

Required Disclosure – Alternative Containers

The Rule stipulates six required disclosures that must be on the General Price List (GPL). The third disclosure, Alternative Containers, deals directly with cremation services. This disclosure declares the following: The third disclosure informs consumers that they may use alternative containers for direct cremations.

This disclosure must read as follows:

If you want to arrange a direct cremation, you can use an alternative container. Alternative containers encase the body and can be made of materials like fiberboard or composition materials (with or without an outside covering). The containers we provide are (specify containers).

You should place this disclosure in immediate conjunction with (directly next to) the price range for direct cremation. At the end of the last sentence, you should describe the specific kind of container(s) that you offer. If you don't arrange direct cremations, you don't need to include this disclosure on the GPL.

The language regarding alternative containers is clear and direct, and the Rule even explains the location of the disclosure. Again, this information has been drafted directly from the FTC document, Complying with the Funeral Rule, with the hope of supporting the compliance of all who read this text.

Required Itemized Price on the GPL – Direct Cremation

One of the cornerstone requirements of the Funeral Rule are itemized prices. The Rule stipulates 16 required itemized prices on the GPL; the third required itemized price is Direct Cremation. It is important to note that this itemized price is one of four on the GPL, that unlike the rest of the goods and services that you must list on the GPL, **must include** any fee that you will charge consumers for the basic professional services of the funeral director and staff.

The FTC manuscript, Complying with the Funeral Rule offers the following: If you offer direct cremations, your GPL must state a price range, make the required disclosure about the availability of an alternative container, and list each of these options within the range:

- a price for direct cremation if the consumer provides the casket or container
- a price for each direct cremation you offer with an alternative container

If you offer **direct cremations**, the Rule requires you to offer at least one alternative container. If you offer direct cremations with more than one alternative container, separately list a description of each container and its price.

Your GPL must describe the services you provide for each direct cremation you offer, such as direct cremation with a memorial service or direct cremation with scattering of ashes.

If you include the cost of cremation in your direct cremation price, **include the words "and cremation"** in your GPL's description of what you provide for direct cremation. However, if you use a crematory that someone else owns, you may treat the cremation charge as a cash advance item. In that case:

- **do not include the words "and cremation"** in your GPL's description of what you provide for direct cremation, and
- clearly explain that the added crematory charge will be estimated or itemized in the Statement of Funeral Goods and Services Selected.

In order to be in compliance with the Funeral Rule, your GPL must include an itemized price for a direct cremation. The language drafted directly from the FTC manual, Complying with the Funeral Rule, is intended to better prepare students of cremation to be within compliance of the Funeral Rule.

Misrepresentation Prohibited by the Rule – Casket for Direct Cremation

The Funeral Rule prohibits specific misrepresentations in six areas; the second area is Casket for Direct Cremation. The verbiage from the FTC document states the following with respect to this prohibited misrepresentation.

You cannot tell consumers that state or local law requires them to buy a casket if they are arranging a direct cremation. (A direct cremation is one that occurs without any formal viewing of the remains or any visitation or ceremony with the body present.) You also must not tell consumers, in the case of direct cremations, that they must buy a casket for any other reason.

If you offer direct cremations, you must make an alternative container available and inform consumers that such containers are available for direct cremations. You do this by including on your GPL the mandatory disclosure about alternative containers.

An "alternative container" is an unfinished wood box or other non-metal receptacle or enclosure, without ornamentation or a fixed interior lining, which is designed for the encasement of human remains. It is made of fiberboard, pressed-wood, composition materials or like materials, with or without an outside covering.

Note: The Rule also prohibits crematories from requiring that a casket be purchased for direct cremation. However, the Rule allows crematories to set standards for the kind of alternative containers that they will accept. For example, a crematory might stipulate that it will accept only rigid containers.

• • •

Conclusion - FTC – Final Thoughts

Compliance with the Federal Trade Commission (FTC) Funeral Rule is a professional standard to which all funeral providers must adhere. It is the responsibility of each and every funeral professional to be aware of these standards and always practice within the guidelines provided by FTC. The Funeral Rule is a detailed document with wide scope and the fundamental goal is to protect consumers. In this chapter, we only explored the items of the Rule that are specific to cremation; this included a brief introduction, who must comply with the rule, a required disclosure, itemized price, and a prohibited misrepresentation. A decision was made to present this material directly from the FTC manuscript with the knowledge this information was current at the time of this publication, but funeral service professionals must remain knowledgeable of any changes to the FTC Funeral Rule. Ultimately, we must all work to adhere to the standards presented by the Rule making it prudent to present information directly as it has been presented by the FTC. It is also important to remember that only a small segment of the elements of the Rule have been presented here, and it is crucial to always remain knowledgeable of the entire Rule and always comply with all standards of the Rule.

> *For Critical Thought...*
>
> - When did the FTC Funeral Rule go into effect?
> - Who must comply with the FTC Funeral Rule?
> - What is the FTC Funeral Rule required disclosure that is directly related to cremation?
> - What is the required FTC Funeral Rule itemized price directly related to cremation?
> - What is the FTC Funeral Rule misrepresentation prohibited that is directly related to cremation?

Chapter 10 – The Arrangement Conference

Chapter Co-Author and Editor: Glenda Stansbury, MAL, CFSP Dean, In-Sight Institute Certified Funeral Celebrant Training & Adjunct Instructor, University of Central Oklahoma

Chapter Learning Objectives

Upon completion of the study of this chapter students should:

- Understand the importance of effective communication when conducting the arrangement conference.
- Be able to communicate the funeral directors' roles in making sure client families are aware of all options.
- Understand the importance of celebrating ceremonies.
- Comprehend the importance of effectively coordinating the arrangement conference, including a strategy that includes: responding to pain, engaging in stories, articulating options, painting the picture, encouraging ceremony, and reviewing and referring.
- Understand necessary bookkeeping, vital statistics and forms utilized during the arrangement conference.
- Understand the importance of following through with the arrangement plan.

• • •

Introduction

Any time you discuss business statistics with funeral home owners and operators it is common to inquire about cremation rates, percentage of families that select embalming, viewing or casket sales, but what we often lose sight of is the one aspect of our business that will always be 100%. The arrangement conference is necessary for each and every family we serve. This meeting is most likely the first opportunity for the funeral director to actually get to know the family and learn more about the life of the deceased, and how they would like to honor their life. This conference is not only an opportunity to establish a trusting relationship with client families, it also provides funeral professionals the opportunity to help grieving families paint a meaningful service. In order to achieve this goal, we must always focus on performing a stellar arrangement conference. This reality should highlight the necessity to evaluate the arrangement processes, study what makes the conference successful, and train both students and seasoned professionals with respect to the art of arranging.

A central impediment to being a successful funeral service professional in the era of cremation may indeed be how the arrangement conference is executed. As was emphasized in chapter three, it is vitally important to understand that all funeral service options are viable options regardless of whether a family selects burial, entombment, or cremation. The seminal question is how will funeral homes handle the reality of increasing cremation rates when conducting the arrangement conference? It is simply unacceptable to look the other way and pretend that cremation rates will level off, and it is just as irresponsible to fail to offer cremation families all of the services and merchandise available to all client families.

Too often, when a family indicates that they would like a cremation, the arranger simply slides the GPL over and points out the "cremation packages" and the conversation is complete. Often families leave without understanding all the options and important ceremonies that are possible because we have treated cremation as a second-class service rather than a choice that a growing percentage of our client families are making.

What we need to understand is, when a family chooses cremation, the funeral home immediately becomes optional. Without the body, they do not necessarily need anything that we have to offer. They can have a gathering, catering, a video tribute and any other elements that are important to them, without us. So, we have to be even more mindful when working with cremation families to exhibit value to the services, merchandise, and ceremonies that we offer. Like burial, cremation requires additional services and merchandise in order to successfully follow through with the families wishes; it is the responsibility of funeral professionals to direct families through this process and assist in the creation of a meaningful service.

Although similarities exist, each arrangement conference ultimately evolves into its own unique consultation and will take on a life of its own. It is difficult, if not impossible, to adequately categorize methodical stages required of the successful arrangement conference, but in an effort to establish and communicate standards of an arrangement; six key areas are identified in this chapter to provide, at minimum, expectations of the arrangement conference. These expectations are presented with the knowledge that it is extremely important to always pay great attention to detail, listen carefully, take great notes, and always be flexible when working with grieving families.

At the beginning of this chapter, it is important to acknowledge that to adequately cover the arrangement conference it would take an entire text; therefore, it is the intention of this chapter to highlight the significance of the arrangement conference, as well as to explore briefly some of the essential elements of a successful conference, especially as related to the cremation consumer. As you read the following suggested steps for the arrangement conference, remain mindful that cremation is a method toward disposition, and like burial, requires the same level of service opportunities for each and every family. Although the following are presented in order, the exact format will rarely follow a specific pattern, beyond the initial greeting and actually meeting the family, the order of the progression is optional, and often driven by family questions, comments, and any pending deadlines that may need to be considered first.

We are going to use the acronym REAPER to help with the conversation that will hopefully be a reminder of the most important aspects of building a relationship with the family.

> **R**espond to the Pain
>
> **E**ngage the Stories
>
> **A**rticulate the Options
>
> **P**aint the Picture
>
> **E**ncourage Ceremony
>
> **R**eview and Refer

Respond to the Pain

It is critical for families to feel that they are the center of attention during the arrangement conference and throughout the funeral process; it all starts with a warm greeting and a relaxed introduction. Scheduling arrangements so that when the family arrives the funeral director and staff are prepared for their arrival and have appropriately prepared the funeral home for their arrival, the facility should be clean, orderly, and the funeral director should have reviewed all available notes and prepared for the meeting. It is best if the funeral director meets the family at the door of the funeral home and welcomes them to the facility; when possible, many directors prefer to actually greet the family in the parking lot and assist them to the door of the facility. Many directors/arrangers offer to take the family on a tour of the building. While a funeral home is our place of business and we are very comfortable with the setting, for some people just walking into a funeral home can be fear inducing. "That's where the dead bodies are." So, giving them a chance to see how welcoming and non-scary it actually is can set worried minds at ease. Once settled into the arrangement office, it is appropriate for the funeral director to conduct formal introductions; it is common at this time for many funeral homes to ask if families would like a coffee, water, or a soft drink prior to starting the actual meeting.

The most important professional skill a funeral director has in the arrangement conference is the ability to acknowledge the initial grief of the loss and to be comfortable with those outward expressions. When a funeral director begins with *just the facts* and begins filling out forms or gathering death certificate information, the opportunity to allow the family to express their feelings has been lost and cannot be retrieved. It can be something as simple as "I'm so sorry about the death of your mother" or "What a shock this must have been for you," or "It was a long road taking care of your dad" or "I can't imagine what this feels like for your family." The words are important but the bigger issue is the opening of communication and allowing the family to respond. Some families will readily take this opportunity to share their experiences, their death story, their emotions and fears. Other families may be more reticent or unable to express their feelings. This should never discourage a funeral director from allowing that time to share.

A helpful suggestion: Have an arrangement ceremony. Invite the family to bring a few items that represent the loved one's life and personality. Put them on the arrangement table and light a candle. Begin with some words such as: We gather today to begin the important work of honoring _____'s life. We hope that our conversation and our planning will focus every thought and effort on the life of _____ and how best to represent and honor the impact that he/she had on each of you here. Everyone has a story and a memory. We will do our best to listen and share and incorporate those special touches in the service that we plan together.

What is a death story? Almost every family has a death story—where they were or what they experienced when the loved one died. "She waited until I could get there." "He waited until we all left the room." "We opened the window and saw a dove as she was dying." These stories have great significance and importance to families, even if they might not mean anything or make sense to anyone else. We often say that the first person who hears the death story is the hero. This is the first person who gets to acknowledge and legitimize that final act. This is the first person who can be a part of the story. The funeral director who takes the time to hear the death story is a caring professional that families will remember.

Engage the Stories

When the family has settled in and the arranger has given plenty of time and space for the initial stories and expressions of loss, it is time for the funeral director to lead them through this difficult process. The funeral professional must remain mindful that most people only go through this process a few times over the course of a lifetime, so it is critically important to speak clearly and explain the procedure step-by-step. The introduction to the arrangement process can be considered profoundly important, as this very time can set the tone regarding the overall satisfaction the family receives from all the services provided. It is at this time that funeral directors can learn about the family and specifically about the deceased, and how they would like to honor his or her life. This is a time to get to know the family, incorporating simple comments such as, "tell me about your father.", "what is one word that describes your mother?", "what hobbies or interests did your son have?" can be significant in learning more about the deceased; gentle probing questions and comments like these can present possible options for the funeral director to personalize services, and create that meaningful memory each family is searching for. Ask open-ended questions, not ones that can be answered "yes" or "no". The question "did your mother like to garden?" will get a single word answer. Instead, "what did your mother do that brought her the most joy?" will encourage a conversation and fuller description of the person.

It is during this initial introduction that we can learn what was important to the deceased, and what defined his or her life. Maybe it was her love for the grandchildren that identified her life, or a church family, quilting, golfing, or an animal rescue program. Nevertheless, these details can bring to the surface items that can be included in the service to make it more personal and more meaningful; the introduction is a great time to learn about the family, the deceased, and the type of services they desire. It has been recommended that funeral directors avoid reaching for their pens and detail sheets during the first 15-30 minutes of the conference. Although this can be a helpful hint, never hesitate to write down a key thought or note, even if it is during that first time of sharing stories, memories, and remembrances. These thoughts can be lost during the meeting if they are not written down at that time.

Articulate Options

After successfully learning rich details about the deceased and his or her family, the funeral director may have a good idea about the services the family desires, but it is extremely important to offer all service options, and verify the actual services and merchandise the family would like to select. It is important to ascertain the types of services, location of services, and the family's desire regarding the officiant of the services. Many families have a church affiliation and it is important that the service reflects this reality. Other families prefer a non-religious option, and may require a funeral celebrant that is not associated with a specific religion, more on this later in the chapter.

It is necessary to remain mindful of the Federal Trade Commission (FTC) General Price List (GPL) requirement when discussing services and prices. You must give the GPL to anyone who asks, in person, about funeral goods, funeral services, or the prices of such goods or services. You must give the GPL to such individuals to keep. Bottom line, you must give the GPL to all persons who inquire about funeral arrangements. This is not only an FTC requirement, but when families have the GPL in their hands, it can help them understand the different aspects of the arrangement process and really serve as an aid throughout the arrangement. Furthermore, if your funeral home does not list the retail price of each casket on your GPL, you must prepare a separate printed or typewritten Casket Price List (CPL). Funeral Directors must show the CPL to anyone who asks in person about the caskets or alternative containers that you offer or inquiries about their prices. Funeral Directors must offer the CPL when you begin discussing caskets or alternative containers, but before showing these items. Consumers must be able to look at the price list before discussing their options or seeing the actual caskets. The same holds true for the Outer Burial Container Price List (OBCPL). If your funeral home sells outer burial containers and you do not list the retail price of each such container on your GPL, funeral homes must prepare a separate printed or typewritten OBCPL. Funeral Directors must show this price to all persons asking about outer burial containers or their prices. You must offer this price list when you begin to discuss outer burial containers, but before showing the containers. Consumers must be able to look at the price list before discussing their options or seeing the actual containers. Bottom line, you must always adhere to the FTC requirements.

Too often, families who are choosing cremation have no idea that they have a wide range of possibilities to honor their loved one. In the public's mind, cremation means no viewing or no service. It is imperative that the funeral professional be comfortable and competent when articulating all of the options. If the family begins the conversation with "we want cremation," then the next statement from the arranger should be something along the lines of: "We've established how we are going to ultimately take care of your mother's body. Now, let's talk about how we are going to honor her life."

Remember, regardless of the decision regarding disposition; burial, entombment, cremation, or other method of disposition, all services of the funeral home remain options. The disposition method alone does not determine if a family desires formal visitation, a funeral service, memorial service, graveside service, memorial gathering, or a committal service at the cemetery or crematory; all are viable alternatives, and must be determined through the interactions between the family and funeral director during the arrangement conference.

As the family and funeral director are working through service details, it is a good idea to have the funeral home detail sheet at hand and make notes as the family reaches decisions. It is not uncommon for families that select cremation to also desire formal visitation and a funeral service with a committal service at the crematory; yet, other families prefer to have a memorial service. Other cremation families prefer only an identification viewing and a memorial gathering, or a graveside service once the cremation has taken place. Still others may ultimately select a direct cremation (disposition of human remains by cremation, without formal viewing, visitation or ceremony with the body present) without other services. Even if this is the final decision, funeral directors must make sure each family is aware of the options available and make an informed decision, one with no regrets. The point here is that all available services are options, and as funeral directors we need to present all options and assist families through the process, working with the family to memorialize and personalize each service.

Yes, it is true that essentially all services are available to the family that selects cremation, but certain available services specific to the cremation consumer warrant further discussion, specifically those services surrounding the identification viewing: How will this viewing be set up? Where will it take place and what container will be utilized?

It is irrefutable that the best verification of identity of human remains is the actual identification viewing performed by the next of kin, or authorized agent(s). If the family selects this option without embalming and visitation, other provisions must be considered. As the remains have not been embalmed, the funeral home/crematory will need to adhere to local and state regulations, as well as specific facility requirements, with respect to viewing remains that have not been embalmed. Typically, the number of people allowed to view as well as the time allotted for such a viewing is limited. It is of key importance for funeral home personnel to make sure these remains are appropriately cleaned, groomed, and otherwise prepared for such a viewing. Recall from chapter three that authorization for minimal preparation is required, and this preparation is extremely important in order for a family to have a positive experience when conducting the identification viewing. If the funeral home/crematory does not make sure the remains are appropriate for viewing, the family will most likely have a negative experience and the long-lasting vision of their loved one will haunt them; and this image will forever be associated with the specific funeral home/crematory.

Each funeral home/crematory should have specific guidelines detailing where the viewing will take place, most common, and most dignified is to have this viewing take place in a slumber (visitation, state) room, although different facilities may have other arrangements made for such a viewing. As indicated in chapter two, this viewing should take place in an area that is standard for viewing remains, not in an isolated area.

Another consideration is how the remains will be presented. Although it is common to have the identification viewing take place in the container selected for the cremation itself, other options exist. The most common is a reposing bed supplied by the funeral home/crematory. A reposing bed can make a nice presentation, but when a reposing bed is utilized, it will require the additional purchase of a cremation container.

The most important part of this discussion with the family is to provide guidance and encouragement about the viewing, helping them understand the power and healing that can occur during that final goodbye. Often, a funeral director will say "You don't want to view do you?" indicating that this seems unnecessary or, (more realistically) a lot of work for the funeral director. Every family should be encouraged to have some type of final viewing, not only from the legal aspects of an ID, but also because it has been proven that the reality of viewing is important in the first steps on a healthy grief journey. (See Chapter 10 Exhibit 1: *The Articulation Factor*)

Paint the Picture

As mentioned above, it is very important that the funeral director provides a wide variety of options to cremation families. It cannot be stated strongly enough that many of our immediate disposition families are created because no one took the time to explain what a service could be.

The other thing to keep in mind is that some families choosing cremation are doing so based upon previous bad experiences with funeral services. Either they were involved in, or attended, an impersonal service that failed to mention the deceased's name, or a hyper-religious event where the officiant/clergy took the opportunity to preach and even offer an invitation. Every funeral director has a host of horror stories where they stood at the back of the chapel or church and watched a funeral go horribly wrong. The minister called the widow by the dog's name. The officiant never acknowledged the deceased by name. The family told the officiant to sit down and they would take over. The family or officiant chose to open the microphone for comments from the audience and it became long or tedious or uncomfortable or even hurtful.

Too often, *cremation-no service*, or *we want a party* is code for families that really means, "I don't want what I've seen before." (See Chapter 10 Exhibit 2: *We Want a Party*)

One of most powerful questions we can ask when a family says *we want a party* or *simple cremation* is "tell me what that looks like for you?" What the family is envisioning may be completely different than what the arranger thinks they are asking for. So, inviting them to expand and explain what would be meaningful for them will help the arranger truly understand what they are looking for. Never assume that their language and their description fit what you are accustomed to offering. "Simple" cremation for some families might mean a full service and a graveside placement. When they say "simple" their understanding is that they will not have a viewing, or a reception or a procession to graveside. When we hear "simple," we assume that they do not want a service and begin to direct the conversation into that space. "Tell me what that looks like for you" can open the doors to a much fuller and robust understanding so the arranger can know exactly which choices they might be looking for.

We must work very hard to paint the picture for the family as to how a well-done, personalized, and unique service will honor the loved one's life and be a healthy first step on the grief journey for the surviving family and friends. This is called *articulating the value of the funeral*. (See Exhibit 1) Every funeral professional should have a well-thought-out belief system that he/she can articulate to the family about the importance of a gathering, the healing elements of remembering, the vital aspects to a service. As you grow through your funeral studies, this should be one of the most important personal steps you should take. If you do not know why we have funerals, then how can you express that to your families?

So, while working through the sometimes-arduous arrangement process it is important to always be connecting these choices back to how they will impact the family and attach meaning to each decision. It is valuable to work out service details, as these decisions often drive merchandise offerings and decisions. The professional funeral director must explain what merchandise selections are required for the services selected and then present all available options. Typical merchandise that will require consideration include: caskets, alternative containers, urns, urn vaults, burial vaults, memorial books, service folders, prayer cards, and memorial videos, to name but a few.

The funeral home data sheet will be useful to determine that all required service information has been acquired. A few of the key elements to determine about the service include the following items:

- Day, date, time, location, and type of the service
- Officiant(s)
- Merchandise selected, including casket, containers, urn, memorial book, service folders, prayer cards, memorial videos, urn vaults/burial vaults
- Pallbearers and Honorary Pallbearers
- Visitation and viewing information
- Cemetery and/or Crematory information

Vital Statistics and Other Specifics

A necessary reality with respect to the services we provide is the collection of vital statistics and other specific information about the deceased and his or her family. Resist the temptation to begin the conference with this task; although you must obtain this information, it is cold and impersonal to begin the arrangement in this fashion. After successfully initiating a relationship with the family it is appropriate to collect the vital statistics required for our business. This information is necessary for documents such as the death certificate, obituary, request for military honors, social security notification, and funeral homes records, to name a few. It is necessary for the funeral director to capture the following information:

- Full name, address, place of death, date of death, date of birth, place of birth, gender, race, social security number, formal education, occupation, and marital status of the deceased
- If married, full name of spouse
- Informants full name, age, address, and telephone number

- Deceased's father's name and birthplace, and deceased's mother's maiden name and birthplace
- The name, address, and phone number of the deceased's attending physician
- If inurnment or entombment is selected, name and location of the cemetery
- Full names of the deceased's children, grandchildren, great-grandchildren and siblings
- If the deceased is a military veteran, a record of their service

The collection of reliable vital statistics is a necessary aspect of our profession. Although this may not be the best time to build rapport with the family, often, the family appreciates the opportunity to take control of an aspect of the arrangement process and will happily assist with the completion of the required vital statistics. As indicated above, several official documents that we process in the funeral service profession requires vital statistics. Always make sure the information obtained is genuine and authentic, it is best practice to wait until the family has knowledge of the absolute correct information when concerning vital statistics, even if this means a short delay in the processing of documents. It is also important to recall that although we look at these forms every day, the families we work with do not, and they are also under a great deal of stress; therefore, as funeral directors, we must be at their side and guide them through this process.

It is also very important that the arranger is aware of the state laws regarding permission to cremate. Each state has a hierarchy of who can grant permission for cremation. If your state requires that all next of kin be contacted, be sure that you have done your due diligence to locate that son that has been estranged from the family or be ready to explain to the family why the cremation cannot take place until all parties sign off.

Required Bookkeeping

The successful business operation must always have impeccable records and archive these proceedings. Certain forms are required every time you serve a family, for example the statement of goods and services selected, while others are only required under certain circumstances, the burial transit permit comes to mind. As indicated at the beginning of this chapter, every arrangement is unique and the specifics of each conference necessitate paperwork, forms, and authorizations that must be completed. Below is a list of many of the common elements that must be completed during or immediately following the arrangement conference to provide you with a small sample.

- Statement of Goods and Services Selected
- Authorization to Cremate
- Application for Cremation Permit Form
- Burial Transit Permit
- Application for Military Honors
- Death Certificate Form and Application
- Authorization to Embalm
- Authorization to Remove Medical Devices
- Funeral Home Detail Sheet

Encourage Ceremony

One of the reasons that people come to funeral homes and pay for our services is that they believe we are the experts when it comes to putting together services. While all the details, minutia, and vital statistics are essential and must be taken care of, if we stop there, then we are nothing more than glorified clerks. We use the term "clipboard jockeys" to describe these funeral directors who only want to deal with death certificates and details.

The best way for people to understand the importance of a funeral, especially for cremation families who have other options just by virtue of the disposition, is to be integrally involved as a consultant and guide when it comes to planning a ceremony. If the family wants to have a service, with or without the body present, the funeral professional should know how to put together a service with music, pictures, displays, the right officiant, and all of the elements that we consider for a funeral service. If that means finding a bingo machine because the deceased loved bingo, then that should happen. If that means putting Mickey Mouse ears on the hearse for a child's last ride, then find someone who has the ability to put that together. If that means playing a favorite music selection at graveside, purchase a Bluetooth speaker and play it from your phone or tablet.

Some of the old guard of funeral directors might turn up their noses and say "I didn't go to school to be an event planner". Honestly, what is a funeral if it is not an event? And today's consumers expect concierge and personalized service at every step. If we are not willing to do whatever it takes, a competitor surely will.

The more challenging situation is when a family does not want what we would consider a traditional service. The most common reaction is to hand the cremated remains to the family and they are on their own to put something together. The way that we stay relevant and worthwhile to these cremation families is to offer a ceremony for whatever they would like to do.

Some of the ceremonies could include:

Cremation/No Service: Have a "returning your loved one ceremony" when the cremated remains are ready to be picked up and tell the family at arrangement that this is a ceremony that your funeral home provides for every family. "You've given us the honor of taking your mother into our care. We will have a ceremony when we place her back into your care". Bring the family into a private area/viewing room/chapel and have candles and flowers on a table. Give them a chance to be settled and then bring in the urn, set it on the table and give the family time to be with the urn or even share stories. Or the funeral director could even say a few words (see box below). Then escort the family and place the urn in the car for the family. This simple ceremony indicates that we have more to offer than the stand-alone cremation only services.

> It is an important day when we gather together to honor a life and mourn a death. Time stands still for just a moment as we stand here to acknowledge that someone has touched our lives, has left an imprint on our hearts and that our souls are eternally changed. _____ left this life on _____ but his/her spirit and his/her living made a difference and will continue to do so as long as each of you remember him/her in your hearts and carry the lessons of his/her life with you.
>
> You now are the representatives and the ambassadors of _____'s legacy. She/He gave you wonderful gifts of kindness, graciousness, strength, acceptance and love. You are her/his future and her/his memories. Be kind and patient with one another and allow each one of your family to experience grief in the way that fits them best. Washington Irving said *"There is sacredness in tears. They are not the mark of weakness, but of power. They speak more eloquently than ten thousand tongues. They are messengers of overwhelming grief...and unspeakable love.* Accept your tears and expressions of loss. Accept the angels in human form who come along with a word, a hug or a memory to share. Help each other during those difficult times, the holidays, the anniversaries, the birthdays, the times when you will miss her/him the most.
>
> **BLESSING:** *May you go forward today with a small flickering of light in your soul. May the memories of your loved one begin to bring comfort rather than pain. May the words, touch and presence of others bring solace. And may you be blessed in your coming in and going out, grateful for a life lived and a legacy left behind. Go in peace.*

Family Wants to Scatter: **Offer to put together a ceremony or a reading that they could take with them when they scatter. Or offer to attend the scattering with them.**

A Story:

Dr. Gary Sokoll was a professor and chair of the Funeral Service Department of University of Central Oklahoma for 20 years. His wife, who lived in San Francisco, died of cancer and had made arrangements to be cremated and scattered through the Neptune Society. When Gary was making arrangements for her service, he went to the Neptune Society to ask about the scattering. She died right before Christmas, so Gary was told that they would not be taking the boat out again until two weeks after the holidays. Gary asked if they did some type of ceremony for the scattering. They were confused and said, "No, we just drive the boat". Gary had asked Glenda Stansbury to be the Funeral Celebrant for his wife's service, so she traveled from Oklahoma City to San Francisco to conduct the service. Gary was very frustrated that there was not going to be a ceremony for the scattering. Glenda told him that she was unable to come back for the scattering but she would write a ceremony that they could experience on the boat. Gary asked one of his friends to read the ceremony as they scattered his wife's cremated remains and was so relieved that someone was willing to help him have the ceremony that he needed.

Scattering At Sea

You can shed tears that she is gone

Or you can smile because she has lived.

You can close your eyes and pray that she'll come back

Or you can open your eyes and see all that she has left.

Your heart can be empty because you can't see her

Or you can be full of the love you shared

You can turn your back on tomorrow and live yesterday

Or you can be happy for tomorrow, because of yesterday

You can remember her and only that she's gone

Or you can cherish her memory and let it live on

And so we come together under this beautiful winter sky, to honor the life that _____ lived. She gathered her friends and family together, gave them the gift of life and love and lived well in the world that she made.

We come to bid her a gentle farewell, to acknowledge the pain of loss and the days of grief that lay ahead for us, her family and friends, and to hallow this spot where she will be sent to lay to rest with _____. Her days of pain and suffering are done and now she can be at peace among the gentle waves of the Bay that she loved sailing with _____.

From this time on, this water will be sacred to you. For it is here that our beloved _____, returns to the earth from which we all came. We can come here to place the orange tulips that she loved and send a wish of remembrance to her spirit.

It is here that we can come to feel the presence and the love shared in life. She left behind such a huge example of living each moment to the fullest, striving to be her best and seeking fun in everything she touched.

It is here that we show honor to the memories of a life that touched us and remains alive in our hearts, for no one is dead until they are forgotten.

May we therefore pledge to keep the example of love and joy of an intentional and determined life with us each day and be eternally grateful that _____ was part of our world and our lives.

The poet wrote:

The cares of the world concern me no longer. I have completed this life. My work is done, the children

of my heart grown. My family is well on their journey and happy and healthy in their pursuits. I have

loved much and well. To those I leave behind, I hope I will remain in their hearts as they will in mine.

Thank you for taking such good care of me and all of you, who have been my friends, thank for teaching

me about life and about love. Go in peace and in blessings for the day.

The Family Wants a Graveside Urn Placement Only: Again, offer to provide words and ceremony at the graveside. Either find a Celebrant to assist, or have one of the funeral directors provide some words to hallow the ground (see box). Have quiet music playing in the background, flowers to put on the place of inurnment, or a family member who can read a poem or a scripture.

> Hallowing the Ground: *A Closing Ceremony to Be Used at the Cemetery*
>
> When an old monk was asked why he cared for the ancient graves and why he cleaned the stones to preserve the writings carved there. His reply was simple, "they still have their names. They will always have their names."
>
> From this day on this place will bear the name of _____. It is here that his/her name will be honored by those who love him. It is here that he/she will be remembered by generations yet unborn. This place means he/she will always have his/her name.
>
> When Chief Crazy Horse was asked where his home was, he replied, my land is where my people are buried. He fought valiant wars to defend the burial grounds of his people. For in those sacred grounds he found a connection with his heritage and felt like he belonged to a family. There he found the hope that he too would be so honored and remembered. In this hope he found the courage to live.
>
> From this time on this land will also be sacred to you. For it is here that the body of _____ returned to the earth from which we all came. It is here that he/she became one with the earth and with the universe.
>
> It is here that generations to come will find a connection to their roots. They will come here and feel the sense of belonging to a greater force called family.
>
> It is here that many will come to feel the presence and the love shared in life. Some will come often. Others may come only on rare occasions; all who come will be blessed. It is here that we show honor to the memories of a life that touched us and remains alive in our hearts.
>
> May we therefore hallow this ground by placing your individual flowers here and, by that act, pledge to remember and honor him/her for as long as you live.
>
> This is now the earthly home of _____, and like Chief Crazy Horse, our home is also where our people are buried. And we are standing on holy ground.

All of these ceremonial words are provided as examples or inspiration for the types of ceremonies that could be provided by the funeral home staff. The important concept is not to adapt the readings, per se; it is to understand that we must find unique and meaningful ways to serve our cremation families so they feel that the money they paid resulted in a professional who knew how to take care of them.

Incorporating an Urn Ark

Too often what is missing in cremation services is the ceremony and honor of the body. Funeral directors are very accustomed to the gravity and dignity that is afforded a casketed body—careful placement at the front of the chapel or church, using pall bearers to honor their family members or friends, processing and recessing and the somber walk to the graveside.

Most cremation services begin and end with the urn sitting at the front on a table, perhaps with flowers and pictures, but this lacks the gravitas that we have historically given to a body in a casket. There is no procession, no pall bearers, the urn just becomes part of the decoration on the table.

Many firms have begun to utilize urn arks. This is a piece of equipment that is designed specifically for bearing an urn. By using an urn ark, the body can be processed and recessed, pall bearers can be used, and it is a much more dignified way to arrive at the inurnment than the funeral director just carrying the urn.

Again, this provides the same type of honor and ceremony that we afford bodies for burial. It allows the firm to give equal treatment to their cremation families and signals to all who attend that every life is special and should receive the same respect and intention.

Image 10.1: Urn Ark.
Image Source: Mercer Adams Funeral Service

Review and Refer

As you begin to wrap up the arrangement conference, a review of all services planned and merchandise selected can be helpful to make sure that you and the client family are on the same page, and have a full understanding of the services that have been selected. It is also very helpful to serve as an aid to assist the family as the stress, and at times sheer exhaustion, of the death experience can cause the details to be foggy or even completely forgotten. It is best to thoroughly and methodically review all details that have been arranged and if adjustments are desired, include these on the final notes. This simple step can reassure families of services and merchandise desired as well as verify for the funeral professional of these items prior to implementing the service plan. This step can not only reassure the family and funeral director, it can also prevent misunderstandings and eliminate miscues associated with serving the family. This may seem routine and like common sense, but this may be the segment of the arrangement that ultimately allows you, the funeral director, to assist the family in painting a meaningful and memorable service to honor their loved one.

Assignment of Tasks

Another useful practice is the actual assignment of tasks, for both the family and the funeral director. It is quite common for loose ends to exist at the conclusion of the arrangement conference; just jotting these items in need of attention for the family can make all of the difference in receiving a timely response as you work to serve the family. For example, you need military discharge paperwork in order to complete the requests for military honors. As you communicate the different items you still need to receive, let the family know that you will be working on the planned services to ensure each detail is addressed as they have requested. Below is a list of some of the common tasks that are helpful to write down for families. Never assume that the family will remember any of the conversation or the things to be done. An arranging family is overwhelmed by grief, by decisions, by family, by the pressure of planning a major event in a brief time. So, have a prepared list that can be filled in or checked off that they can take with them. Of course, each arrangement is unique, and a list of this nature can never be considered cumulative. Here are a few common items families may still need to get to the funeral home after the initial conference:

- Burial Clothing
- Photographs for hair and cosmetics
- Photographs for memorial video
- Obituary for Publication
- Photo for Obituary
- Military Discharge Paperwork
- Missing vital statistics; social security number, family names, and the list goes on…
- Selection of poem or verse for the memorial folder
- List of Pallbearers or Honorary Pallbearers
- Full list of Survivors

Refer

Sometimes the best thing we can know is who we know. A funeral professional should understand what the families of today need and want and have a contingent of professionals for referral. Be informed and knowledgeable about musicians, tribute videos, florists, caterers (if the firm does not offer that in-house) and any other professional that might be needed for the service. Everything that the funeral director can offer to take care of makes that firm more valuable to the family who is paying for our services. If we tell the family to take care of those details, then they question why they are paying your professional service fee.

Most funeral homes have a list of clergy who are willing to do services for families who are not members of a church or do not have an officiant. In some cases, that is the best option. However, the funeral director should be vigilant about listening to those services and assuring that the minister is meeting the needs of the family, not repeating the same service he/she did last week. When "rent-a-ministers" use *Funeral Sermon #3, insert name here*, or when they take the opportunity to preach and proselytize, often, the family is left with a meaningless or hurtful event. And, from a business standpoint, when a family walks away unhappy or unfulfilled, they are not angry at the minister. They are angry at the funeral home, and future business just walked out of the door. If your firm has a minister(s) who will not meet the needs of each family, then it is in the best interest of the funeral home to quit referring services to that individual.

With the advent of Funeral Celebrants in North America in 1999, there is an option available for most funeral homes to refer a family to a trained professional who will meet with the family and create a personalized and one-of-a-kind service for the family. Celebrants meet with the family for 2-3 hours to gather the stories and then write a service that fits the deceased and the family. They are specifically trained in the value of the funeral, the impact of the grieving experience, and each Celebrant has invested time and energy into training to be prepared to consult, coordinate, and create a meaningful and special service.

As fewer people define themselves as church affiliated (see box below), the demand for an officiant who can handle secular or spiritual or non-denominational services is growing. There is also a proven correlation between church affiliation and cremation rates. In those states where cremation rates are highest (e.g. Nevada, Washington, Oregon, Hawaii, Maine), church affiliation or attendance is the lowest. Therefore, it is imperative that funeral professionals become familiar with Celebrants and become adept at offering their services for those families who need them.

Fewer than half of U.S. adults say they belong to a church, synagogue or mosque, according to a new Gallup survey that highlights a dramatic trend away from religious affiliation in recent years among all age groups.

A Gallup Poll recently indicated that religious membership in the U.S. has fallen to just 47% among those surveyed — representing less than half of the adult population for the first time since Gallup began asking the question more than 80 years ago.

In 2018, 50% of adults polled said they belonged to a religious congregation, down sharply from the 70% who said so as recently as 1999. That figure fluctuated only a few percentage points over a period of six decades beginning in 1937 — the first year of the survey — when 73% of U.S. adults said they belonged to a church, synagogue or mosque.

For years, demographers have cited millennials as being on the cusp of "the rise of the 'nones' " — a group defined as atheists, agnostics and those who say they have no religious preference. But, as Gallup points out, more Americans of every age bracket — including "traditionalists" born before 1946 – say they are among this group.

Scott Neuman – NPR – March 30, 2021

Conclusion - Follow Through

The most successful arrangement conference will ultimately fail if the funeral director does not follow through! Great attention to detail during the conference is a great first step, providing the ability to follow through with the exact wishes of the client family.

Checking and double checking that all necessary information has been obtained and is on the funeral home permanent record. Ordering and verifying that all necessary merchandise and services have been ordered and secured. Verifying all necessary contacts have been made and required details communicated. You must provide every service and merchandise item arranged during the conference in order to successfully serve the family. It takes work, practice, and talent to become a great arranging funeral director, but this skill is only one aspect of the successful funeral, impeccable communication and dedicated follow though is essential.

> *For Critical Thought...*
>
> - At the start of an arrangement conference a family indicates that they desire a cremation, but they are unsure about any other details. What options should be offered to this family?
> - What is the first element of a successful arrangement conference?
> - What are the required steps to successfully completing an arrangement conference?
> - What acronym is used to represent the required elements of a successful arrangement conference?
> - What does each letter represent?

Chapter 10, Exhibit 1

"Reprinted from the October 2012 edition of *ICCFA Magazine* with permission of the International Cemetery, Cremation and Funeral Association in Sterling, Virginia. Copyright © 2012."

by Glenda Stansbury

glenda@insightbooks.com

ICCFA Magazine author spotlight

➤ Glenda Stansbury, CFSP, is vice president of marketing for In-Sight Books, Oklahoma City, Oklahoma.
www.insightbooks.com

➤ She is a licensed funeral director and embalmer and trains funeral directors, cemeterians and others as Certified Celebrants who meet with families to talk about their loved ones and plan personalized funeral services.

➤ She and her father, Doug Manning, conduct celebrant training as professors in the College of 21st Century Services at ICCFA University and at other locations across the country through the Insight Institute.

• ICCFAU 2013 will be July 19-24 at the Fogelman Conference Center, Memphis, Tennessee. Call 1.800.645.7700 or go to www.iccfa.com for more information.
• Contact Stansbury or go to the In-Sight Books website for information about celebrant training sessions scheduled around the country.

➤ Stansbury is adjunct faculty with the funeral service department at the University of Central Oklahoma, where she teaches courses in funeral service communication and the psychology of grief and oversees practicum students.

Editor's note

The ICCFA believes in celebrant training for funeral directors and cemeterians who wish to better help families and to be successful in the 21st century. In addition to articles by celebrant trainer Glenda Stansbury, ICCFA Magazine will be running, as a regular feature, stories by celebrants about specific services they put together for families.

Contact ICCFA Magazine Managing Editor Susan Loving, sloving@iccfa.com:
• if you are a celebrant with a story about a service that the family involved is willing to let you share in order to inspire others

or

• if you have any tips for celebrant services such as the ones from Tanya Scotece on page 18.

CELEBRANTS

Do you believe in the value of what you offer families? Then why are so many of your families choosing 'cremation, no services'? Maybe it's because you're waiting until the arrangement conference to make your case, and by then it's probably too late.

The articulation factor: What we must learn to say to families

My favorite show on television for the past three years has been "The Big Bang Theory." The writing is wickedly funny and there is something endearing about incredibly intelligent scientists who understand and revel in concepts, equations and theories that we mortals have no chance of grasping trying to find love and acceptance in a world that doesn't embrace them and relegates them to nerd status.

One of the best parts of the show is the title. Each week the episode is titled in very scientific geek-speak to describe a mundane everyday experience. Some recent ones: "The Speckerman Reccurence" was about one of the characters dealing with a bully from his high school days; "The Good Guy Fluctuation" dealt with a cheating boyfriend; "The Isolation Permutation" showed one of the female leads becoming jealous because the two other girls went wedding shopping without her. It just makes you feel smarter to read the titles, even if the script is basic situation comedy fare with a physicist twist.

And so, in thinking about the topic I'm addressing in this article, I decided to title it, a la Big Bang, "The Articulation Factor."

I hope we can discuss an issue that presents possibly the biggest dilemma and source of frustration for funeral homes and cemeteries across the country and feel like extremely smart people while doing so.

We hear it constantly. How do we convince people who have decided to have an immediate cremation with no viewing, no service, no burial—nothing—to consider the alternative? Why do people not want what we have to offer? Why are so many of our customers walking out the door with an alternative container in their hands, never to be seen again?

At conferences, conventions, meetings or wherever two or more funeral directors are gathered together, the conversation inevitably turns to this conundrum. The call load for cremation may be increasing, but the revenue and income per service is decreasing.

Families are convinced that cheaper and quicker is better, and we are left nodding our heads while they walk out saying to themselves, "I showed them. I didn't let them talk me into anything!" How do we combat that? Should we combat it? What will the future hold if we do not combat it?

Funeral directors have three very powerful tools: ears, knowledge and a voice. We sometime forget that we are the paid professionals the family has chosen to help them through this life experience and that we truly are the smartest people in the room when it comes to all aspects of the funeral process. We need to learn how to embrace that confidence, that passion and that belief.

First we need to learn how to listen, to hear the stories of the family, to hear the importance of a life lived and how the family would like to honor that life. And then we need to learn how to open our mouths and express it to the very people who need to hear it. We need to articulate the value of the funeral and how each element of a funeral can assist the family in their grief journey.

I'm going to make some suggestions in a chronological and experiential way to show you the opportunities we have for "the articulation factor."

➤ to page 14

CELEBRANTS

**Go! Do not send your apprentice, your part-timer or your driver.
Even if you use a call service for removal, the funeral director needs to be there.**

▶ *from page 12*

The first call

We could write an entire article on first calls, about the importance and power of being there at that very first step in the journey. For the purposes of this article, there is only one thing to say about first call: Go! Do not send your apprentice, your part-timer or your driver.

Even if you use a call service for removal, the funeral director needs to be there. If our profession can't figure that out, all the rest of these thoughts will ultimately be moot.

Before the arrangement

You may have read this before, but it bears repeating. We are firm advocates of touching base with the family during the "gap" between removal and arrangement. It is when the family is left alone with their questions, concerns and fears that they make decisions with little information or surf the Web to find out what their options are.

Therefore, it greatly benefits the family as well as your company when the funeral director takes the time to answer many of the inevitable questions before the family even gets to the arrangement room. This is especially imperative if the funeral director is not present at first call (see first call discussion above).

A visit to the home or, at the minimum, a phone call to let the family know that the director is available for whatever they may need, is vital and a valuable use of time and staff. Those hours between when the removal car drives away and the family sits down in the arrangement room can either be the time when the family decides, on its own and to its own detriment, to forgo services, or when the family learns, thanks to an informed and caring funeral professional, about the many options available for honoring their loved one.

During "the gap," the funeral director has an opportunity to widen the family's thinking about options. The alternative is to leave the family to their own devices. That's when the computer comes on, Google appears and off the family goes on a search for information, pricing and alternatives to choices they do not want to have to make in the first place.

Without some guidance, the family will come into the arrangement conference with decisions set in concrete based upon no information, horror stories from the Internet or reactions to bad funerals previously experienced, and the funeral director can do little to sway their thinking or offer alternatives.

The funeral director could stop by the home with some coffee and donuts, a few sub sandwiches or some paper goods, along with a funeral planner or packet of information. This tells the family that you are there to meet their needs, whatever they might be. What do you say when making this "gap" visit? You can start out with something like this:

"I just wanted to stop by to check in on you, see how you are doing and see if there is anything you need or any questions I could answer before we get together later today (or whenever the arrangement conference is scheduled).

"I'm sure you have a hundred thoughts flying around and it is difficult to concentrate on any of them. I want to assure you that we will work together to take care of all of those important decisions, details and arrangements and I'm more than happy to clear up any concerns you may have right now."

The discussion then might include, but does not need to be limited to, the value of having a viewing before cremation, a celebrant service or personalized tribute that fits their loved one and family, the importance of a funeral experience for family and friends, etc. The information you drop off certainly should let them know about their options.

Even if they look at you standing at their front door and say they have nothing to ask right now, never underestimate the power of just making that effort, the long-lasting effect of articulating your care and your expertise.

Please notice that I clearly said "the funeral director" should do this. This is not the place for a concierge or an apprentice or a part-timer who is sent on an errand to deliver coffee and cookies.

The first call and the "gap" meeting are the most important times you can spend with the family. I cannot say this enough times or in enough different ways. Unless we touch the family from the beginning, we are playing catch up, and we never get a second chance to make that first impression.

After a recent shoulder surgery, I was lying on the couch trying to overcome the effects of the meds and the pain of the incision and wondering why I thought this was such a good idea.

The phone rang; it was my surgeon. It was not the nurse or the physician's assistant or the secretary. It was the professional I had chosen calling to see how I was, whether I had any questions or if I needed anything.

I was overwhelmed and thankful. I didn't have any questions, but I felt better that he had made the effort to touch base with me. A few weeks ago, a friend of mine asked me to recommend a surgeon. Who do you think I told her was the very best doctor in the city?

Do you see the connection?

The arrangement room

In a perfect world, funeral directors would return to the days of making arrangements in the home. People were comfortable in their own setting and it seemed less like a business arrangement and more like a meeting with an honored friend invited to help the family in a time of need.

I realize this probably is not going to happen anytime in the near future. Therefore, we need to give a great deal of thought to the location and setting of our arrangement rooms.

Ask yourself: Are you more comfortable sitting at a long wooden conference table or on an overstuffed couch with a coffee table you can put your feet on? The answer should be obvious.

It's time to make the arrangement room look more like a living room and less like an attorney's office or a furniture store. Most arrangement rooms today have way too much "stuff" lying around and are intimidating to people who are already overwhelmed by grief and probably operating with little sleep or food.

Every piece of furniture, brochure, book or sample in an arrangement room should

CELEBRANTS

I am also a firm advocate of creating an atmosphere of "ceremony" every time you interact with the family, including the arrangement experience.

be reexamined, not from the standpoint of "Does this help us sell something?" but rather from the standpoint of "How does someone who has been up all night after losing a husband of 52 years feel when sitting here?"

The principles of simplicity, comfort and a welcoming atmosphere should guide you as you set up an arrangement room. The location of the coffee pot and the bottled water with the funeral home logo on it is of much less importance than the ability of the funeral director to sit next to the grieving widow and pat her hand if needed.

The "stuff" will get sold only after we have heard their hearts.

The arrangement ceremony

I am also a firm advocate of creating an atmosphere of "ceremony" every time you interact with the family, including the arrangement experience.

This could mean asking the family to bring some special items or pictures of the loved one and placing them on the table, lighting a candle and beginning by saying something like this:

"We are here to honor _____, and want to take a moment to acknowledge the importance of a life lived as we come together to plan a fitting tribute to honor _____'s life among you."

That can go miles toward calming upset and angry minds and helping the family focus. It also says to the family that the funeral director is not just there to take their money but is very much attuned to the occasion and the loss and will be a guide for them.

Even if the family does not bring anything with them, the pausing, the acknowledging—the ceremony—is vital in setting a tone of remembrance for the family.

The arrangement bucket

For several years, Doug Manning and I have used the concept of buckets when talking to funeral directors in training settings. We try to help funeral directors visualize the family sitting in front of them as having walked in with a bucket full of feelings, fears, hurts and uncertainties. Nothing that is said to that family will make a difference until they feel someone has heard what is in their bucket.

This is where funeral directors have failed miserably for years. The arranger is so intent on getting down to business and getting the GPL on the table that feelings and needs are ignored and families walk out of the arrangement room feeling they have been taken for an expensive ride and no one cared how they felt, what they needed to say or who their loved one was.

It is imperative that the first thing you do with every family is acknowledge their loss and let them talk about their loved one. It might be saying something as simple as:

"This must have been such a shock for you," or

"What a long journey this has been for your family," or

"I can't imagine what it feels like to lose a young child," or

"What a great long life your mother lived. I'll bet you have some wonderful stories and memories of her," or

"This must really hurt."

The words are not the magic. The act of stopping to acknowledge their feelings and opening the door to hear their story is powerful and life changing. Almost everyone will have a "death story" about where they were when the death occurred: "She waited until I could get there"; "He waited until we all left the room"; "I whispered that it was OK for him to let go, and he died."

Almost everyone wants to share their death story and, in our opinion, the first person who listens to that story is a hero in the family's eyes.

You will encounter some families who don't want to talk much or to share, but the majority will be extremely grateful that the professional they chose to accompany them on this unfamiliar journey is interested and compassionate and willing to be lend an ear, or a shoulder to cry on.

The arrangement consultant

For several years there has been much discussion about changing the "order taker" mentality, but not a lot has been done to encourage or provide training in effective new behavior. The usual approach funeral directors take is to mildly offer options, then sit back and hope the family didn't think they were too pushy or trying to up-sell. This has resulted in some pretty awful funerals, as well as loss of revenue for the funeral homes.

The family hires the funeral director to be their expert, to be the professional. A person who walks into the office of a neurosurgeon, an attorney or a wedding planner expects to be dealing with a confident professional who knows what he/she is doing, not one who apologizes for the cost or the procedures involved.

It is way past time for the funeral profession to truly believe in the value of what they have to offer, to explain with pride and conviction that the experience of a funeral is an important first step for families in grief. That means taking ownership in articulating:

- The value of viewing, regardless of the means of disposition
- The value of ceremony and gathering for some type of service
- The value of accepting expressions of sympathy and honor from friends and family
- The value of a well-planned and well-executed funeral service containing elements that make sense and are a meaningful part of the whole service.
- The value of having a final resting place as an important part of the grief experience.

If you as a professional cannot clearly define and verbalize to someone else why each of these elements is important—dare I say vital—for a healthy funeral and grieving experience, I suggest you stop reading this article right now and go spend some time working that out for yourself. Don't worry, the article will be here when you get back.

All of these points should be made with each family to be sure that they have fully explored all the options as presented by their professional. Too often the family says "cremation" or "no service," and the pen goes down and the folder closes.

Even if the family decides not to take advantage of any of the wide array of options presented, the funeral director will

CELEBRANTS

The location of the coffee pot and the bottled water with the funeral home logo on it is of much less importance than the ability of the funeral director to sit next to the grieving widow and pat her hand if needed. The "stuff" will get sold only after we have heard their hearts.

have done his/her job as a professional, ensuring the family is making informed decisions rather than knee-jerk or avoidance decisions.

The funeral director must assume the role of an experienced guide with a strong conviction that these are important decisions to be made. A few examples:

The family says "no viewing":
"It is my responsibility as a funeral professional to not only be trained to care for the dead, but also to be a guardian of the living. Studies and writings by experts in the field of grief recovery tell us that having an opportunity for a final viewing is extremely important for a healthy grief journey, even if it is a private family gathering time.

"It will give each family member a chance to face their new reality while sharing the comfort that comes from being among others also searching for ways to cope with the loss. We would strongly encourage you to consider giving the gift of goodbye to your family and your loved one.'

Or:
"While the law requires that we have at least one family view the body for identification, we believe this is an important, sacred moment of goodbye. We will have your loved one on our beautiful reposing bed and give your family members a chance to say their final goodbyes. What time tomorrow would be good for your family?"

The family chooses to scatter:
"There are many wonderful ways to honor the life of your loved one and to carry on his memory and legacy. While there may be a very meaningful spot or location that your loved one chose for scattering, it has been our experience that at some point families need a place of remembrance.

"For some families, the ability to physically visit a grave or have a memorial marker where the urn is buried or even a tree planted in a special place can be most important in dealing with their grief.

"May I suggest that you take some time to consider all the options before you make a final decision and, if you scatter, think about saving some of the cremated remains for a memorial spot at a later time? And when you are ready to make those decisions, please know that we are ready and able to help you create a ceremony for that final tribute and farewell."

The family doesn't want any type of service:
"We believe that every life deserves to be honored in a wonderful and fitting way. Our firm has trained professional life tribute specialists called celebrants who can work with you to put together a service that gives voice to your memories.

"The celebrant will take your stories and weave them into a gathering experience that will tell the story of your loved one's life and times and give each person attending special remembrances to take away with them.

"The service can be as religious or non-religious as is appropriate for you and your family and your loved one. In our experience, a well done personalized tribute that honors the life is the most important first step in the grief journey.

The family just wants family and friends to get up and speak at the service:
"In my experience, when you just open up the microphone for speakers from the floor, it can get too long and sometimes uncomfortable or even embarrassing.

"If you would like to have several family members and friends speak during the service, one of our professional celebrants or funeral directors will work with you as a master of ceremonies to help organize all the speakers, talking to each one ahead of time to make sure the stories do not overlap and to give a sense of continuity and framework to the service.

"We want to do everything possible to ensure that every part of the funeral service is meaningful and comforting."

The family wants to have a private ceremony away from the funeral home:
"We take our responsibility as your funeral professional very seriously and want to be available to help you with the ceremony so that you do not have to worry. This is your time to welcome the comfort and presence of your friends and family, not a time to be dealing with the details.

"We will provide one of our staff members to be present to make sure everything is set up and that everything runs smoothly. The cost will be minimal and it will take such a burden off you and the family."

These are merely brief examples illustrating many of the decisions made during arrangements in which a director needs to be a guiding voice, a professional who knows what grieving people need and a confident planner who knows how to help the family create the service they want.

Your goal should be to hear everyone who uses your funeral home say, "I couldn't have done it without you."

This approach does not come naturally or easily to many. The first step is to actually believe in the value of the funeral as outlined above. Then it requires a vision and commitment from the owner and the entire firm that no family will walk out of an arrangement room without being given options, guidance and assistance geared to help them plan a healthy and healing funeral experience.

It takes practice to get comfortable listening, articulating and offering. It may take role-playing, videotaping or partnering with a mentor, but we all need to learn how to master the articulation factor.

We need to own the fact that we are the smartest people in the room when it comes to planning a meaningful, touching and lasting ceremony in honor of the deceased and for the family. We need to release our inner funeral geek, claim the power of knowledge and experience and be confident in how we approach each family.

Learning and putting into practice the approach is time-consuming, but it may be the only thing that will save funeral service in the coming years. People who find meaning and value in an experience will return and be willing to pay for that experience again. Just ask Disney.

Chapter 10, Exhibit 2

"Reprinted with permission from the February 2013 edition of *The Director*, a publication of the National Funeral Directors Association."

Glenda Stansbury

WE WANT A PARTY

She was dying. Her hospital bed was set up in the sunroom of her parent's home. Her husband sat on one side, her hospice nurse on the other, and her parents, who had invited her to move back home after her ovarian cancer diagnosis, hovered in the background, helpless and hurt as they watched their daughter suffer the agonies of this cruel disease. The day I was asked to come to the home, she had just days to live.

So why was a celebrant coming to meet with a family before the death? They had some very specific ideas about how to have a service for this wonderful woman and wanted to talk about them while she could still have input and offer her feelings. They'd been referred to me by one of their friends who had attended a service I had the privilege of doing a few months before. She told them, "She will honor her life and tell her story. You must call her."

> *Give families what they want in honoring their loved one's life but also what they need – a time to grieve before the celebration commences.*

I sat down next to her bed with my celebrant notebook at the ready. Before I could get my pen out, the husband said, "We are going to have two parties. One just for close friends and family, with wine, lots of pictures and music and people telling stories. Then, the next day, we will have another party for anyone who wants to come, catered food and wine, lots of pictures and music and let everyone tell stories." He went on, "And then we are going to do the exact same thing back in Maryland, where we live."

They were in their mid-50s, well-educated professionals, she a high school history teacher working on her doctorate and he a real-life rocket scientist who worked for NASA. Religion or embalming or traditional funeral elements were not even topics of discussion.

My first thought was, "So why am I here?" If a family wishes to have a storytelling party, then they probably do not want a celebrant. I was confused.

My second thought was, "So this is the new face of funerals?" – people so determined not to have what is considered the expected funeral experience that they will bend over backward to not use a firm, not have a service, not embrace anything that feels funereal. *We want a party.*

As we continued to talk, I tried very hard to listen to what was being said and also what was not being said. It was clear that the mother and father were really struggling with the idea of not having that one moment, that one experience that they could call a funeral service for their daughter. The son-in-law was adamant that he didn't want anything to do with funerals. The woman who lay there waiting for the inevitable had no real opinion. She was focused on her pain and her breathing from one minute to the next and truly did not care what happened, as long as there were lots of candles and some of her favorite songs.

I finally offered, "Stories and sharing from family and friends are wonderful, and those stories will be cherished. But in my experience, on down the road in your grief journey, I think it will be important that you have some organized and cohesive collection of memories, a life tribute if you will, that you can look back on." I went on to explain that I would meet with them and gather all of the stories and put them together in a service that would share her life and her personality and her spirit. If they wished to choose a few people to speak in the course of the service, they would be an integral and coordinated part of the entire tribute rather than random stories offered from around the room. (Anyone who has been to a celebrant training can attest to the fact that

I'm neither a fan nor an advocate of "open mic night at the karaoke bar.")

You could feel the tension subside. They had no idea what to do, and so the good old "celebration of life party" concept became the only frame of reference upon which to build. But now they were hearing that there *was* a way to have a service without having *a service*. Here was someone who was willing to work with them to have the type of gathering that was meaningful for them while still being a professional guide who would offer suggestions and experience that would be important as they began to grieve together.

While sitting in that sunroom watching this exhausted, brave woman live out her remaining days surrounded by people who adored her and who would miss her beyond comprehension, it struck me: These truly are our next customers, the growing number of families that wish to use the funeral home only as a removal and disposal service. Please take care of the body because we don't want to. Outside of that, we see no need for you. You are so yesterday, so black suits and somber faces, so impersonal and disinterested officiants, so limited options and burdensome traditions. *We want a party.*

There are two grave concerns about this next phase of funeral avoidance as we consider the changing face of our profession that I hope we can consider in this discussion.

The Wedding Planner Isn't Just a Bad Movie

Some of us are old enough to remember the 1950s and early '60s. It was a time of conformity, of acceptance by anonymity, of doing exactly what our neighbors did so people wouldn't talk about us. Weddings during those decades were all cut from the same organza. The dresses were modest and always white, the music was *I Love You Truly* and *The Lord's Prayer*, the flower girl was a darling niece or the child of a friend, florists took care of all of the details, the reception was cake and punch and nuts, and everyone got married in a church. Those few daring ones who went to Vegas or eloped were certainly gossiped about in the grocery store.

Similarly, funerals were all very predictable. Everyone went to the funeral home, everyone was embalmed and buried, most had services in the church and then went to the house where the

> The question must be asked: What do we have to offer those families that completely reject any and all forms of our business model? Are we allowing surmountable obstacles to be our excuse for not climbing out of the traditional chasm?

neighbor ladies had brought casseroles and cakes to last a month. A few brave souls opted for cremation, but it was so rare that most adults of this era had never seen an urn.

Then weddings began to change. The songs evolved from John Denver to Bare Naked Ladies; the flower girl is the daughter of the bride and groom; the dresses have become bold fashion statements; receptions are sit-down meals with champagne and plenty of alcohol, which means that very few are held in churches; elaborate gifts and cakes are the norm; and everyone wants a destination wedding with a theme. And out of this metamorphosis, a new profession was born.

In the 1990s, event planners realized that there was a void in the wedding business. Florists had given up the role as coordinator, and the ceremonies – and budgets – were ballooning. Someone needed to step in and help these poor brides spend their money and realize their vision. There are now wedding planners in every city, the Wedding Channel on cable TV, a national Association of Bridal Consultants and multiple training schools for becoming a wedding planner.

Just as weddings have evolved, so have funerals. The implication for the funeral business is that people are turning away in droves from our beautiful buildings, our chapels with pews and stained glass, our impressive cars, our quiet halls, the same-service-different-day ministers and our dignified staff. They want a place to feel comfortable, to have the type of service that fits them, which includes an officiant who tells the story of their loved one, food, alcohol, multimedia pictures, good music and lots of time to visit.

I've heard so many funeral directors snort in derision at the idea of becoming an event planner. "I'll never do that. I'm a funeral director." Well, the fact of the matter is that we can quickly become as obsolete as the florist who refused to adapt to the changing consumer.

Sure, florists still sell flowers for weddings, but they are not an integral part of the experience and are not realizing the financial gains from the new reality.

Sure, funeral directors can still do removals and embalm or cremate bodies, but if we are not willing to embrace the new expectations of the families we serve, we can sit at home while the service is taking place someplace else with someone else running the event.

The question must be asked: What do we have to offer those families that completely reject any and all forms of our business model? How do we answer those families that ask if you can arrange for catering, for wine, for a place to have a gathering? What do we say to those families who say, "We want a party"?

Some readers can shake their heads because they are limited *at their location* by state statutes and regulations. But even in those states that allow food and drink in the funeral home, how many of us are truly taking advantage of accepting the role of funeral *director*? Have firms in states that prohibit food and drink been proactive in seeking out other ways to serve families or do they simply shrug and say, "Sorry, the law won't let us." Once we get beyond selling boxes, books and DVDs, how equipped are we to walk with a family that needs and wants something completely different than what we are comfortable offering? Are we allowing surmountable obstacles to be our excuse for not climbing out of the traditional chasm?

Reality Show Candidates

The second concern/danger in this type of change is that grieving people really don't need a "party." Just like the family with which I met, they believe that the opposite of a boring, meaningless, impersonal funeral experience is a party. What we need to be ready to help them understand is that grief ignored is grief compounded and that it is vital to their mental health that they stop and acknowledge the death while honoring the life. *These families need a service.* They need a service that fits them and allows them to grieve in the way that is right for them.

I'm an avid fan of the *Hoarders* reality TV shows. There is an incredible level of interest and intrigue with this sad segment of the population that struggles with a debilitating disorder. But, contrary to what my husband says as he smirks while I watch, I do not watch these episodes out of train wreck fascination. I'm doing grief research.

You can't watch a single episode without hearing, "Everything was fine until..." until a baby died, until a parent died, until a divorce happened, until a trauma occurred. Each of these people suffered a loss of some type and none of them were given the chance to grieve that loss in a healthy and appropriate way. And so, to protect themselves from losing something again, they began to keep everything.

It has been well documented by a host of grief and bereavement experts that an ignored death becomes a problem death. When people are not given the opportunity – or they avoid the opportunity – to grasp the reality of the death and to say goodbyes in a safe and structured setting, there are huge boulders waiting for them on the road back to health.

By failing to help people understand the power and importance of a personalized, unique and special service to commemorate the death, we are creating more people who might show up on reality shows. TLC and A&E are very grateful.

And Now... What?

Our future holds a twofold challenge and responsibility: to be expert and vocal consultants on grief and how the funeral experience plays a vital role in that experience and to be expert and vocal consultants on planning events that incorporate all of the elements our new client is looking for.

How do we do that? Of course, given my particular interest, I'm going to say that the first step is to have funeral celebrants available to offer at all times. Whether you have a celebrant on staff or utilize independent contractors, using celebrants as your first option rather than your last-gasp effort will keep many families from walking out the door after deciding that you have nothing to offer. When they hear that you have a trained professional who will work with them to capture the story and the essence of their loved one, they will know they have come to the right professional to guide them through their planning.

Second is location, location, location. If your firm isn't conducive to having events because of space or regulatory or staffing limitations, then become the expert on what *is* available in your city. Where are the event centers, the hotel ballrooms, the wedding chapels, the open-air spots where a tribute service could be held? What equipment do we need to have in portable setups for these sites? A projector and screen for DVD tributes? A self-contained sound system and podium? Do we need to provide seating?

What are the expenses for time, coordination and use of the hall or center? Who are the caterers we can work with or do we need to hire and train our own staff? What are the requirements for serving wine, beer or other alcohol?

Are we willing to change our vision of who we are in order to stay relevant and in business? Are we willing to change our pricing structure and how we charge for our professional services to meet the needs of the next generation? If we are not, then a whole new profession of event planners will be more than happy to step in and fill that void. Just ask your florists.

One Week Later
Exactly a week after I met with the family, the woman died. I went back to the house and they shared the endearing and special stories of this adventurous and amazing daughter, wife and mother. We discussed what they wanted included in the tribute and they selected three people to speak at the service that I would incorporate into the eulogy.

They spoke highly of their time at the funeral home and the staff there but saw the funeral home's role only as the cremator of the body and dispenser of death certificates. They did not expect – nor did they receive – any other help from the funeral professionals they had chosen.

Then they spent three days frantically searching for a place to have a service. It was December 19 and many of the venues were already booked or were charging outrageous fees for the use of their facility. Since the family knew the funeral home did not have the ability to do what they wanted, they were on their own to navigate the waters of putting together the event. Finally, they decided to hold it at a friend's home on a Sunday evening.

The family and friends put together a DVD that was played. They glued together a picture board and borrowed an easel from a friend. They went to Kinko's and printed service folders on purple paper, her favorite color. They brought snowmen to hand out to all of the attendees. They hired caterers and purchased cases of wine. They took care of every detail, believing this was their only option.

That night, about 60 people arrived and crowded together in the various rooms so they could hear and try to see the service. It was not ideal – it was a little uncomfortable – but I stood up in front of the fireplace in the den, with family and friends sitting on couches and chairs around the house, and we had a service that told the story of Liz. We lit candles, honored her life and acknowledged the pain of the loss; two of her friends briefly spoke about her touch on their lives; and I closed by giving everyone a word-find game with important words from Liz's life experiences.

> Are we willing to change our vision of who we are in order to meet the needs of the next generation, to stay relevant and in business?

After our time together, which took about 40 minutes, the caterers served dinner, the wine flowed and they all shared stories over the rest of the evening. Before I left, the husband and mother both hugged me and said that it was exactly what they had hoped for.

A few days later, the mother of the deceased called. She said, "I just have to tell you how perfect that service was. It was elegant and so much more than I expected." I was a bit impressed – I'd never been called elegant before! But what she was trying to say was the service flowed together, made sense, told the story and captured memories in a way that will be meaningful for her in the hard days and weeks to come in a way a random smattering of stories over dinner could not.

They *thought they wanted a party,* but what they *needed* was a sacred space of remembrance *before* the party. That's the missing element and the one piece we as funeral professionals can offer.

Just as the wedding of today is not how your mother or grandmother got married, this is no longer your grandfather's funeral business. We must find out what our customers need and want and then find a way to fulfill it or we will be alone in our beautiful buildings, with empty pews and unemployed staff and driving around without purpose in our impressive cars while families are having services without us and paying someone else to plan the event. It's up to us to decide how this party ends. ✦

Glenda Stansbury, MAL, CFSP, a practicing funeral celebrant, has worked as marketing and development director for In-Sight Books for 16 years and as dean of In-Sight Institute Certified Funeral Celebrant Training for 12 years. She is a licensed funeral director and embalmer and an adjunct professor in the University of Central Oklahoma's funeral service department. She can be contacted at glenda@insightbooks.com or 405-810-9501.

Chapter 11 – Alkaline Hydrolysis

Chapter Author: Lucia Dickinson

Chapter Learning Objectives

Upon completion of the study of this chapter students should:

- Demonstrate knowledge with respect to alkaline hydrolysis.
- Understand the legal aspects that impact alkaline hydrolysis.
- Be able to discuss various alkaline hydrolysis manufacturers and machines.
- Understand how the alkaline hydrolysis process works.
- Be able to identify pros and cons associated with alkaline hydrolysis.

• • •

Introduction

Innovation and ingenuity allow for new ideas to emerge. As consumers grow more concerned with the environment and want more "green" options, the newest method of disposition arose: alkaline hydrolysis. In 2010, the Cremation Association of North America (CANA) elected to include processes like Alkaline Hydrolysis (AH) in its definition of cremation as "the mechanical and/or thermal or other dissolution process that reduces human remains to bone fragments" (para. 1). Others describe AH as a dissolution process by which tissues are dissolved in a heated and sometimes pressurized solution of water with strong alkaline chemicals, such as potassium hydroxide or sodium hydroxide, to accelerate natural decomposition (Ross, 2010; Olson, 2014; CANA 2020; Terreri, n.d.). It is an alternative to flame-based cremation and sometimes referred to as flameless cremation, natural water cremation, green cremation, chemical cremation, aquamation, biocremation™, or Resomation™ (CANA, 2020). Much of the public that chooses this method of disposition do so as they perceive water cremation to be "gentler" than flame. Independent studies have shown that the process is much less impactful on the environment than flame-based cremation and burial; therefore, seen as an ecological alternative to burial and flame cremation. Some stakeholders have varying views on whether these claims are valid, and thus, this disruptive, game-changing innovative process elicits solid arguments for and in opposition to.

History

Amos Herbert Hobson, an English farmer, developed the idea of Alkaline Hydrolysis (AH) in 1888 and it was originally patented to process animal carcasses into plant food. Researchers saw a need for an effective and inexpensive way to dispose of laboratory animal remains containing low-level radioisotopes. The first commercial system was developed and installed at Albany Medical College in 1993 to dispose of human cadavers (CANA 2020; Olson 2014). The process continued to be adopted by universities and hospitals over the next ten years. The development of single body AH systems began in the early 2000s, and the Mayo Clinic in Rochester, Minnesota, was the first to put into commercial operation in 2005. In 2011, the process was first used in the funeral industry by two different funeral homes – one in Ohio and one in Florida. Several other states followed suit in 2012, such as Maine, Minnesota, and Illinois, and offered it to consumers.

Laws

As defined by CANA, cremation covers a variety of technologies that may be applied to achieve reduction to bone fragments, including traditional flame-based cremation, calcination, and Alkaline Hydrolysis. The primary reason for adopting this language was that state and provincial laws were already in place that determined Alkaline Hydrolysis could be marketed as cremation, and redefining already established laws is an easier tactic than enacting a whole new form of disposition. Presenting as a new disposition method would require proposing an open bill and making considerable change through committees and lobbying processes. This method also requires licensing to own these certain chemicals and possible certification depending on state law. This was the exact direction Washington State decided to go. On May 1, 2020, it became the first state to recognize Alkaline Hydrolysis and natural organic reduction, otherwise known as "composting", as separate forms of disposition. CANA suggests "when considering legislation or regulation concerning alkaline hydrolysis, it is important to understand that current cremation laws and regulations may be sufficient to address matters including, but not limited to transportation, storage, identification, authorization or disposition." (Para 4). From a consumer perspective, the result is the same; the differences, however, lie in the technical processes like equipment used, the technological instrumentation, and interaction with municipal agencies. It is up to the state whether to redefine its definition of cremation or legalize it as its own form of disposition.

In the United States, state and local laws continue to evolve. Manufacturers, practitioners, and regulators are left to work collaboratively to make Alkaline Hydrolysis commercially available. Just because it is legal in a state does not mean that it is available to the public; "there are still local water sanitation permits to obtain, standard operating procedures to write and OSHA regulations to follow" (Fisher, 2012, p.34). There are 20 states in which it is legal and actively practiced in 10; in total, there are about 35 AH machines (low and high-temperature designs) in use in the United States.

Manufacturers and Machines

Currently, two companies manufacture and sell Alkaline Hydrolysis machines in the United States: Resomation, Ltd. And Bio-Response Solutions, Inc.

Resomation, Ltd. is a Scottish registered company that manufactures in Leeds, England, and has a North American office in Minnesota. They refer to the process as "water cremation," but its trademarked name is Resomation® and was founded by Sandy Sullivan in early 2007. The Resomator looks much like traditional cremation retorts and is a high-pressure, high-temperature model, operating at a pressure of 65 psi and 302 degrees Fahrenheit. The process takes an average of 4 hours. It has a US/EU patented Focused Agitation Cranial Targeting (FACT) design aspect that ensures all brain tissue is broken down every cycle. Body donation programs such as the Mayo Clinic, Minnesota and UCLA Los Angeles currently use this kind of technology.

Image 11.1: Image Courtesy of Resomation, Ltd.

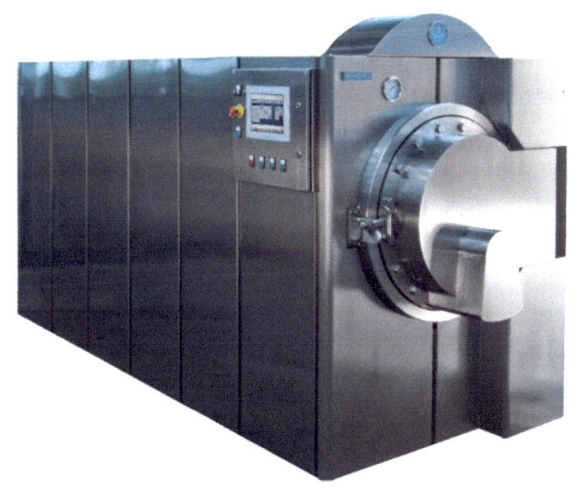

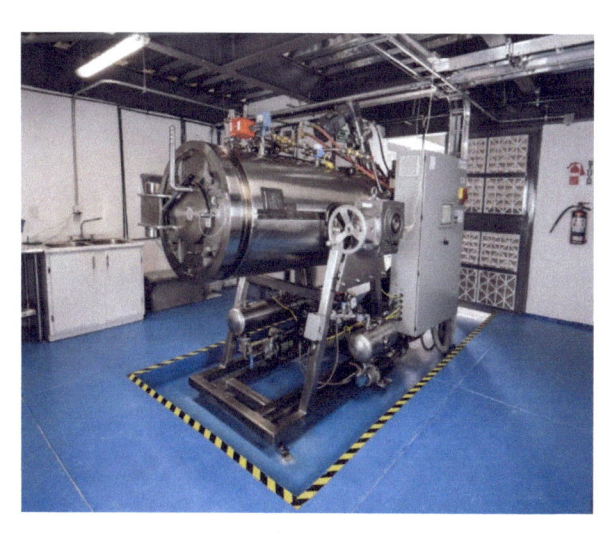

Image 11.2: Image Courtesy of Bio- Response Solutions, Inc.

The other is Bio-Response Solutions, Inc, and they refer to the process as Aquamation. This company is located in Danville, Indiana and this model was developed by Joe Wilson, his son Luke Wilson, and daughter Sam Seiber. Together they engineered two machines: one that operates at atmospheric pressure-low heat model (204 - 208 degrees F) and needs 14 -18 hours to process and the other, a high pressure- high heat model (302 degrees), less than 65 psi, and needs 6-8 hours to process (Bio Response Solutions, 2020). These machines do not resemble traditional retorts as the body is loaded in a horizontal position and tipped back.

Process

As described above, the process requires unique equipment and training. AH entails placing the body in a [stainless steel] chamber filled with water and strong alkaline chemicals that fill the chamber. Sex, body mass, weight, and whether or not the deceased was embalmed will determine the amount of water and alkaline chemicals that will be needed to fulfill the process. Through a mixture of heat, agitation, and/or pressure (varying with equipment), the body's tissues are hydrolyzed (CANA, 2020; Gilligan & Stueve, 2011: Olson, 2014). In other words, the body's compounds are broken down into smaller molecules by way of reaction between alkaline chemicals and water. In addition to the human body, pathogens and prions, including embalming chemicals, are broken down and eliminated.

Once AH is complete, calcified bone fragments and a sterile liquid containing amino acids, peptides, sugar, and soap are otherwise known as effluent or hydrolysate, are left behind (CANA, 2020). System developers have demonstrated via independent testing and claim that the process destroys all RNA, DNA, and pathogens (including infectious prions), and breaks down embalming fluids, cytotoxic agents, and biological and chemical warfare agents into harmless materials (Olson, 2014) and therefore these basic organic compounds known as effluent may be disposed of through the sewer system once cooled, and the pH is adjusted (Gilligan & Stueve, 2011). According to CANA Manual (2020), the water's pH must be brought down to at least an 11 to be discharged down the sewer system, though each local municipality has the final say. An operator may neutralize the pH by adding sulfuric acid or citric acid or injecting carbon dioxide.

What is left behind are fragile bone fragments, now called cremated remains or hydrolyzed remains, which appear pure white in color (CANA, 2020). Because the process uses water, the remains need to dry before pulverization. The process results in approximately 25- 30% more cremated remains than flame-based cremation and may require a larger urn. (CANA, 2020). The overall process is similar to flame-based or "traditional" cremation, except that pacemakers and other implants do not need to be removed prior to the process, except where required by law. And from the consumer's perspective, the processes and results are similar.

Image 11.3: Image Courtesy of Bio-Response Solutions, Inc.

Debated Pros and Cons

The process is regarded as an environmentally friendly green alternative to flame-based cremation and traditional burial (CANA, 2020; Ross, 2010). It is described as a clean manner of disposition that does not produce smoke or ashes, uses with less energy by using significantly less fuel and has a lower carbon footprint, and by allowing less mercury emissions into the atmosphere and ecosystem (Olson, 2014; Ross 2010 Rumble et al.,2014; Stall, 2017; Terreri, n.d.). Consumers have become more environmentally conscious, therefore there is a growing interest. Some other pros include a reduced need for cemetery land use, less maintenance than incinerators because of its specific American Society of Mechanical Engineers (ASME) design, and finally, the product the families receive is safe and viable.

On the contrary, many death-related entities — like funeral professionals, biomedical researchers, lawmakers and regulators, associations, religious leaders, environmentalists, and funeral consumers remain skeptical regarding this method of disposition. For example, many religious objections believe that it is disrespectful to dispose of remains in this manner. No one entity can agree if its categorization under cremation or classification as its own category is best. Another concern is that of the public's health and safety; some perceive that AH's liquid result is too unsanitary to be going down the drain and processed normally (Olson, 2014). Independent studies have shown the effluent to be harmless and totally safe to go down the drain. As stated previously, regulatory challenges will occur at the local level, where regulatory approvals occur through zoning boards and water treatment agency permits (Ross, 2010).

Some funeral directors fear that this divisive and still misunderstood practice could confuse or mislead clients, leading to litigation (Olson, 2014). Another real reported concern is it cutting into the well-understood cremation business (Stall, 2017). Alkaline Hydrolysis machinery can range from $200,000 to $400,000 (Terreri, n.d.) The cost of equipment and longer completion time is enough reason to question this form of disposition. For funeral home owner's time is money; the AH machine funeral home owners invest in will determine how many water-based cremations a funeral home can do in one day, mainly since only one body will be processed at a time. As indicated above, a fully processed AH can take anywhere from 3- 18 hours; consequently, it may take longer to make an initial profit (Olson, 2014). On the other side of that coin, funeral professionals believe that this environmentally sound option will allow funeral homes to charge more for this service type.

• • •

Conclusion

It remains to be seen how rapidly this disposition method will grow in the US death care and how regulations surrounding it will change or evolve. It is a matter of time before it is accepted worldwide; countries such as Canada, China, Japan, South Africa, Brazil, Australia, the Netherlands, and the UK are considering adopting this method of disposition or are actively using it. Alkaline Hydrolysis is undoubtedly a revolutionary change and has the potential to succeed, however, it needs to be better understood not only by the consumers but within the industry. Many varying numbers exist within the literature on the number of emissions produced and how much less energy it uses than traditional flame-based cremation; therefore, continued studies are necessary. While some funeral professionals are eager to tap this new market, others resist out of concern for lost revenues from service and merchandise sales, including embalming services, casket, and vault sales. (Olson, 2014). Although still relatively unknown to the public, Alkaline Hydrolysis' acceptance continues to grow, and it may be just a matter of time before this newest offering is available to consumers in the majority of the United States.

Chapter 12 – Understanding and Interpreting Cremation Statistics

Chapter Author: Cremation Association of North America (CANA) – Barbara Kemmis

Chapter Learning Objectives

Upon completion of the study of this chapter students should:

- Demonstrate knowledge of cremation statistics.
- Be able to discuss the milestone project.
- Understand the key learnings related to cremation statistics research.

• • •

Introduction - The Cremation Landscape

The fist cremation in the United States took place in 1876 in Washington, Pennsylvania. Nearly 100 years later, the national cremation rate had only reached 5%. However, only forty-five years after that, the national cremation rate exceeded 50%. During that period of growth, from 1972 to 2016, the cremation rate grew predictably and steadily, ranging between 1% and 2% a year. Consumer demand has fueled this upward trend in recent history and funeral professionals have tried to keep up with the changing preferences of the families they serve.

Because consumers are entirely responsible for driving this change, it is important to understand why they are choosing cremation and what their experience with cremation has been and might be in the future. The following is a summary of recent CANA research on cremation topics.

- Annual Cremation Statistics
- Milestone Project
- Cremation Velocity
- Roaming and Rooted

The most recent statistics are available here: https://www.CremationAssociation.org/Teach

Annual Cremation Statistics

Over the years, many funeral directors and cemeterians have cited "cremation" as the primary threat to their businesses; however, cremation is simply a form of disposition. Whether it has any ramifications beyond that is determined by societal practices and the response of the death care profession. Funeral professionals who blame cremation for disrupting their businesses are referencing a business model that assumes "traditional" is best. That perspective is built on many biases and false assumptions, including the idea that cremation is equivalent to "direct cremation" or that cremation families seek only the lowest price and don't care about their loved ones. A traditional business model is dependent on casket sales, visitations, and burials—options that have subsidized as a result of cremation services. As cremation rates climb toward and surpass 50% of call volume, businesses that do not adjust their practices will continue to experience declining revenue and profits.

How can you tell if your business is adaptable and ready for change? Know your numbers.

Statistics – the practice or science of collecting and analyzing numerical data in large quantities, especially for the purpose of inferring proportions in a whole from those of a representative sample.

CANA has a proven history of over two decades of tracking, projecting and just plain getting it right when it comes to statistics. We collect data every year from the vital statistics department or other designated regulatory agency in each state and province. It can take up to three years following the close of the calendar year for these agencies to prepare final data. CANA takes all of this data and publishes it in a report that is available on an annual basis to CANA members.

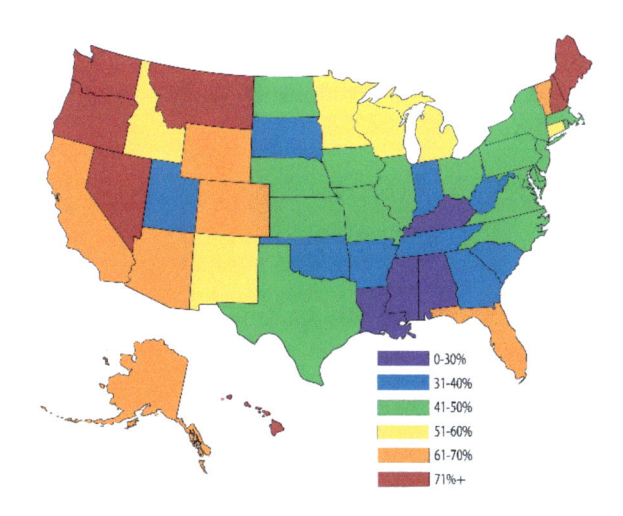

Image 12.1: US Cremation Percentages, 2015

One of the things we provide in our report is a five-year comparison, presented in map format. Instead of showing the statistic for each state individually, we look at them in ranges. We produce a color-coded heat map that makes it easier to see the changes that are occurring over time. The maps also highlight particular geographic regions where cremation rates are concentrated in certain ranges.

For example, in 2015 the west coast was a cremation hot bed, with the exception of the lone state of Utah. This isn't news, but looking at the map raises questions. Why does this area of the country have higher cremation rates than elsewhere? Why is Utah different? How is the map relevant to your business? You will find some of the answers to these questions in this chapter, but ultimately each of you will have to research your own answers.

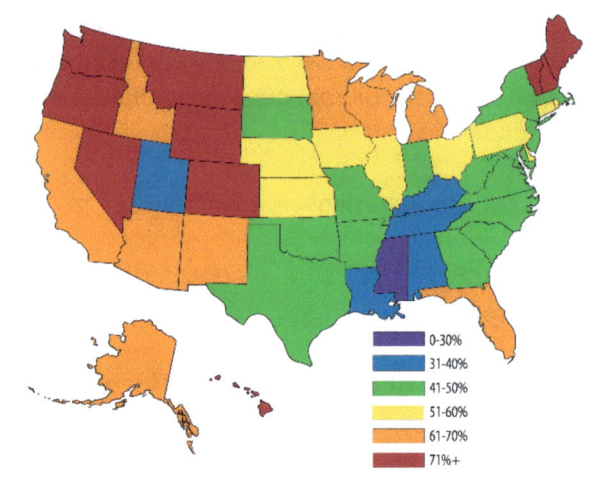

Image 12.2: US Cremation Percentages. 2019

If we go forward five years, from 2015 to 2019, what has changed? When you compare the maps, you find more orange and red states in the west and many blue states turning green in other regions. Cremation rates are growing across the country.

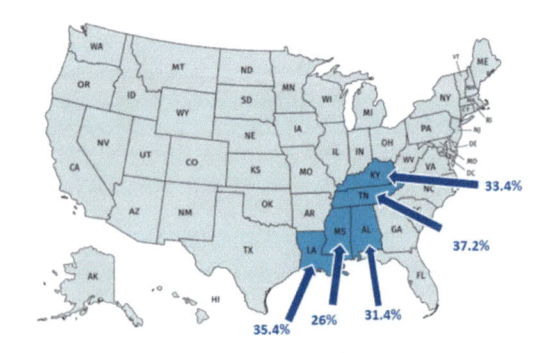

Image 12.3: Bottom Five States by Percentage of Cremation, 2019

When we examine all of the states in rank order in terms of their cremation percentages [find the most recent data in the link provided within the chapter], there is a wide range of cremation rates. These are the bottom five states and they've been at the bottom five for a couple years now.

Top Five States 2019
% of Cremations

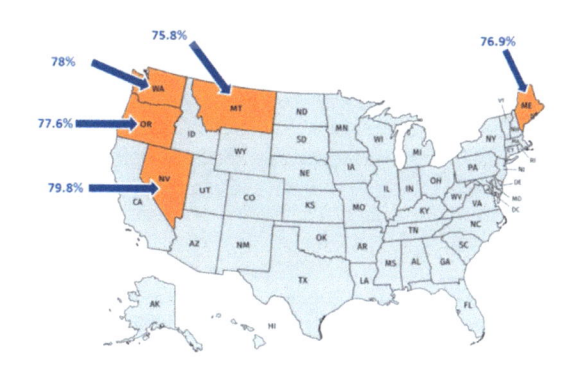

Image 12.4: Top Five States by Percentage of Cremation, 2019

The highest cremation rates are found in the west coast and in Maine.

Benchmarking is the primary use of statistics such as these. Business owners compare their state rate to their own business's sales and call volume to measure market share and track the competition. These data can also be useful when seeking financing for growth or setting the value of a business.

It's important to remember that cremation rates and numbers are only part of the picture and raise new questions.

Milestone Project

A few years ago, as the national cremation rate began approaching 50%, CANA embarked on new research to learn more about the meaning behind the numbers. There were two parts to the project. The first was to examine why cremation percentages grow at different rates in different parts of the country. The second was to examine which demographic characteristics drive cremation growth speed.

We will start with some basic numbers and then look at the US cremation rate as a whole. This chart shows the national cremation rate in roughly five-year increments. Over a 19-year time period, the cremation rate doubled, such rapid change taking place over such a relatively short time has left the profession reeling to some extent. Many businesses were not prepared for this big shift and they weren't able to adapt at a speed that matched the growth.

If we delve into that growth rate a little bit more, this is what we find. Remember that it took about 100 years to get to the 5% mark. Once we got there, the growth rate really started to take off. Analyzing past growth at the state and national levels, CANA learned that growth from 5% up to about 20% will take about 15-25 years. This precise number of years in a given location depends on the community, the customer base, the clustering of states, and what's happening around them.

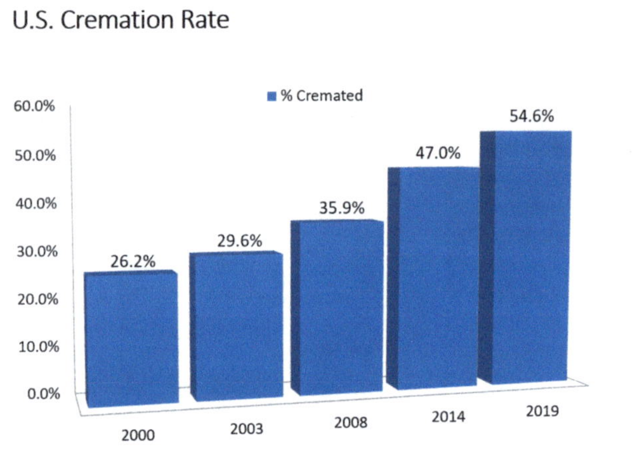

U.S. Cremation Rate

Year	% Cremated
2000	26.2%
2003	29.6%
2008	35.9%
2014	47.0%
2019	54.6%

Image 12.5: US Cremation Rate Growth over time

To go from 20% to 40% takes another 15-25 years. Once we hit 40%, we really start to pick up speed. To go from 40% to 60% will only take about 15-18 years. It's a much narrower and faster range. At 80% we expect the cremation rate to slow. Not to decrease, but to slow. We don't know how long it will take to get to 95%, but that's about where we think it will top out. It will never be 100%.

The main area to focus on in terms of business survival is that 40 to 60% range. Because that is when the most rapid growth rate is occurring, businesses already need to be in a position to serve cremation families. They don't have a lot of time to make changes if they haven't already before they hit 40%. If they don't act quickly, it's unlikely they will be able to remain profitable and successful during this period.

We can look at the growth rate as a whole using the speedometer approach. Keep in mind that every business operates in the context of an individual community. This means your rate may vary slightly compared to another business in the next town or in the next state over, but these are good estimates to keep you in your lane and inform where you're going.

The Acceleration period is preparation time. With a 40% cremation rate, you should be ready to embrace cremation and serve families. Most of the country is in Rapid Growth or Deceleration at this point, so it may be too late to regain cremation market share in some areas of the country.

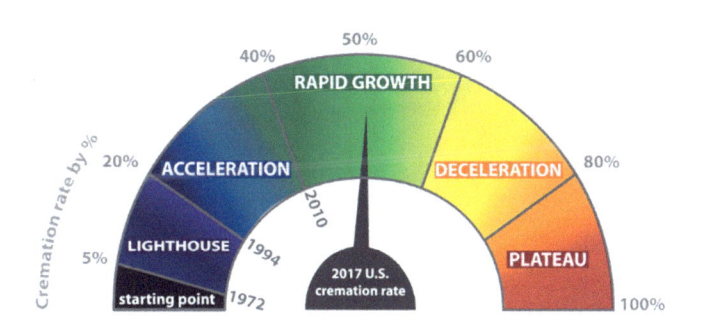

Image 12.6: Velocity of Cremation Rate Speedometer

Roaming and Rooted

In the second part of the Milestone Project, we evaluated consumer trends and used US census data, demographics, and the Pew Religious Landscape Study (https://www.pewforum.org/religious-landscape-study/) and overlaid that data with the cremation rates in every state. Because comparable census data from Canada was not available, we focused solely on the US.

The Pew Religious Landscape Study illustrated what appeared to be a correlation with cremation. The fastest growing portion of Americans was those who claimed no affiliation with organized religion. They answered "none" when asked for their affiliation and have been referred to as *Nones* ever since.

Anecdotally, we have long believed that having no/weak religious affiliation drives cremation. But could we prove this? Yes. This research helped us to understand why some people might adopt cremation more quickly or more slowly than others in the same community.

CANA dove into demographic data and was able to identify two distinctly different communities, which we labeled Rooted and Roaming. By comparing 2010 census data with 2012 cremation rates, CANA's consultant ran algorithms to see how demographic components correlate with each other—and an informative picture emerged.

If we look at the characteristics of the rooted cremation communities, we find that they tend to be areas with high home ownership, many manufacturing businesses, higher rates of affiliation with Christianity, and lower income and education levels. These families are not moving. They are staying in the area, living near other family members, and probably more rooted in traditions practiced by past generations. While they are choosing cremation, they still value tradition. They may want to do something to make the experience unique or different for their family, while still incorporating familiar liturgies or ceremonies. They may add cremation to traditional aspects of the service. They will probably not be interested in a lot of merchandise but they will be interested in the services.

Rooted Cremation Community

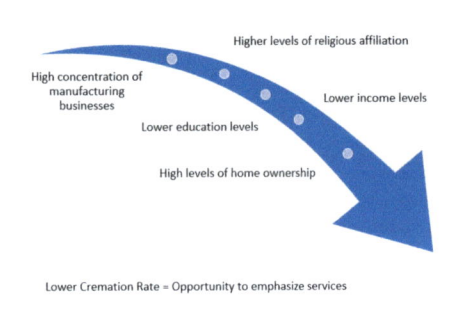

Image 12.7: Rooted Community

Roaming community members tend to be the ones who move around a lot. These communities have a lot of women-owned small businesses, lower levels of home ownership, higher education levels, and higher income. Cremation rates have grown faster in these areas, which are often found in large cities or college towns. These cremation customers may want to create new traditions and ceremonies. Give them what they want—something that is important to them and personal. They will do a gathering of some kind, but this group is far more likely to hold an event somewhere other than the funeral home, perhaps at a country club or hold a catered event at home. If they don't like what is offered through the funeral home, they will do it themselves. It is important to listen carefully and work with these families to develop a personalized experience.

Roaming Cremation Community

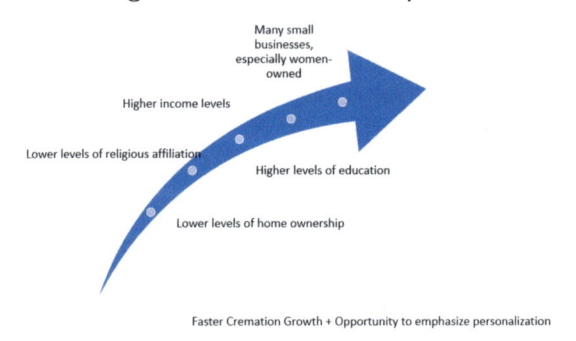

Image 12.8: Roaming Community

What it boils down to is simple. The roaming communities will have a faster rate of growth for cremation than the rooted communities.

Both communities coexist in your market and you will serve families exhibiting these characteristics in whichever setting you work. This is a marketing and service challenge. The mission of your business might be to have a beautiful, updated building designed to hold visitations and services. Advertising may focus on church bulletins, billboards and local cable commercials. Which community will benefit from those efforts? If your business also has a website with a virtual tour, prices listed, and informative text about memorialization options, what new markets might you reach? Successful marketing depends on knowing your audiences and targeting your messages specifically to them. There are a wide variety of cremation providers now, so differentiate yourself and stand out from the crowd with a clear mission, well-chosen service offerings, and communication with your audiences based on who they are. The Roaming and Rooted research provided a model for marketing and service offering discussions.

•••

Conclusion

In conclusion, this research pointed to several key learnings for further discussion and study.

1. Everyone does it. Everyone cremates regardless of gender, race, or religion. You cannot judge what families will want based on how they roll up to the funeral home. You can prepare based on your community and your typical family, but you always have to listen and challenge your biases. Your past preneed customers won't be the same as the current or future customers.

2. Direct cremation is an American phenomenon. When cremation started to become popular in the 1970s, funeral directors did not want to deal with families who wanted cremation and sent them down the street to the cremation societies who were happy to help them. The cremation societies and funeral homes who embraced cremation and cremation families thrived. We could talk for a long time about how direct cremation became so big. The important thing is that we need to educate families on why funerals are so important. Not because it's a way to make money but because it's the right thing to do. We don't send our direct burial families home with the body, so why do we do that with the urn? Consider this question as you progress through your degree program.

3. CANA was founded by cemeterians who believed that cremation was preparation for memorialization. These founders opposed scattering—and even pulverizing—cremated remains until the 1950s. The pendulum of history has swung widely in the other directions now and the profession has separated cremation from memorialization. A philosophical question that you want to ask yourself is "Should cremated remains rest in peace?" Decide how you feel about this question.

Many people believe the answer is yes, while some haven't really thought about it or don't care. So, when a family says that they're going to take the remains home with them, it is your duty to ask them the 5, 15, 50 question – where are the remains going to be in five years? How about 15 years? What about 50 years? Are the remains still going to be sitting on a shelf at home? Will they have been relegated to a closet? Will they end up in a garage sale? Unfortunately, that happens all too frequently. People end up with a great-grandparent in an urn—someone they had no personal connection with— and have no idea what to do with the remains. Do they pass the urn along to their own kids?

4. The last thing to keep in mind when working with cremation families is that they do not know what cremation really means—they just know they want it. It has become clear as we work with our members that when families ask for cremation they aren't quite sure why they are asking for it. They know it's the new tradition and everybody does it, but they don't know why or what it means. Sometimes they do it because it's cheaper or easier—or so they think.

As a funeral director, it is your job to educate consumers on all the things that cremation can be. It does not have to be a direct cremation. They do not have to just "cremate me" and be done with it; they can and should have some sort of service or gathering. It is really important to the grief process, as you will learn in the rest of your program. Please think about your own philosophy so you can guide families into making the decision that is best for **them** and one that **they** will be comfortable with.

Chapter 13 – Contemporary Trends

Chapter Learning Objectives

Upon completion of the study of this chapter students should:

- Be able to identify reasons people select cremation including consumer preferences and rising costs.
- Be able to discuss various green alternatives.
- Understand the impact of religion related to selecting cremation.
- Comprehend general consumer preferences.
- Understand the impact of increased educational levels with respect to selecting cremation.
- Be able to discuss the impact of greater life expectancy related to contemporary trends.
- Understand expanded funeral options.
- Comprehend the effect of increased migration as related to cremation.
- Understand the reality that cremation is more socially accepted in modern society.
- Recognize the significance of pet cremation.

• • •

Introduction

The funeral service industry is finally embracing cremation as a real, rather than a perceived or passing, influence on the American funeralization process. Results from the 2012 Citrin Cooperman Funeral Directors Survey found "funeral directors are increasingly embracing the inevitable changes in the industry rather than fighting them…the specter of cremation did not appear as the biggest issue or the most negative change affecting the industry [as in previous years]" (Defort, 2013). Although there are varied suppositions as to the increase of cremation in the United States, it is important for funeral service professionals to have awareness of the trends surrounding the rise in cremation. It should be emphasized that achieving awareness is half the battle, and it is imperative that funeral directors embrace changing consumer needs by providing the variety of services and products necessary to fulfill client desires. The acknowledgement that cremation is a significant force affecting the funeral process can be seen in today's marketing, arrangements facilitation, facility architecture and construction, merchandise and memorial product offerings. Finally, enter the unprecedented COVID-19 pandemic and the mandated restrictions placed on funeral service which overnight caused families to consider radical alternatives and funeral service personnel to meet family expectations.

Consumer Preferences Toward Cremation

It is not enough to assume that the popularity of cremation is the result of an overall love affair with the process or a simple dismissal of traditional values. Instead, it is important to dig deep into available data (and explore past data), perhaps done at the local level by a canvass of clients served, to discover the complexities of why cremation is utilized at such growing levels. In this chapter we will take somewhat of a longitudinal approach to explore the evolution of cremations' popularity into the 21st century and identify recent developments that continue to shape this increasingly favored selection. In a 1995 article on cremation in *The Southern Funeral Director*, the "new family" was described as, "highly mobile, values oriented, less driven by previous traditions, and a greater sense of time urgency" ("Tom Snyder," 1995). Perhaps this may begin to explain why in segments of the country once considered "traditional", strongholds are changing in favor of cremation. The National Funeral Directors Association (NFDA) 2014 Cremation Report noted:

There is a growing trend to select direct cremation because it is, in general, more cost-effective for consumers. It is often followed by some type of memorialization event with family and friends – but frequently without the services of a funeral home. (p. 1)

The 2020 NFDA Consumer Awareness and Preference study revealed that 72 percent of respondents believed it was important or somewhat important to have cremated remains or the body present at a funeral service. In the previous year study, consumers expressed a desire to have their own funeral or the funeral of a loved one that included the following elements: photos, personalized music, a gathering of family and friends, and all done in an affordable manner (Gillespie & Defort, 2020).

The changing landscape surrounding the popularity of cremation has witnessed a dramatic shift from the "traditional" funeral. However, this does not mean that cremation-preferring clients are abandoning the desire for a ceremony for their deceased loved one. According to data gathered by the 2015 Funeral and Memorial Information Council (FAMIC) Study of American Attitudes Toward Ritualization and Memorialization included in the 2020 NFDA Burial & Cremation Report, more than 26 percent of respondents who prefer cremation revealed they would have a visitation and a service with a casketed body present prior to cremation. The same study discovered 23-32 percent would have cremated remains present in an urn. In 2010, this study revealed 40 percent would not have the body present at all. While only 2 percent of respondents specified a desire for no ceremony (Defort, 2011). As consumers continue to express interest in some type of ceremony, funeral directors should view this as a tremendous opportunity to provide continued service to their communities.

Rising Costs

The poor economy which plagued the United States after the recession of 2008 was once thought to be one of the contributing factors in the rise and popularity of cremation. The 2010 FAMIC study revealed the number one reason (33 percent) participants would choose cremation is because it saves money (Johnson, 2010). The FAMIC Study (formerly the Wirthlin Group Study) has been conducted approximately every five years since 1990 (subsequent studies were conducted in 1995, 1999, 2004, 2010 and 2015), and has consistently revealed the primary reason families choose cremation is cost (this has been the overwhelming choice by a consistent large percentage). Current studies, including the annual NFDA Cremation and Burial Report, continue to identify perceived cost savings as a primary reason families choose cremation. Even traditional news outlets, such as the New York Times and CNN, are bringing attention to the rise in cremation and often cite cost as a driving force in the popularity of cremation (Carrns, 2019; LaMotte, 2020).

According to the Federated Funeral Directors of America, the average adult funeral in 2013, which included the service and casket, cost $6741.85 (CFSAA, 2014). In 2019, according to NFDA's *Member General Price List Study*, that cost had risen to $7640.00. In comparison, NFDA estimated that in 2019, funeral homes charged an average of $2395.00 for a direct cremation (which included the crematory fee and alternative container). The addition of a memorial service (with no formal viewing) saw the price increase to $3667.00. The appeal of the cost-effective aspect of a direct cremation (followed by a memorial event usually without the assistance of the funeral home) was confirmed by the 2019 NFDA Study (NFDA, 2019). In 2001, a Baptist pastor in religiously conservative Texas expressed the sentiments of those in his congregation for whom he assisted in making funeral preparations, "many people are opting for cremation. It's less expensive, and burial costs have gotten so high. My own counsel with them is it's something they have to feel right about" (Wingfield, 2001, p. 7).

Green Alternatives-Environmentally Responsible Funeral Practices

Since the first FAMIC Study was conducted in 1990, the second most consistent response as to the primary reason for choosing cremation has been: "saves land." Consumers today are flocking to businesses that offer environmentally responsible or eco-friendly choices (and they are willing to open their wallets in the process, sometimes at a premium) to reduce their carbon foot print, and the funeral industry is no exception. Today's Gen X and Millennial consumers, those with the greatest disposable incomes, have an overwhelming concern for environmental impact and not only believe they should do business with environmentally responsible companies, but those companies are in particular favor when offering goods and services to match (McQueen, 2021). Disposable income is an important factor in determining what a consumer will actually spend on funeral related services. In an interview for the *American Funeral Director* magazine in 2011, Patrick E. Lynch, Past President of the National Funeral Directors Association, acknowledged, "the issues of alkaline hydrolysis and green burial are beginning to be viewed as legitimate forms rather than an affront on traditional funeral service" (Bartsche, 2011, p. 40). These two issues reflect the segment of consumers who place a personal value on their impact upon the environment. In fact, after burial and cremation, the top preferences for body disposition now include: green burial, human composting and alkaline hydrolysis (Gillespie & Defort, 2020).

Still relatively unknown to the general public, only 7.5% of respondents to the 2019 NFDA Consumer Awareness study were aware the process existed, alkaline hydrolysis (or resomation) represents one of the newest offerings to consumers who are seeking an alternative to flame-based cremation and traditional burial.

According to the Green Burial Council (GBC) website, green (or natural) burial is described as:

...a way of caring for the dead with minimal environmental impact that aids in the conservation of natural resources, reduction of carbon emissions, protection of worker health, and the restoration and/or preservation of habitat. Green burial necessitates the use of non-toxic and biodegradable materials, such as caskets, shrouds, and urns (Green Burial, n.d., para. 1).

The concept of green burial denotes the growing trend and desire for eco-friendly choices when it comes to funeral practices, funeral merchandise and body disposition.

While some have touted cremation as a green practice, primarily due to the limited impact of upon-the-land space, GBC and others have not yet committed themselves to this premise. With fossil fuels being utilized for flame-based cremation and ensuing emissions from crematory facilities, questions remain whether this is indeed a green process. Using one-fifth the energy of flame-based cremation while releasing no air emissions in the process, alkaline hydrolysis has been marketed as a green alternative to traditional cremation (Ross, 2010). Companies marketing alkaline hydrolysis as an eco-friendly procedure have promoted the terms "Bio Cremation" and "Green Cremation" (Burn, 2011). It would be wise for funeral directors to take notice of those interested in exploring green funeral options as those identified in NFDA's 2019 Cremation and Burial Report reached 51.6% (Gillespe & Defort, 2019) while NFDA's 2020 Burial and Cremation Report has the number at 61.8%.

Since passing a law in 2019, Washington State was the first state to allow natural organic reduction or "human composting" as a legal form of disposition. A process used by Herland Forest Cemetery, unaided by any industrial equipment, includes several steps in the phases of body decomposition and ultimately returns the body to the earth naturally as useable soil. The procedure takes time, and depending on climate conditions, can take up to a year to complete (Patrick, 2019). Consumer demand for this type of disposition choice seems somewhat slow at this time, however 4.1 percent of respondents to the NFDA 2020 Consumer Awareness and Preferences Survey preferred human composting as a disposition option. Other unique green options are emerging in the realm of being environmentally responsible when it comes to deathcare, such as mushroom suits, burial in organic pods, promession (freezing the body with liquid nitrogen followed by pulverization by vibration), using cremated remains to create an artificial reef, etc. Widespread popularity of these green options (and others) is emerging and the actual impact remains to be seen as these represent more recent offerings. Once again, funeral directors should be careful to dismiss these developing green options as mere fads since consumer demand may give an opportunity to grow and differentiate business.

Religion – Fewer Ties and Greater Acceptance

Americans have fewer ties to religion than any time in recent history. Only 35.4% of participants in the NFDA 2019 Consumer Awareness and Preferences Survey believed it was very important to have religion as a part of the funeral service (Gillespe & Defort, 2019). Cremation is more likely to be selected by those who do not have an association with an organized religion or strong religious ties. In areas of the country with lower participation rates in church there tends to a corresponding increase in cremation. According to the NFDA 2019 Cremation and Burial Report, the Eastern states represent an area of the country where cremation consumers (over the age of 40) have a greater preference (32 percent) toward a ceremony with the body present prior to cremation, while the western United States represents a strong preference (20 percent) for a ceremony without the body present (Gillespe & Defort, 2019). Organized religions themselves are becoming more tolerant and accepting of the use of cremation. Such acceptance may be an attempt to try and meet the demands of a dwindling membership, or possibly due to more highly educated congregations who seem to be embracing the concept of spiritualism over religion (Kenevich, 2010). Although it should be mentioned that as more religions are accepting of the use of cremation, there are some religions, Orthodox Judaism, Greek Orthodox Church, and Islam, that demonstrate continued reluctance to the idea.

As ties to religion continue to decline, the use of celebrants to officiate or emcee a memorial event is seeing favor among families. According to the NFDA 2020 Consumer Awareness and Preferences Survey, just over 44% of respondents attended funeral services where someone other than a clergyperson presided. Funeral directors are increasingly relying upon the services of these specially trained officiants to create a very warm, personalized funeral experience, without regard to religious affiliation. As families seek new ways to memorialize their loved ones that forego traditional funeral rites, celebrants seem to offer value for a meaningful experience. It should be noted the services offered by celebrants are not without their critics. Dr. Thomas G. Long, author of *Accompany Them with Singing: the Christian Funeral*, is skeptical that some families may be utilizing celebrant services to the detriment of their emotional health (Kenevich, 2010). The 2020 NFDA Consumer Awareness and Preference Study revealed that almost 39 percent of respondents would consider using a celebrant. While more funeral homes are encouraging staff to seek certification as celebrants, many continue to outsource this asset.

Rapidly Changing Consumer Preferences - Event Planning/Facility Design

The funeral service industry must take notice of data being revealed by studies spanning a period of time that not only are consumers utilizing facilities for end of life services exclusive of the funeral home setting, they are also looking to others outside of funeral service to assist with arrangements (Lambert & Kleese, 2011). Nearly 70 percent of respondents to the 2020 NFDA Consumer Awareness and Preferences Survey admitted to attending a funeral at a location far from a house of worship or funeral home. Venues such as the home, an outdoor setting, banquet hall or setting, and a cemetery are just a few places listed. This should not be a surprise, when as far back as 2010, the FAMIC Study revealed the top two places to hold a memorial event or funerals were: "park/theater" and "hotel/event place." Churches and funeral homes (which took the top two spots in the 2004 study) did not even make it into the top three, finishing fourth and fifth place respectively (Gober & Seyler, 2012). This should have been acknowledged by an industry at the time as to where funeral service was headed, and now we have arrived at a place in time whereby the funeral home and the funeral director are in some instances continuing to fight for their relevancy in a sea of options.

In 2014, The NFDA Cremation Report detailed the type of experience funeral consumers were seeking: Details of most importance to consumers for their own funeral or the funeral of a loved one: a gathering of family and friends, honoring the wishes or prearrangements of a loved one and having a life celebration with an uplifting atmosphere. They also want personalized music and a ceremony or tribute to the deceased. (p. 6)

This should be a stark wake–up call for funeral service providers as families turn to wedding and hospitality planners to fulfill service needs. Gould (2012) even suggested families may be better served by "unlicensed, college-educated arrangers" functioning as event planners rather than "licensed funeral directors because they would not have preconceived notions of how a funeral should be conducted" (p. 42). Certainly a provocative commentary, it does bring forth the notion that funeral service providers in certain areas have missed a seminal moment of opportunity, while others are subject to follow suit if the needs of this market are not addressed. The 2019 NFDA Consumer Awareness and Preferences Survey revealed that 53% of respondents did not require a funeral director as they could direct their own memorial service or funeral (Nixon, 2020).

Funeral service trade journals are ever-increasing in their coverage of funeral home design which incorporates an inviting familiar space which encourages families to plan meaningful celebrations. New funeral home designs, whether new construction or remodeling, include replacing the traditional funeral home chapel with comfortable seating and eating areas, encouraging families to stay. In years past, funeral home design seemed to follow a grand facility philosophy, however scaling down the large funeral home footprint to become more flexible in meeting families' needs means a 5,000 to 7,000 square foot structure may be optimal. For example, consider the space allotted to the display or showroom that can now be placed quite effectively on a laptop computer or electronic tablet (Isard, 2020). In many cases, new funeral facilities are designed specifically to not resemble a traditional funeral home, and instead a visitor may end up entering a facility reminiscent of an upscale resort or that which is as inviting and homey as their own living room. Gober and Seyler (2012) suggested an opportunity for the innovative funeral director:

If consumers are willing, even eager, to embrace non-traditional funeral venues, why not build or buy one? It could share the funeral home's name and brand, but it wouldn't have to. It could be physically connected to the funeral home or it could be in another part of town, in markets the firm otherwise couldn't reach. It could be equipped to handle traditional services but could also be designed to handle events that are completely different – happy, noisy events that families now take to providers. (p. 76)

Increasing Education Levels, Technology and the Educated Consumer

Americans have always possessed a spirit of inquiry. In the formal sense, the Pew Research Center confirms that Americans have attained education at record levels. In fact, a milestone was reached in 2012 when, for the first time, one-third of the nation's 25- to 29-year-olds completed at least a bachelor's degree (Fry & Parker, 2012). The U. S. Census Bureau revealed that in 2019, 36 percent of those age 25 and older attained a bachelor's degree (Census, 2020). Education level has been identified as a factor corresponding to those who select cremation. Informally, consumers are doing their homework outside of the classroom and satisfying their inquisitive nature through powerful technological tools, chief among these is the internet. Funeral consumers are increasingly going online to find a funeral home, read obituaries and participate in virtual memorialization activities (NFDA Bulletin, 2010).

Consider this: only 65 percent of respondents to the 2010 FAMIC Study said they would look to a funeral home or a funeral director for information on making arrangements (Lambert & Kleese, 2011). This should cause funeral service providers to pause and give considerable thought as to where or to whom funeral consumers are turning to for arrangement resources. Fast forward to 2021 and the technology availability that is so pervasive, powerful, and reliable that Americans have developed an overwhelming reliance on the information obtained from its use. Social media and comprehensive internet resources have enhanced the ability of consumers to research products, select services, read customer reviews, and do it all in the palm of their hand even while sitting across from the funeral professional during the arrangement conference. Nearly 68 percent of participants in the 2020 NFDA Consumer Awareness and Preferences Study revealed they had previously visited a funeral homes' website. Also, consumers are using technology to check funeral home prices, check out their Facebook and other social media websites, write condolences, and look for obituary information. In short, consumers arrive at the funeral home educated and many times have explored available cremation and memorialization options. Funeral arrangers should take the time to venture into the virtual world and educate themselves about the available information prospective clients are accessing. In the past, funeral directors have been guarded about sharing too much information to families beforehand. The GPL is a prime example whereby, fearing it was the competition; suspicion seemed to be at the forefront when telephone inquiries were made regarding funeral pricing. In today's world where consumers demand immediate information for decision making (at 3:00 AM from the nursing home where a loved one just died), the funeral home that does not have published prices runs the risk of a family moving on to the next firm that is information accessible. Publishing all content, including pricing, that a family might need to make a decision might be a wise decision as the funeral home is in charge of helping make the decision and not the next user-friendly firm down the block or across town.

The use of, and harnessing the power of, technology is without a doubt a keystone in today's successful funeral service firms. One estimate finds that 85 percent of families begin funeral planning by going online. And it is not just the millennial generation going online as older generations are increasing their time behind the computer screen (Sagel & Bloomfield, 2018). Today's funeral service trade journals are replete with articles on leveraging the benefits of technology, whether it's how to reach consumers via marketing, how to harness the desire of consumers who want to make arrangements without being physically present in the funeral home, or those who want to utilize technologies' benefits to enhance services or reach a wider audience. For example, live streaming of a funeral or memorial service is an ever-increasing option that families are being offered, and now often expected as a standard service offering. The consumer actively willing and seeking the ability to arrange a cremation online is increasing. E-commerce sales of all varieties is exploding, and stay at home orders during the COVID-19 pandemic only accelerated the comfort and ease of conducting business this way; even funeral business. Looking ahead it is not certain what the lasting effects of the COVID-19 pandemic will be to the industry, but the following assessment by Weigel (2020) provides a summation:

This pandemic has been a stimulus that thrust our profession ahead by more than a decade overnight. No one could have seen the instant transformation of the funeral profession coming so quickly, but it's here. What once was the norm – having families sit in your arrangement office for hours going over every detail – has been replaced with the click of a mouse and an online meeting. (p. 55)

Many firms have expressed families' appreciation for the ability to plan funerals remotely at a time when mobility was limited and in-person gatherings were discouraged or not allowed (Isard, 2021).

Greater Life Expectancy

The Centers for Disease Control (CDC) estimated the 2018 U. S. life expectancy at 78.7 years (76.2 for males; 81.2 years for females). When compared to 1940 life expectancy of 62.9 (60.8 for males; 65.2 for females), the evidence is clear: Americans are living longer (CDC, n.d.). Advancements in health care and pharmaceuticals; new tools for disease prevention and diagnosis; and, increased safety awareness (mandatory seatbelt use, less environmental pollution, greater workplace safety, etc.) have all served to extend our lives into old age. Such news is welcomed as Americans spend billions of dollars each year to ward off the inevitable, instead favoring health and a quest for continued youthfulness.

The U.S. population ages 65 and over is expected to reach 73 million people by the year 2030 (Federal Interagency Forum on Aging-Related Statistics, 2020). The age group 85 and older is now the fastest growing segment in the population (ICAA, 2009). As we age, our circle of friends and family may diminish, as well as financial resources. Others may be left with the monetary burden when faced with final arrangements. As discussed, the fear of rising funeral costs along with geographic distance from one's hometown may be a factor in the decision to utilize the affordability and portability of cremation. This older segment of the population should not be ignored or dismissed as being out of touch when it comes to reaching them via technology. The ability to reach those 65 and older has never been greater as 75% those who live in households have internet access while 80% have access to a computer (Roberts, et al., 2018).

Expanded Options Offerings

Cremation allows tremendous flexibility and greater options when compared to traditional earth burial or entombment. Families were forced to discover this during the COVID-19 pandemic when funeral options were limited and gatherings were not allowed. In the article "Cremation Makes Portable Memories," Mark Wingfield (2001) explained the many options available to families for cremated remains:

[They] may be placed in wind chimes, stored in drawers beneath a home-size eternal flame, mixed in paint used to create a unique piece of framed art for the home or mixed with concrete to form hand-made reefs strategically placed on the ocean floor to help keep nature in alignment. (p. 8)

Since 2001, the options for cremated remains have only expanded and become more creative. In 2019, it was revealed that 42% of cremated remains are returned to families (the remainder are interred in a cemetery (35.2%); placed in a columbarium niche at church (8.1%); or scattered (16%). With the expected continued rise of cremation, the selections for non-burial options of cremated remains are likely to grow. Chapter eight offers detailed insight into the numerous merchandise options available for consumers who choose cremation. As families look toward personalizing the memorialization experience, options extend far beyond merchandise and into abundant service opportunities which, as discussed, are all available at the click of a button.

Abundant opportunities exist to capitalize on and provide direction to the families that have no direction regarding a final destination of cremated remains, as well as avenues to memorialize a loved one who is being cremated. It is important to remember that, according to one study, only 7.1% of families who select cremation do not associate it with any type of ceremony. Therefore, there is a large number of those choosing cremation who desire or believe that some type of service is associated with the selection of cremation. Funeral professionals must be able to meet the demands beyond a direct cremation with adequate merchandise and service options. And further, be able to deliver these options to consumers in a variety of ways. Once again, the funeral director is being placed in the position of being an educator to the funeral consumer regarding all available options that many families may not have had any awareness of prior to the time of having to make arrangements.

Increased Migration to Retirement Locations

Baby Boomers are beginning to rapidly reach age 65 (by 2030 all Boomers will have reached 65) and may be considering a phase in life that includes retirement. There is no law or requirement that those reaching the age of retirement must relocate. In fact, a substantial number of retirees make no decision to move, especially those involving long distances. However, it seems to be part of the American cultural identity that one works a lifetime, enjoys a party complete with a gift of a gold watch and then it's off to the sunshine of Miami Beach. While this stereotype is just that...a stereotype, the prevalence of senior retirement communities in hospitable climates is becoming increasingly big business in the United States. Those who choose to relocate at some point during retirement may be drawn to new areas for various reasons, as provided by the following explanation:

Low cost of living and warm weather are prime draws for retirees. They tend to move from colder or high cost states such as New York, Illinois, New Jersey, Michigan and California, in search of warmer and lower cost states including Florida, Arizona, North and South Carolina and Texas. (Henderson, 2014, para. 8)

One study seems to support the continued exodus of those aged 60 and older from high cost of living states to more climate friendly and tax tolerant locations. Nearly 930,000 people in this demographic packed up and headed across state lines in 2018. While California and New York both witnessed negative net migration, Florida and Arizona retained the top two spots respectively for the 60 and older crowd moving in state (Horan, 2020).

Mobility has now become an important factor and may be directly tied to the rise in cremations as people are dying away from home with "no emotional attachment to where they left or to where they are"

(Springer, 2003). Families have discovered that "cremation enables them to return cremated remains from wherever their loved one has moved to wherever their loved one still considers 'home'" (CANA, 2014, p. 8).

More Socially Acceptable Than in the Past

Cremation is no longer considered a taboo practice in the United States. As more people attend and participate in a memorial service or some type of a non-traditional celebration of life, a sense of normalcy may begin to develop. Those who have been reluctant to consider cremation, and anything other than the traditional route for a funeral, are being exposed to non-traditional alternatives which serve to change their minds and attitudes, and is having them seek out more personalized celebrations (LaMotte, 2020). Families are less bound by traditions prescribed to them by the church as in years past, and instead are deciding to begin their own unique traditions. No longer are survivors concerned about the scrutiny from friends and neighbors about the quality of casket wheeled down the center aisle at church. Add to this the prevalence of the family plot declining, as people are rapidly moving from their hometowns to seek their fortune. Older Americans are following suit, either retiring to warmer climates or choosing to be closer to children and grandchildren.

Many of the choices for memorialization today center on the personal nature that is becoming expected in the ceremony. Baby Boomers, those born between 1946 and 1964, an estimated 73 million strong as of 2019. In fact, everyday about 10,000 Boomers turn 65 and are now firmly in control of making decisions for their own funerals (Census Bureau, 2019; ICAA, 2009). Boomers have scrutinized traditional rituals and concluded them to be lacking and inadequate (Bondor, 2003). Although somewhat lengthy, the following narrative provides a robust explanation of the Baby Boomer experience which has provided the foundation for change in the acceptance of cremation:

Universities opened up to the public, giving more people a broader view of the world, loosening the grip of family and community traditions. Women, ethnic minorities and gays achieved more civil rights and became outspoken about their views and opinions. Death and sex were no longer taboo subjects, and natural childbirth and midwives became preferred over hospital- controlled births. At the same time, mainstream religious affiliation declined, and people took on a more holistic view and concern for the natural world.

As women began participating more in the work force, convenience and saving time became their mantra. Rural America saw families move from small, unprofitable farms to the suburbs of larger cities. Immigration patterns began to change. Most immigrants in the early part of the last century came from Europe. Later, most immigrants came from Asia and Latin America. This shift in culture is transforming our country (Bondor, 2003, p. 10).

Additionally, Baby Boomers have significant resources and available discretionary income. They know what they want and are not afraid to spend money as long as they perceive value for dollars spent. Boomers are particularly interested in personalization of their funeral or memorial services which in itself is contrary to some of the more traditional funeral rites.

One singular 20th century event brought the attention of an entire nation to the significance of the traditional funeral service. The assassination of President John F. Kennedy in 1963 and his subsequent state funeral, which included Catholic funeral rites, became engrained in the memories of many Baby Boomers and those that lived through the event. These same individuals, now reaching the age of planning for their own funerals and those of their parents, witnessed the events surrounding the tragic death of John F. Kennedy, Jr. in 1999. In this instance, the son of President Kennedy was cremated and received full Catholic funeral rites before his cremated remains were scattered at sea (Maxwell, 1999). These two events seem to encapsulate the shift we are experiencing today in American funeral practices.

Pet Cremation and Memorialization

The pet industry is a juggernaut in the U. S. economy, no matter the economic climate. According to the American Pet Products Association, in 2019 it estimated that $100 billion was spent on pets in the U.S. (Tyler, 2020). Some states and cities have gone so far as to legally change the term of the caretaker of pets from owner to guardian; giving the relationship a deeper legal attachment. A growing number of state legislatures have also changed or enacted laws that allow pets and humans to be buried together in a cemetery (Lemasters, 2017). In fact, Americans love affair with their pets goes far beyond what has been traditionally accepted as the role of our furry friends. Kenevich (2010) aptly sums up the status of our relationship with household pets:

Dogs, cats and other household pets used to be seen as just that, pets. Today, these beloved animals aren't just pets; they are part of the family. Our furry friends are given pet-sized clothes to wear, the best toys available and the highest-quality food on the market. (p. 46)

It is no surprise that the funeral service industry in recent years has taken keen notice of the special relationship.

Today, a simple search of the internet reveals the plethora of providers offering service for those who have experienced pet loss. In years past, stand-alone pet cremation facilities existed through close relationships with veterinarian offices. Many in funeral service were more than pleased to distance themselves from these less-dignified facilities. With the dramatic change in American perception of pets as part of the family, funeral service has embraced compassionate pet loss services. According to the 2019 NFDA Member General Price List Study, 11.4% of funeral homes have their own pet care services business, with this segment only expected to see continued growth in the coming years.

• • •

Conclusion

It should be without question now that the prevalence of cremation is not by accident. The American funeral consumer is becoming comfortable with the choice of selecting cremation for their loved ones and themselves. Whether greater acceptance for the practice is due to the tremendous choices associated with the process, the attraction of portability, greater recognition by religious authorities or the perceived lower costs, it seems certain that cremation is being embraced and is here to stay. In providing their summation of the 2010 FAMIC study, Lambert and Kleese (2011) concluded:

There is no denying that consumer preferences for celebrating the lives of the deceased are changing. Funeral professionals must feel compelled to understand what consumers want and not only adapt, but actively promote, that they are willing and able to meet these demands. (p. 3)

The ability for funeral service professionals to find the pulse of the communities they serve may very well directly impact future revenue and more importantly the ability to function into the future. Funeral professionals must continue adapting to meet changing client needs as the only certainty toward the future is: what is important to families today will look much different as generations' age and identify new rituals of importance.

Glossary

Alkaline Hydrolysis (Resomation or Green Cremation): The reduction of human remains to essential elements through a water-based dissolution process using alkaline chemicals, heat, agitation, and pressure

Alternative Container: An enclosure for human remains in preparation for cremation. The container is composed of an appropriate combustible material; rigid enough for handling ease; assure the protection of the health and safety of the crematory operator as well as provide appropriate covering for the remains

Authorizing Agent(s): The person(s) legally entitled to control the disposition of human remains

Burial: The interment of dead human remains in the earth

Casket: A rigid container designed to hold human remains, typically constructed of wood, metal, or like materials and ornamented and lined with various fabrics, which may or may not be combustible

Casting (Scattering): The free release of cremated remains over land, through the air, or over water as allowed by state and local law

Ceremonial (Rental) Casket: An exterior casket shell with a removable insert. The insert, which is removed from the exterior shell for cremation, includes all parts of the interior that may come in contact with the remains, including a removable and disposable pillow, extendover, overlay, and overlay skirt. Following all visitation and funeral ceremonies, the insert is removed and covered with the included container enclosure in preparation for cremation. A new insert is then placed in the casket shell preparing the unit for reuse

Charging Door: Door to the primary chamber, typically electronically or hydraulically operated

Combustion: The interaction of fuel with oxygen accompanied by a well-defined flame releasing heat; a high-temperature exothermic chemical reaction between a fuel and an oxidant

Coniferous Tree: Any gymnospermous tree or shrub bearing cones

Columbarium: A structure, room, or other space in a building or structure containing niches for permanent inurnment of cremated remains

Commingling: To combine, intentionally or otherwise, the cremated remains of more than one person

Cremated Remains: All the remains of the cremated human body recovered after the completion of the cremation process, including pulverization which leaves only bone fragments reduced to consist of unidentifiable dimensions and may possibly include the residue of any foreign matter including casket or container material, bridgework, or eye glasses that were cremated with the human remains. Cremated remains are sometimes referred to as Human Cremated Remains

Cremation: The mechanical and/or thermal or other dissolution process that reduces human remains to bone fragments. Cremation includes the processing and usually includes pulverization of the bone fragments

Cremation Casket: Casket manufactured for cremation. These units encase the remains, are combustible (interior and exterior), rigid in order to assist in the loading process, and contain less than 0.5% chlorinated plastic of total weight. The goal is to take steps to ensure a successful cremation, eliminate toxic and hazardous elements as well protect the machine and the environment. Common materials used for the construction of containers appropriate for cremation include corrugated cardboard, particleboard, and wood

Cremation Container: The case in which the human body is delivered to the crematory and in which it is cremated. General requirements for the container includes that it is composed of combustible materials, it is rigid enough for handling ease, assures protection of the health and safety of the operator, and provides proper covering for the remains

Cremation Pan: Specially designed cremation tray to contain infant and stillbirth cremated remains in a smaller area in order to improve the possibility of retrieval

Cremation Shroud: Simple or ornate material constructed and designed to wrap human remains as they are placed into a crematory

Cremator: The total mechanical unit for the cremation process. Inside it is lined with a heavy refractory tile or brick, with a layer of insulation between the inside surface and the outside protective housing or casing

Deciduous Trees: Trees and shrubs that lose their leaves seasonably

Direct Cremation: Disposition of human remains by cremation, without formal viewing, visitation or ceremony with the body present, or other services

Due Diligence: An investigation of a business prior to signing a contract, or an act with a certain standard of care. It can be a legal obligation, but the term more commonly applies to voluntary investigations

Durable Power of Attorney: When a person executes a power of attorney which will become or remain effective in the event he or she should later become disabled

Entombment: The placement of the remains in a columbarium niche, these may be located in cemeteries (indoor and outdoor options exist) and it is also common for churches and now even funeral homes to offer a columbarium for the entombment of cremated remains. This term is also commonly associated with the placement of casketed remains in a mausoleum

Ferrous Metal: Metals that contain iron

Final Disposition: Final resting place of human remains

FTC Funeral Rule: Requires you to give consumers accurate, itemized price information and various other disclosures about funeral goods and services, and prohibits specific misrepresentations

Funeral Provider: You sell or offer to sell both funeral goods and funeral services to the public

Grave Liner: Outer burial container without a lining or sealing properties

Green Burial (Natural Burial): A method of final disposition of a body with fewer environmental impacts than traditional burial or cremation

Hearth: A solid surface upon which waste material with high moisture content or liquids or waste material may turn to liquid before burning

Human Remains: The body of a deceased person, or part of a body or limb that has been removed from a living person, including the body, part of body, or limb in any stage of decomposition

Indemnity: A duty to make good any loss, damage, or liability incurred by another.

Interment: The act or ceremony of burying human remains in the earth, including cremated remains

Insert: A cremation container designed to encase human remains while placed in the shell of a ceremonial (rental) casket. This container includes all necessary material and bedding for a dignified viewing

Inurnment: The act or ceremony of burying an urn containing cremated remains

Keepsake: Also known as "mini urns", these containers are specifically designed so that families that select cremation have the opportunity to divide cremated remains and retain a small portion of the remains while the majority of the remains are interred, entombed, scattered or disposed of by other means

Memorial Service: A service without the body present

Next of Kin: Denotes the persons nearest of kindred to the decedent

Niche: A compartment or cubicle for the memorialization or permanent placement of an urn containing cremated remains

Non-Ferrous Metal: Metal that does not contain iron and are not magnetic

Opacity: The degree to which light is reduced when viewed through a smoke plume or visible emissions

Ossuary: A depository for cremated remains. Typically, these are designed for the commingling of the cremated remains of numerous people

Outer Burial Container: A container constructed for placement in the earth around a casket or urn, including but not limited to, containers commonly known as vaults, grave boxes, and grave liners

Particleboard: also known as chipboard, is an engineered wood product manufactured from wood chips, sawmill shavings, or even sawdust, and a synthetic resin or other suitable binder, which is pressed and extruded

Permanent (Cinerary urn) Container: A container which will permanently house cremated remains

Power of Attorney: An instrument in writing whereby one person, as principal, appoints another as his agent and confers authority to perform certain specified acts or kinds of acts on behalf of a principal

Primacy: Primary, preeminent, or more important with respect to declaring the authorizing agent

Primary Chamber: Chamber in within a cremator where primary ignition and burning of the case occurs

Processing: Pre-pulverization, removing foreign materials (non-body) from cremated remains in the preparation for pulverization

Pulverization: The reduction of identifiable bone fragments after the completion of the cremation and processing to granulated particles by manual or mechanical means

Raking: Cremated remains are dispensed onto the ground and raked into the earth

Refractory Material: Special lining for the firebox to provide insulation to retain the heat and prevent it from escaping

Retort: A specific crematory design in which the air flow is from front to back, then underneath the hearth prior to exiting through the stack

Right of Disposition: Having authority to determine the method of final disposition of human remains

Scattering: See Casting

Scattering Urn: Urns designed to hold the cremated remains for a brief period of time between the cremation and the scattering of the remains. These urns are more durable than a standard temporary container, usually constructed of wood or wood by-products or spun bronze

Secondary Chamber: Chamber within a cremator where unburned combustible gases from the primary chamber are completely burned

Sift-Proof: Designed so that loose powder cannot sift out during transit

Somatic Death: Death of the entire body

Stack: The final discharge point where the products of combustion are released to the environment

Thermocouple: A heat-sensing device, typically crematories have two one in each chamber

Temporary Container: A receptacle for cremated remains usually made of cardboard, plastic, or similar material designed to hold the cremated remains until an urn or other permanent container is acquired

Third Party Crematory: A crematory that offers to contact with funeral homes to perform cremation services

Trenching: Shallow trench dug in the earth and cremated remains are placed in the trench. The trench in then covered with soil. The trench may be dug in a design that is significant to the deceased in order to add additional meaning to the placement of the remains

Urn: A receptacle designed to permanently encase the cremated remains

Urn Grave Liner: An outer burial container designed to encase an urn that is interred in the ground. This container is not lined, nor does it seal. This container will support the weight of the earth

Urn Vault: An outer burial container designed to encase an urn that is interred in the ground. This container is lined, and has sealing properties. This container will also support the weight of the earth load

Witnessing of Cremation: When the authorized agent(s), or others designated by the agent(s) are present for the beginning of the cremation process

REFERENCES

America Counts. (2019, December 10). By 2030, all baby boomers will be age 65 or older. U. S. Census Bureau. Retrieved from https://www.census.gov/library/stories/2019/12/by-2030-all-baby-boomers-will-be-age-65-or-older.html

American Pet Products Association. (n.d.). *Pet Industry Market Size & Ownership Statistics*. Retrieved from http://www.americanpetproducts.org/press_industrytrends.asp

Bartsche, P. M. (2011, December). Business outlook 2012: What will the new year bring for the funeral industry? *American Funeral Director* 134(12), 36-45.

Bio Response Solutions. (2020). Aquamation. Retrieved December 13, 2020, from https://aquamationinfo.com/

B & L Cremation Systems (n.d.). *Crematory Operator Training Program Manual*. Largo, Florida: B & L Cremation Systems, Inc.

Black, H.C. (1990). *Black's law dictionary, with pronunciations* (6th ed.). St. Paul, MN: West Publishing Company.

Bohdan, B., Blais, M., Vandierendonck, R. & Driedger. (1998, September). Radiation Safety When A Patient Dies After Therapy. *Journal of Nuclear Medicine Technology*, 26(3), 206-207.

Bondor, P. (2003 Sept/October). Why Cremation? *The Independent*, 5(5), 10-11.

Canadian Nuclear Safety Commission (2018, June). *Radiation Protection Guidelines for Safe Handling of Decedents* (REGDOC-2.7.3). http://nuclearsafety.gc.ca/eng/acts-and-regulations/regulatory-documents/published/html/regdoc2-7-3/index.cfm

Carrns, A. (2019, July 26). What to know when choosing cremation. *New York Times*. Retrieved from https://www.nytimes.com/2019/07/26/your-money/funeral-cremation-burial.html

Casket and Funeral Supply Association of America (2014, June 03). FFDA Releases 2013 Data. Retrieved from http://www.cfsaa.org/news/175981/FFDA-Releases-2013-Data.htm

Centers for Disease Control (2020, November 17). *United States Life Tables*, 2018. *National Vital Statistics Reports* 69(12). National Vital Statistics System.

Cincinnati Cremation Company Historic Collection, National Museum of Funeral History, Houston, Texas.

Cobb, Augustus Gardiner. *Earth Burial and Cremation*. Knickerbocker Press; 1892.

Cremation Association of North America (2020). *CANA Annual Statistics Report* 2020. Wheeling, Illinois: Cremation Association of North America.

Cremation Association of North America, *Model cremation law and explanation*, approved by CANA Board of Directors, November 16, 2017.

Cremation Association of North America (2020). Alkaline Hydrolysis. Retrieved December 2, 2020 from https://www.cremationassociation.org/page/alkalinehydrolysis

Cremation Association of North America (2020). *The CANA Crematory Operations Certification Program + Alkaline Hydrolysis Manual*. (1st Ed.) Cremation Association of North America.

Cremation Association of North America, http://www.cremationassociation.org/

Cremation Association of North America
- Annual Convention Proceedings 1925 – 1965
- National Cremation Magazine 1965 – 1976

DeArmond, P.R. (2003). *Funeral service merchandising: An introductory text for students*. Cincinnati, OH: The Cincinnati Foundation for Mortuary Education.

Defort, E. J. (2013, January). Funeral home owners look to stem the tide of eroding profitability: Latest data from the annual Citrin Cooperman survey. *The Director*, 85(1), 46-49.

Defort, E. J. (2011, July) Cremation A - Z. *The Director*, 83(7), 40-43.

Defort, E. J. (2013, January). Funeral home owners look to stem the tide of eroding profitability: Latest data from the annual Citrin Cooperman survey. *The Director*, 85(1), 46-49.

Defort, E. J. (2011, July) Cremation A - Z. *The Director*, 83(7), 40-43.

Defort, E. J. (2019, August). Focus on cremation: "I don't want two songs and a sermon." *The Director*, 91(8), 38-44.

Editorial: Tom Snyder discusses cremation and the new family. [Editorial]. (1995, July). *The Southern Funeral Director*, 151(7), 22.

Engler Cremation Collection, National Museum of Funeral History, Houston, Texas.

Erichsen, Hugo. *The Cremation of the Dead*. D.O. Haynes & Co, Detroit, MI; 1887

Federal Interagency Forum on Aging-Related Statistics. (2020). *Older Americans 2020: Key indicators of well-being.* Washington, DC: U.S. Government Printing Office.

Federal Trade Commission (2019). *Complying with the funeral rule.* Washington, DC: Federal Trade Commission.

Federal Trade Commission. (2021). *FTC Publishes Inflation-Adjusted Civil Penalty Amounts for 2021.* [online] Available at: <https://www.ftc.gov/news-events/press- releases/2021/01/ftc-publishes-inflation-adjusted-civil-penalty-amounts-2021> [Accessed 3 February 2021].

Fisher, D. (2012, January). Creating policy and legislation for alkaline Hydrolysis. *The Director.* 84(1), 34-36.

Fry, R., & Parker, K. (2012, November 5). *Record Shares of Young Adults Have Finished Both High School and College.* Retrieved from Pew Research Center Social Trends website: http://www.pewsocialtrends.org/2012/11/05/record-shares-of-young-adults-have-finished-both-high-school-and-college/#overview

Gillespie, D. & Defort, E. J. (2019, September). 2019 Consumer Awareness and Preferences Survey: The people's voice. *The Director*, 91(9), 44-63.

Gillespie, D. & Defort, E. J. (2020, September). NFDA 2020 consumer awareness and preferences survey: A younger and more diverse demographic in 2020 provides some surprises in our annual consumer survey. *The Director*, 92(9), 28-46.

Gilligan, T.S., & Stueve, T.F.H. (2011). *Mortuary law* (11th ed.), Cincinnati, Ohio: The Cincinnati Foundation for Mortuary Education.

Gober, D., & Seyler, P. (2012, December). Thinking outside the traditional. *The Director*, 84(12), 76-77.

Gould, G. (2012, March). Marketing in the new economy. *The Director*, 84(3), 40-42.

Green Burial. (n.d.). In Green Burial Council website. Retrieved from http://greenburialcouncil.org/home/what-is-green-burial/

Henderson, T. (2014, June 16). Retirement moves make a comeback. *USA Today.* Retrieved from: http://www.usatoday.com/story/money/personalfinance /2014/06/16/stateline -retirement-moving/10575961/

Horan, S. (2020, March 10). Where Retirees Are Moving – 2020 Edition. *SmartAsset.* Retrieved from https://smartasset.com/financial-advisor/where-retirees-are-moving-2020

International Council on Active Aging. (2009). *The Business Case for Wellness Programs in Retirement Communities and Seniors Housing, A white paper.* Retrieved from http://www.icaa.cc/business/whitepapers/ icaabusinesscase-wp.pdf

Isard, D. (2020, February). When traditional isn't the tradition anymore. *The Director*, 92(2), 46-48.

Isard, D. (2021, February). Finance 201: Memorialization since COVID-19. *The Director*, 93(2), 22-24.

Johnson, B. (2010, November). 2010 FAMIC Study: Findings and surprises. *American Cemetery*, 82(11), 22-27.

Kenevich, T. (2010, February). Religious reform. *American Funeral Director*, 133(2), 22-25.

Klein, C.M., Nicodemus, M.W., & Watkins, M.J. (2014). *Cremation standards for Funeral Service professionals.* Brookfield, Wisconsin: National Funeral directors Association.

Kubasak, M. & Lamers, W.M. (2007). *Traversing the minefield, best practice: Reducing risk in funeral cremation service.* Pasadena, California: The Castle Press.

Kubasak, M.W. (1990). Cremation and the funeral director: Successfully meeting the challenge. Malibu, California: The Avalon Press.

Lambert, D., & Kleese, P. (2011, October). 2010 FAMIC Study Reaction: Interpreting the data to ensure success. *American Funeral Director*, 134(10), 62-66.

Lambert, D., & Kleese, P. (2011). FAMIC Research Reveals Opportunities and Threats. Retrieved from http://www.homesteaderslife.com/userdocs/FAMIC-Opportunities_Threats.pdf

Lapin, H.I. (2005). Avoiding cremation liability. *American Cemetery*, 77(4), 16-17, 34-35.

Lemasters, P. (2015, Autumn). Another wrongful cremation. Really? 3 ways on HOW to get others involved in identification. *Lemasters Parliament*, 6(1), 7-12.

Lemasters, P. (2018, October). Online cremation arrangements: Not as easy as 'Just click here.' *ICCFA Magazine*, 78(8), 12-15.

Lemasters, P. (2014). Get proof of identification when dealing with out-of-town clients. *ICCFA Magazine*, 74(6), 54-56.

Lemasters, P. (2018, October). Online cremation arrangements: Not as easy as 'Just click here.' *ICCFA Magazine*, 78(8), 12-15.

Lemasters, P. (2017, Autumn). The world of pets in deathcare is changing isn't it? *Parliament*, 7(3), 13-17.

LaMotte, S. (2020, January 23). Cremation has replaced traditional burials in popularity in America and people are getting creative with those ashes. *CNN Health*. Retrieved from https://www.cnn.com/2020/01/22/health/cremation-trends-wellness/index.html

Maxwell, P. (1999, July 28). Kennedy cremated in Duxbury. *The Duxbury Clipper*, pp. 1, 4.

Mayer, J.S. (1980). *Restorative art*. Dallas: Professional Training Schools, Inc.

Mayer, R.G. (2012). *Embalming: History, theory, and practice* (5th ed.). NY: McGraw-Hill.

McQueen, J. (2021, February). The future of green. *The Director*, 93(2), 32-34; 36.

Memorial Business Journal (2019, March 21). *Know the radiation protection guidelines*, 10(12), 1-2.

Nardi, N. (2018, May). The more things change, the more they stay the same. *ICCFA Magazine*, 78(4), 16-18.

National Funeral Directors Association. (2014, September). *The NFDA Cremation and Burial Report: Research, Statistics and Projections*. Retrieved from http://nfda.org/surveys-a-reports businessmangement/cat_view/223-other-documents/240-cremation.html

National Funeral Directors Association, (2019). *Cremation standards for funeral service Professionals, 2nd ed*. Brookfield, WI: National Funeral Directors Association of the United States, Inc.

National Funeral Directors Association. (2019, September). *2019 NFDA Member General Price List Study*. Brookfield, WI.

National Funeral Directors Association. (2020, July). *The NFDA Cremation and Burial Report: Statistics, projections and analysis of consumer preference for cremation and burial in the United States, Canada and worldwide*. Brookfield, WI

National Museum of Funeral History, Houston, Texas.

Neuman, S. (2021) Fewer than half of U.S. adults belong to a religious congregation, new poll shows. Npr.org retrieved April 12, 2021

New FAMIC Study Shows Americans Clearly Recognize the Importance and Value of Memorialization. (2010, September 20). *NFDA Bulletin*. Retrieved from http://www.msfda.net/sitemaker/sites/Maryla1/images/Website%20NFDA%20Bulletin%20Memorialization%20Survey%20Results%209-21-10.pdf

Nixon, D. (2020, Jan). How long will my burial business last? *The Director*, (92) 1, 32-35.

Olcott, Henry Steel. (1895). *Old Diary Leaves*. Theosophical Publishing House.

Olson, P.R. (2014). Flush and bone: Funeralizing alkaline hydrolysis in the United States. *Science, Technology, & Human Values*, 39(5), 666- 693. https://doi.org/ 10.1177/0162243914530475

Parting stone: https://partingstone.com/products/human-solidified-remains. Retrieved April 12, 2021

Patrick, W. (2019, May 20). Natural Organic Reduction aka "Human Composting". *Windward Education and Research Center*. Retrieved from http://www.herlandforest.org/human-composting/

Pearson, M.P. (1999). *The archaeology of death and burial*. College Station, Texas: Texas A&M Press.

Prothero, S. (2001). *Purified by fire: A history of cremation in America*. Berkeley, California: University of California Press.

Que, W. (2001, Summer). Radiation Safety Issues Regrading the Cremation of the Body of an I-125 Prostate Implant Patient. *Journal of Applied Clinical Medical Physics*, 2(3), 174-177.

Roberts, A., Ogunwole, S, Blakeslee, L. & Rabe, M. (2018, October 30). *Most older adults lived in households with computer and internet access*. U. S. Census Bureau. Retrieved from https://www.census.gov/library/stories/2018/10/snapshot-fast-growing-us-older-population.html

Rosen, F. (2004). *Cremation in America*. Amherst, New York: Prometheus Books

Ross, J. (2010, July). Cremation: Alkaline Hydrolysis. *The Director*. 82(7), 46-48.

Rumble, H., Troyer, J., Walter, T., & Woodthorpe, K. (2014). Disposal or dispersal? Environmentalism and final treatment of the british dead. *Mortality*, 19 (3)243 – 260, http://dx.doi.org/10.1080/13576275.2014.920315

Sagel, E. & Bloomfield, A. (2018, Aug./Sept.). Online funeral planning a hit for customers, owners. *ICCFA Magazine*, 78(7), 40-43.

Smith, T., Gitsham, P., Donell, S., Rose, D., Hing, C. (2012). The potential dangers of medical devices with current cremation practices. *The Journal of European Geriatric Medicine*, 3(2), 97-102.

Springer, J. M. (2003 Sept./Oct.). Study shows significant increase in cremation rate. *The Independent*, 5(5), 13.

Stall, S. (2017). Bucking the yuck factor. *Indianapolis Business Journal*, 38(14), 22.

Stansbury, G. (2013, February). We want a party. *The Director*, 85(2) 34-38.

Stansbury, G. (2012, October). The articulation factor: What we must learn to say to families. *ICCFA Magazine,* 72(8) 12-18.

State of California Department of Consumer Affairs (2017). *Cremated remains disposers booklet: Complying with California law*, Sacramento, CA: Cemetery and Funeral Bureau.

Starks, J. (2014, October). How to properly manage remains before, during, & after cremation. *ICCFA Magazine*, 74(8), 24-29.

Stueve, T.F.H, (1966). *Mortuary law* (4th ed.), Cincinnati, Ohio: The Cincinnati College of Mortuary Science.

Terreri, C.(n.d.) Alkaline Hydrolysis: A greener option? *Cremationist*. 47(3), 1-5.

The Cremationist Magazine 1976 – Present.

Transportation Security Administration (2018). *Ways to travel with cremated remains* Retrieved from *tsa.gov*

Tyler, J. (2020, March 3). US pet spending nears $100 billion in 2019. Pet Food Processing Newsletter. Retrieved from https://www.petfoodprocessing.net/articles/13660-us-pet-spending-nears-100-billion-in-2019

U.S. Census Bureau (2020, March 30). *U.S. Census Bureau Releases New Educational Attainment Data.* U.S. Census Bureau Release Number CB20-TPS.09. Retrieved from https://www.census.gov/newsroom/press-releases/2020/educational-attainment.html

United States Postal Service, (2019). *How to package and ship cremated remains*, Publication 139. September 2019.

Wagemann, D. (2020, March). Is funeral home loyalty dying out? *The Director*, 92(3), 36-39.

Washington County Historical Society, Washington, Pennsylvania.

Weigel, J. (2020, September). Death by cremation? Will cremation be funeral service's demise? Even after the pandemic, I think not. *The Director*, 92(9), 54-55.

Wingfield, M. (January 22, 2001). Trends in dying: Ashes to ashes. *Baptist Standard*, 113(4), pp. 1, 7.

Yu N., Rule, W., Sio, T., Ashman, J., & Nelson K. (2019 Feb. 26). Radiation Contamination Following Cremation of a Deceased Patient Treated with a Radiopharmaceutical. *Journal of the American Medical Association*, 321(8), 803-804.

∙ ∙ ∙

INDEX

A

Alkaline Hydrolysis: 157, 158, 159, 161, 172, 173

Alternative Container: 106, 110, 114, 115, 116, 117, 126, 127, 128, 129, 135, 138, 173

Authorizing Agent: 26, 27, 28, 29, 30, 31, 32, 33, 34, 35, 36, 38, 40, 42, 43, 44, 45, 46, 66, 71, 72, 73, 74, 82, 83, 86, 99, 101, 112

C

Casting: 74, 75

Ceremonial Casket: 54, 111, 112

Charging Door: 93, 102, 103

Combustion: 91, 92, 93, 94, 102, 103, 105, 106

Columbarium: 3, 10, 14, 15, 16, 17, 18, 19, 20, 23, 24, 74, 118, 119, 125, 178

Commingling: 58, 72, 75, 104

Cremation Casket: 50, 110, 112, 113, 114, 116, 117

Cremation Container: 26, 29, 46, 85, 87, 90, 95, 98, 99, 100, 101, 102, 103, 106, 109, 110, 111, 114, 116, 117, 137

Cremation Pan: 95, 106

Cremation Shroud: 115

D

Deciduous Trees: 112

Direct Cremation: 21, 61, 62, 126, 127, 128, 129, 136, 163, 169, 170, 172, 173, 179

Due Diligence: 28, 42, 62, 84, 85, 86, 88, 89, 139

Durable Power of Attorney: 38, 40

E

Entombment: 69, 74, 118, 132, 136, 139, 178

F

Ferrous Metal: 83, 100, 171,

Final Disposition: 1, 2, 3, 5, 7, 9, 22, 24, 25, 27, 28, 35, 36, 37, 51, 55, 56, 57, 58, 59, 60, 61, 62, 66, 67, 68, 70, 78, 87, 93, 105, 106, 108, 109, 113, 115, 160, 172, 174

FTC Funeral Rule: 61, 62, 126, 127, 129, 130

Funeral Provider: 29, 30, 34, 110, 116, 120, 121, 124, 127, 129

G

Grave Liner: 116, 123, 124

Greek: 2, 13, 16, 175

Green Burial: 115, 173, 174

H

Hearth: 93, 94

I

Indemnity: 34

Interment: 18, 70, 74

Insert: 113, 115, 146,

Inurnment: 13 ,16, 18, 74, 120, 139, 143, 144

K

Keepsake: 25, 46, 75, 77, 108, 117, 121, 122, 124

L

LeMoyne: 5, 6, 7

M

Memorial Service: 36, 42, 69, 128, 136, 173, 176, 177, 180

N

Next of Kin: 30, 39, 40, 42, 64, ,72, 136, 139

Niche: 14, 16, 17, 23, 24, 74, 118, 125, 178

Non-Ferrous Metal: 103, 112

O

Opacity: 92, 94, 103

Ossuary: 72, 75

Outer Burial Container: 117, 123, 124, 135

P

Particleboard: 99, 114, 115

Permanent Container: 117, 118, 120, 121, 124

Power of Attorney: 38, 39, 40

Primacy: 40

Primary Chamber: 91, 93, 94, 102, 103, 106, 109

Processing: 22, 28, 45, 48, 50, 52, 76, 87, 89, 90, 94, 96, 97, 103, 104, 108, 112, 139, 143

Pulverization: 73, 104, 107, 160, 174

R

Raking: 75

Rental Casket: 110, 112, 113, 114, 115, 116

Refractory Material: 94, 95, 97, 102, 103

Retort: 6, 23, 93, 107, 158, 159

Right of Disposition: 36, 37, 39, 40, 41, 42, 43, 44, 68

Roman: 2, 3, 13, 16

S

Scattering: 16, 20, 22, 71, 72, 73, 74, 75, 108, 118, 119, 121, 128, 141, 142, 169

Scattering Urn: 118, 119

Secondary Chamber: 91, 92, 94, 102, 105, 106, 109

Sift-Proof: 77, 78

Stack: 91, 93, 94, 97, 103, 106

T

Thermocouple: 94, 97

Temporary Container: 19, 80, 96, 98, 117, 118, 119, 120

Third Party Crematory: 27, 28, 38, 43, 85, 86, 88

Trenching: 75

U

Urn Grave Liner: 117, 124

Urn vault: 74, 117, 120, 124, 138,